RADICAL BRILLIANCE

The Anatomy of How and Why People Have Original Life-Changing Ideas

ARJUNA ARDAGH

Nevada City, CA
2018

Press Inquiries to media@radicalbrilliance.com

Published by Self X Press
An Imprint of Awakening World LLC
420 Nursery St, Nevada City CA 95959

radicalbrilliance.com

ISBN: 978-1-890909-44-4

DEDICATION

To the indelible memory of
Leonard Cohen.
In respect, gratitude, and awe.
And to the grandchildren
Of my grandchildren:
We have done our best to pave the way.

OTHER BOOKS BY ARJUNA ARDAGH

Relaxing into Clear Seeing (1997)

How About Now (1998)

The Last Laugh (2003)

The Translucent Revolution (2005)

Leap Before You Look (2007)

Let Yourself Go (2008)

Better than Sex (2013)

Conscious Men (2015) with John Gray

TABLE OF CONTENTS

FREE INTERACTIVE SITE

This is a book.

We have done all we can to cram as much brilliant information as possible between its covers, whether those covers are made of paper or bytes. But there were many useful things we could not include. Some needed video or audio, some were lists that exceeded our available space, and some things get updated so frequently that a website worked better.

Since you have purchased this book, please now go to

radicalbrilliance.com/register

and register your copy. This will give you immediate access to much more material in many different media.

PART ONE

THE MAP

I went for a walk in the Arctic Circle without map or compass. Fortunately, I was only lost for hours, not days.

—John Burnside

CHAPTER ONE
MY LIFE AS A MISFIT

Whenever I stumble upon a new book, or podcast, or anybody wanting to tell me something new, I don't just want to know "What do you have to teach me?" I want to know "Who are you? What is your life like? Tell me about the personal journey that has led you to feel you have something important to say. What challenges have you overcome along the way? Tell me about your triumphs."

Just in case you have similar criteria before you read on, here are my credentials.

This book is the fruit of my lifelong experience of feeling like a misfit. I was born to very intellectual and also very neurotic parents in London in the 1950s. The world of my childhood was scattered everywhere with books. For my first birthday, when kids today might get a stuffed animal or a squeaky toy, I got *The Complete works of William Shakespeare* and *The Oxford Book of English Verse*. My parents and their friends discussed movies, novels and philosophy. A person's worth was not measured by their capacity to love, or their financial stability, but by their intellectual and creative acuity... by knowing what the word "acuity" means. With tremendous pressure to achieve and produce in this arena myself, I got good at the game, and earned a first-class degree from Cambridge University in English Literature. But I also felt empty, that this world of the intellect was not my real tribe. There was something missing.

This feeling of emptiness started in my teens. I went to the King's School in Canterbury, one of the oldest schools in England, nestled under the shadow of Canterbury Cathedral. While walking one day through the cloisters, dressed in the uniform of a wing collar, black jacket, and boater hat, I met a Hare Krishna monk sitting just a few feet from the wall of the Cathedral. "*Hare Krishna, Hare Krishna, Krishna Krishna, Hare Hare,*" he was chanting. I was fascinated. I waited patiently till he was finished, and then shyly approached him. "Excuse me, sir, do you speak any English?" I timidly asked the Indian-looking holy man. "Yeah mate, sit down 'ere. I'll tell yer ol abadit: Krishna ... reincarnation ... enlightenment." My monk was a cockney from the East End of London.

I was overjoyed. Everything he said made perfect sense. The real purpose of life was spiritual liberation. That night I called my mother from the red phone box just outside the school walls. "Great news, Mummy," I said. "I've found my real calling in life. I'm going to become a Hare Krishna!" She knew something about them, because they had been chanting up and down Oxford Street in London, to everyone's dismay. My mother promptly threatened to commit suicide, which was her default setting when faced with unwelcome news. We had to forge a quick compromise. Instead I would learn Transcendental Meditation.

Various flavors of spiritual seeking became a central part of my life for the next twenty years. I meditated, I went on long retreats, I traveled many times to India. I learned yoga, and mudras, I changed my diet, I wore beads. I adopted an oriental name. But there was still the feeling of something missing. Making your life about Nirvana, "snuffing out the candle," dedicated to emptiness, also felt incomplete. I noticed that most of the spiritually oriented people I knew – more advanced than me – were still waiting for the carrot of Enlightenment, dangled at the end of the stick. Everyone was on a path; no one had arrived. Again, I did not feel completely at home in the spiritual crowd.

Spirituality is often about leaving behind the personal, bypassing your humanity, but it can also put us in touch with the shadow. I realized that I was carrying wounds from childhood, and that I was unconsciously causing both myself and other people unnecessary pain. This caused me to align with yet another subculture: psychotherapy and the world of "working on yourself." Have you ever seen those magazines that you sometimes find in coffee shops? In the Bay Area it is called *Common Ground*, but you see them everywhere. They usually have a couple of articles, but then they also have seemingly endless advertisements for Rolfing, chakra balancing, past life regression, dolphin channeling, you name it. Over time I did just about every one of the strange woo-woo things advertised in those magazines. If it is available as a way to heal yourself, or fix yourself, or improve yourself, I have probably done it. But in just the same way, after years and years of diligent attempts at self-improvement,

I also came to feel that there had to be something more. While it was invaluably important to self-reflect, for me this also became another endless hamster wheel.

Finally, in my late twenties, I realized that I had spent most of my life up to that point meditating and introspecting. I also needed to get my sh*t together, and make some money. So I got familiar with another subculture: with the people who love to get things done. Be productive, manifest, create abundance, activate the Law of Attraction, and be healthy, wealthy, and influential. It was actually not so difficult. In 1987 I founded a school in Seattle to train psychotherapists how to integrate hypnotherapy into their practices. I trained more than 300 people in three years. I also bought a house that doubled in value, so for $12.5K down, it yielded about $150K when I sold it. In three years I had accumulated enough to stop working, if I could live simply. Making money and being "successful" also quickly became an empty goal. As my clients made very obvious, winning at the material game did not lead to any kind of reliable happiness.

Throughout all these different phases, I have always also had a strong sense of political and social activism. I'll easily donate my voice, and my time, and my dollars to environmental causes, advocating for women's rights, indigenous people, and many other worthy pursuits. Important as all those things are, activism also left me questioning: how much of a difference can I really expect to make? Even if we do save some trees, or enact new legislation, is that going to allow me to feel that I've led my brief life intelligently?

In fact I have discovered that all of these things – intellectual and artistic creativity, spiritual practice, self-reflection, productivity, and social and political action – are all important components of a brilliant life. But none of them on its own was the central key.

My lifelong exploration of what it truly takes to live a life of no regret is what follows in these pages.

CHAPTER TWO
THE MAGIC SWITCH

Why are you reading this book? What do you hope to gain from it? This book probably loosely falls into the category of "self-improvement," or "self-help." Have you read other books that also fall under this umbrella? Have you downloaded podcasts, watched videos, taken online courses, or even attended live seminars? The *Small Business Chronicle* writes: "The self-improvement industry is an umbrella that encompasses all aspects of self-improvement — how to build self-esteem, lose weight, get rich, meet the love of your life, become successful and be physically fit. All of this information comes in diverse media — books, seminars, CDs, DVDs, webinars, seminars and online courses. Self-help is big business, and the industry will continue to grow." With revenue of $10.8 billion a year, self-improvement activities are forecast to continue growing at a rate of 6% per year.

But why do we do all this? Why do we put so much time and energy into trying to improve ourselves in some way? As far as we know, out of the 8.3 million species on this planet, we are the only ones who preoccupy themselves in this way. My cat, Angel, is seventeen years old. We have lived together her whole life. She lies in the sun, she eats her food, she takes lots of naps, and occasionally she climbs trees. She does all the things cats do. We have never seen any evidence that Angel is spending time pondering, "*I know I could be a better cat. I know I could excel. I know that if I really go for it, I have greater cat potential.*" I don't think that fleas attend motivational seminars to get pumped up to suck more blood, or that penguins seek for greater name recognition among their peers.

We have this preoccupation with improving ourselves because of the development of the pre-frontal cortex, which gives us a dynamic tension between cognitive awareness of two opposing things. On the one hand, we have the capacity to summarize and evaluate our present condition. *Well, I'm in my forties, I'm putting on a little extra weight around the middle. I know I don't exercise enough, and my diet could be better. My marriage is okay, -ish, but I know we could have more sex and have more fun. I do my best as a parent, but I don't know if the kids can really feel how much I love them.* At the same time, all of us have an intuitive sense of our potential: how we could be, and how life could be, with a little more focus and better habits. *I know that a few trips to the gym each week would take the weight off, and the trainer explained to me how I could improve my diet. I read this book about relationship by John Gray, and now I feel inspired. It's never too late to rekindle romance.* These two things together — the capacity to evaluate how things are, alongside the awareness of how things could be — creates the dynamic tension. Just like there is energy between two poles of a magnet, or between two electric cables, so this dynamic tension that exists in all of us provokes a force called "human evolution."

This intuition we all share of our potential creates something like an itch. It is a longing for something which your mind cannot quite articulate, but your heart will not let you forget. It is as though you are homesick, but you can't remember where you live. From having coached people for so long, as well as having trained so many coaches, I have discovered that we all have a sense of one pivotal decision we could each make that would transform everything else. We have an instinct of a magic switch, which when activated will illuminate all the lights on the Christmas tree, all at once. The desire to find this magic switch, as well as the instinct that it exists, is more or less universal.

Because we cannot quite pin down exactly what it is we are longing for, we also do not know the fastest path to get there. We come to rely upon outside sources to tell us where we are going, and what we need to do to advance. Hence the self-improvement industry. We read books, we hire consultants and coaches, we go to seminars, we listen to podcasts, all the time in search of the magic switch. But what makes all this confusing and sometimes frustrating is that everybody has a different suggestion about what that magic switch is, and what we should do to activate it.

It is really, really, important for us to have this conversation together, you and I, before we go any further. There is no benefit to running with great determination down a path which is going in the wrong direction. So let's review some of the most popular assumptions about what it will take to satisfy this longing for true fulfillment.

Very popular back in the 1980s and 1990s was the assumption that money can buy you everything. The market was flooded with books about success. The good life required a Ferrari, a yacht, a mansion, and designer jewelry. We have all of us lingered sometimes at the checkout line at the supermarket, staring at glossy magazine covers that display the lives of the rich and famous.

Another very popular mythology, deeply embedded in the self-improvement industry, is the Holy Grail quest to find your soulmate. The idea is that somewhere out there, in the confusing and overwhelming sea of humanity, there is one perfect person for you. The only reason you feel miserable, and lonely, and terrible about yourself, is because you have not yet found this one person who knows how to love you in the way that you want to be loved, so that you can finally be happy.

Yet another mythology is the quest for perfect health, longevity, and physical beauty. The Internet is overflowing with websites that will tell you which of the latest supplements to take, not only to live in perfect health, but also to feed your brain in such a way that you are at peak performance all the time. Many of these supplements are sold through multilevel marketing schemes, so they have proven quite effective boosts for the bank balance of the distributors.

We could go on and on. Every year thousands of books and online courses are published offering the latest and greatest ultimate key to real and lasting happiness. The big kahuna of pivotal life-changing interventions is spirituality, and the quest for enlightenment. This was the particular drug that had me hooked for a good part of my adult life. It is based on the idea that you are "trapped in your ego," and if you just meditate enough/retreat enough/sit with the teacher enough/get mindful enough, you will finally reach the giddy peaks of Nirvana, and then you can relax and be blissful and free... all the time.

Once we step into any of these mythologies, we very quickly lose the ability to fact-check how well they work. I have a friend who got involved in multilevel marketing some nutritional supplements a few years ago. My buddy has never been a very healthy guy, a bit of a couch potato. He never cared much about what he ate, and never did any exercise. But once he got hooked up with his multilevel marketing vitamins, and the smell of the big bucks, all he talked about was his health. He said he felt so alive now, had so much energy, that his sex drive was through the roof, that his hair had started to grow back. But after some months he didn't enroll as many people as he had hoped. Soon after, he stopped taking the supplements. "What about all the health benefits you were experiencing?" I asked him. He shrugged, looked a little embarrassed, and took another swig from his can of beer before reaching for the Doritos.

We all hypnotize ourselves with our own mythologies about what works, and then these "alternative facts" supersede any interest in reality. So let's go back now over some of the popular mythologies of the self-improvement industry, and do a little fact-checking together.

By now, there has been a fantastic amount of research done on the relationship between well-being and money. Several sociology studies have now demonstrated that money and well-being relate to each other on something like a bell curve. It means that if you're making $25,000 a year, and your income increases to $30,000, your well-being does increase. This continues to be true up to the top of the bell curve. In America this is about $75,000 a year, but less in countries that have nationalized medicine and higher education.

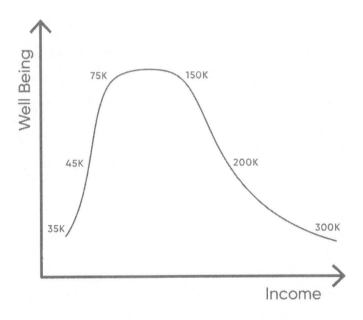

After you reach the top of the curve, increasing your income further makes relatively little difference. But here's the big shocker: above certain income levels, increasing your annual income actually causes your well-being to go down. That means that if you are making $250,000 a year and it goes up to $300,000, the likelihood of drug abuse, divorce, stress related illness, estrangement from your family, and a host of other barriers to well-being actually increases. Who would have guessed?

We could fact-check each and every one of the mythologies of self-improvement. In fact, we need to! What happens when you make relationship with one particular person the center of your well-being? Have you ever done that? Have you seen people do that? You meet someone and you say, "This is it. This is 'the one.' Now we will be happy together forever." You know what happens, don't you? It's called the romance cycle. You go through a few months in a euphoric sex-induced honeymoon... and then cracks appear in the veneer. The other person starts to do things and say things that no longer fit your idea of what will make you happy. Then the adoration changes to resentment, a sense of betrayal, and you can feel just as passionately about wanting to get rid of this person as you did about wanting to stay together forever.

The spirituality mythology also rarely stands up to rigorous examination. The great majority of people who identify themselves as "spiritual" have an idea of a future state of arrival. It is usually projected into an imaginary time in their own future, or onto a teacher whom they do not know personally. Making spirituality the center point of your life can easily become something like a hamster on a wheel. *I'm working hard, I'm working hard, I'm working hard ... but I'm not quite there yet.* The question I always like to ask people who are on a spiritual path is: "How does your spirituality affect your breakfast?" They frown, looking a little confused. "Excuse me?"

"This belief which you have described in a future state of enlightenment, which you are working hard to achieve, how does it affect enjoying your breakfast? Does it help you to enjoy the taste of the strawberries on the pancake?"

It is an important question for us to ask ourselves. Holding on to any idea of not yet being complete, or not yet being completely healed, or not yet having met "the one," or not yet being enlightened, but still striving for something better in the future: how does it affect your ability to enjoy a simple kiss? Or the sunlight pouring through the trees?

All of these mythologies prove themselves to be somewhat unstable. We create the idea of an insufficient, inadequate, unsatisfactory present moment relative to something that could be better. We work hard to get there, at the same time blinding ourselves to whether we have any proof that it will work for us, or that it has really worked for anyone else.

At this point, we might be feeling quite despondent, and ready to give up in a Jean-Paul Sartre-style malaise, doomed to mediocrity and repeating and consuming the things we have been told to. But hold your horses, people, because the truth is that there *are* lots of extremely fulfilled, happy people in the world for whom just about everything *is* working. At the risk of sounding a little self-aggrandizing, I would count myself among them... and my wife... and most of my friends for that matter. There are lots and lots of people alive today for whom everything has fallen into place. Relationships are loving, health is balanced, money flows in and out quite well but is not an obsession, and spiritual practice and experience has found its role in our lives, but is not the centerpiece.

We have all of us had at least moments in our lives where we feel completely fulfilled. We have all of us met people who were glowing with well-being. If we talk about a "fulfilled" person, you understand what I mean by the word. You recognize it from your own experience. So what is the reliable precursor to a truly well-lived life, to a life of no regret? I have made this question more or less the central inquiry of my life. Over the last two decades I have interviewed hundreds and hundreds of people, sometimes in great depth over many hours, who display an above average level of fulfillment, energy, and meaning in their lives. You can find a list of some of these people in the appendix at the end of this book. I wanted to find out: what is the common denominator that all these people share?

In a moment, I'm going to tell you what that is. But first I'd like to suggest you put this book down for a few minutes and contemplate the question for yourself. If highly fulfilled, energized, motivated, happy people have something in common, what do you think it might be? Please jot down a few notes on your own now, and then we will compare your answer with what all these people have told me.

*****

The research I have conducted was quite conclusive. Of all the hundreds of highly fulfilled people I have interviewed, not all of them were happily married. Some were single, and many were in relationships that have ups and downs. Not all of them were in perfect health. Some were very wealthy, but many were not, and the money didn't really seem to make any difference to the fulfillment. Definitely not everyone practiced meditation, or prayer or yoga. Not all were vegetarian, or vegan, and not everyone hit the gym.

Here are some of the answers which I have heard over the years to the question "What is the most important element to living a life of deep fulfillment, energy, and meaning?"

Having a sense of mission. Being on fire.

Living your passion.

Knowing what I'm here to do, and doing it every day.

Living authentically.

Surrendering to something bigger than myself.

Feeling taken over by a creative force which I can either resist — and create suffering — or flow with.

Feeling so excited by what I have to offer that I stop thinking about myself.

Feeling taken over by something greater than self-preoccupation.

I call this "brilliance." It means the irreversible, deep, abiding recognition that you are not actually here on planet Earth to get something for yourself at all. You are not here primarily to accumulate money, to get love, or sex, or pleasure, or fame, or power. The acquisitive relationship to life is, in fact, one big misunderstanding. You are actually here to make a contribution that flows uniquely through you. When you discover that gift, and make it central to your life, you become naturally brilliant and everything else falls into place.

Imagine that planet Earth is one enormous potluck gathering. Everyone has been allocated a dish to bring, and if each of us complies and shows up with our offering, it will create the ultimate all-time greatest celebration that could possibly be.

But here's the rub. Although I have no doubt left in me whatsoever by now that everyone has a unique, sparkling, extraordinary gift to share, very few people manage to create a life in which that gift can truly shine. A few people, like Albert Einstein, and Steve Jobs, and the singer Maggie Rogers (who I just discovered...) knock it right out of the ballpark and amaze us all. But many people just live lives of quiet repetition and imitation. Why?

It has been widely assumed that the kind of brilliance we are talking about is the result of genetic accident or just pure luck. A few people are destined to make a huge difference, and the rest of us are left to stand on the sidelines and politely applaud. I beg to disagree. I have spent the last thirty years coaching people and training coaches in how to become radically brilliant and to support others to do the same. I have learned a thing or two along the way. I have learned that there are certain very specific components which need to coexist in order for life to light up and become brilliant. Each and every one of these components can be activated through conscious and deliberate practice.

Every great book, every new movie, every album, every new App, every new invention and innovation has to begin somewhere with an event in consciousness — a thought — inside of someone's mind. Let's begin there.

CHAPTER THREE
NOT ALL THOUGHTS ARE CREATED EQUAL

Everything great and inspiring and true, everything which has forwarded the evolution of humanity, had to begin with an event in consciousness — a thought. The Eiffel Tower, Beethoven's 9th Symphony, the iPhone... everything we can reference as great in any dimension had to be preceded by an event in someone's mind.

Everyone can recognize a picture of the Eiffel Tower. It was an engineering marvel at the time, unprecedented in architecture and design. It has been duplicated and copied countless times since. But the original in Paris was not a copy of anything: it was an example of Radical Brilliance. Of course, before work could begin on the tower, it was necessary to have detailed engineering plans. Those plans were drawn up by Gustave Eiffel and his colleagues. Prior to the detailed plans, Monsieur Eiffel created rough sketches in his notebook. Prior to those sketches, he was able to visualize — to imagine — the tower in his mind. Because this was not a copy of anything else, his visualization came not from imitation, but from within himself.

Exactly the same is true of Beethoven's 9th Symphony, which he composed when he was deaf. Almost everyone can recognize the refrain. In just the same way: before an orchestra could play the music, it was written as a score. Before the notes were written onto the paper in Vienna in 1823, the Maestro had to hear the refrain in his mind. But he was not remembering something he had heard before. It was an event in consciousness that had no precedent.

Not every event in consciousness creates the Eiffel Tower, or a great symphony, or the icon-based system on the Macintosh computer. Research done at the Laboratory for Neuro-Imaging at the University of Southern California estimates that we each have approximately 48 thoughts per minute. That's about 2880 thoughts per hour — 70,000 thoughts a day — if we assume, as they do, that these events in consciousness continue in some way during sleep. With 7 billion people on the planet, it means that 483,840 billion thoughts are being generated every day. 176,601 trillion events in human consciousness happen every year. How many of those thoughts would you imagine turn into radically brilliant, life-changing ideas? How many become great music, cutting-edge technology, great art or architecture? How many of those events in consciousness eradicate suffering or contribute to our shared evolution? Obviously, the answer is very, very few. When I have asked participants in seminars this question, people guess that it must be much less than .0001%, or one in a million. Even that is probably hopelessly optimistic. Based on that wild guess, it means that 99.9999% of the thoughts that pass through our minds are actually not original, life-changing, or brilliant.

I want to suggest to you now that there are in fact two kinds of thought. They look very much the same on the surface, in the sense that both kinds of thought could turn into speech, and writing, and action, and visible material results. But the source of each kind of thought is very different.

One kind of thought, infinitely the most common, we could call "recycled thought." These are thoughts that are imitative, repeated from something which has been heard, or read, and then remembered. For example, during the day, you open up Facebook on your phone and casually scroll through your timeline. You find one of those inspiring quotes: "Before you complain about anything, remember all the blessings in your life." This kind of statement is often superimposed upon a sunset, or a very, very wrinkly old person's hand holding a baby's hand, or a gentleman in a business suit inexplicably jumping off a rock in the desert with his arms outstretched. Later that day, your partner returns home. "How was your day?" you ask. "Terrible," your partner replies. "I got stuck in traffic this morning on the way to work. I was late for a meeting, and when I got there everyone stared at me. I didn't get my report in on time and my boss told me my job is on the line. I've had a terrible headache, back pain, and then on the way home I got a flat tire." Just at that moment, you remember the quote you read on Facebook that inspired you so much earlier in the day. With a smile on your face you say to your partner, "Well, honey, before you complain, remember all the blessings in your life." But now this is not a fresh, alive response to life. It is repackaged, secondhand, borrowed. It was repeated from something you heard before. It is recycled brilliance, and may not necessarily lift your partner's mood at all.

Most thoughts are like that: repetition of something we have heard before. Every great world religion is composed of the recycled thoughts and statements of its founder. Most education (mercifully, not all) is dedicated to passing on recycled thoughts. So is most philosophy, the majority of art, the way people do business, and the way they create technology. The way we have relationships, the way we parent our children, the way we spend money, and the ways we earn money are all based on accepting and acting on recycled thoughts: beliefs we adopt from someone else and then obediently regurgitate into a predictable life.

At one point, every recycled thought was original, fresh, new, and brilliant. There had to be a time when it was thought for the first time, without a precedent. For example, if you grew up with Christianity as the religion in your family, you probably often heard the phrase "Consider the lilies how they grow: they toil not, they spin not; and yet I say unto you, that Solomon in all his glory was not arrayed like one of these." These words are from the Sermon on the Mount. How many times do you think they have been repeated and quoted since the King James Bible was printed in 1611? There was a day, back in about 30 A.D., when Jesus was sitting on a hillside with his disciples. Then, quite out of the blue, he started speaking.

"Blessed are the poor in spirit, for theirs is the Kingdom of Heaven."

"I like it, Josh," replied Simon. "Keep going..."

Then Jesus threw in another jewel, about mourning.

"Excellent!" said Andrew.

"Awesome!" said James.

"Blessed are the meek," Jesus went on, feeling encouraged. Now John and Philip perked up too. "Yeah. It's good. Don't stop."

"For they shall inherit the earth."

"All right!!" they chimed in together.

Jesus continued to challenge the conventional way we think of meekness, mercy, and purity of heart, while all twelve disciples and other friends became increasingly and loudly enthusiastic. So you can imagine, when Jesus got to the bit about the lilies, the crowd went wild. Hollering, clapping, and whistling. This must have been a completely, incomparably, brilliant moment. Probably breathtaking. But once you have heard it repeated hundreds of thousands of times, it gets to be a little dusty. The very repetition kills the brilliance. In just the same way, at the end of his life, Buddha said to his friend and student, Ananda, "Be a light unto yourself." You might imagine Ananda feeling completely transformed by those words in that moment. But once the phrase is recycled enough times, the power is lost.

Obviously, not all thought is repetition, because there is a moment when an event in consciousness happens for the first time, without any precedent. When a thought is not repeated, or recycled, where did it come from? When I have taught this in Radical Brilliance seminars, we use a diagram to make things clear. You could imagine recycled thoughts as being horizontal, like small bubbles floating on the surface of the pond. One thought causes another, which causes another, which causes another. Each thought is precipitated by a previous thought.

Original thought does not originate on the surface of the pond, but from the depth. We could call it a vertical thought. It starts at the bottom of the pond and bubbles its way up to the surface. Thoughts which originate in this way begin as very, very subtle and fine impulses, but as they bubble up to the surface, they become more vivid and pronounced.

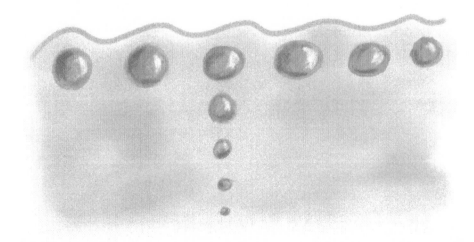

Perception and Conception

Once we begin to accept the difference between these two kinds of thought, we might begin to wonder why anyone would choose to imitate and repeat, when we all also have the possibility to innovate. Barnet Bain is a film producer, director, and the author of *The Book of Doing and Being*. He teaches a class on *Artistry and Personal Spirituality* at Columbia. Barnet feels that we are, all of us, inherently capable of innovation. He told me, "The ability to develop oneself so that we can perceive and conceive, so that we can develop our creativity, is innate in all of us: it is baked into what it is to be a human being. Because of the way we are raised and conditioned, particularly early in life, we become encoded with other people's thoughts and feelings, choices and patterns and beliefs, with other people's music and art, and pronouncements as to what creativity is. As a consequence, our vast relationship to perception and conception gets shoehorned into a very tiny outlook that is called 'creative,' a pursuit that is reserved only for certain kinds of people. We are led to believe that creativity is a limited range of expression, primarily in the seven fine arts.

"But creativity is consciousness's work: there is no act or thought, or feeling, or choice, or decision, or attitude that is an uncreative act. By virtue of how we are patterned, we simply silo ourselves off from truly innovative explorations. We rush to be 'the first in line to be second', and to mimic others' art. We limit both our perceiving and conceiving to the way we have seen it done around us.

"It is a giant leap of consciousness to even understand that what we take for free will and possibility is actually the product of conditioning of inputs from outside the self. Only then we can begin to explore real perception, real conception, and to ask, 'What can I conceive of beyond my patterned beliefs, my patterned systems, my conditioned ideas, beyond what has already been given to me by others?'"

WHERE DO THE BUBBLES COME FROM?

Where does thought originate from when it has no precedent in another thought? If we can penetrate together into this question, we will have a much clearer understanding of the mechanics of Radical Brilliance.

I remember, when I was about seven years old I won a prize at school for reading poetry. I still have that book which I won on my shelf today. My mother was so proud of me after the prize-giving ceremony that she took me out to *Dionysus*, our local Greek restaurant, to have a baklava pastry and a Coca-Cola. Back in the early 1960s, Coca-Cola was not such a common thing in England. It was more American, and I had never had one before. This was a big treat. My mother and I were sitting at a glass table with no tablecloth. The waiter brought the glass of Coca-Cola and placed it on the table. I can still remember looking at my glass, and noticing the bubbles rising up and bursting on the surface. They started off at the bottom of the glass, very small, and became bigger as they rose up. I didn't like the drink very much. In fact, I got sick that night and I've never drunk a Coca-Cola since! But I was fascinated with where those bubbles were coming from. I looked underneath the glass table. There was nothing there, there was no way for the bubbles to get into the glass from under the table. Where did the bubbles come from?

Inquiring into the origin of an original brilliant life-changing thought is very similar. On the surface, there are words and images and music and new inventions bursting into life. Below the surface, there are thoughts — events in consciousness — quite well-formed. Deeper down, there are finer, more subtle thoughts. Deeper still are just the finest impulses, hardly detectable. And deeper than that is the source from which those impulses are arising. Just like my Coca-Cola at Dionysus restaurant, the source of those finest impulses remains mysterious and fascinating. If we have a way to become more conscious and sensitive to what is happening at these finest levels of activity, we become more masterful at harnessing the power of authentic creativity at its source. We have a deeper understanding of, and greater access to, the origin of Radical Brilliance.

EVERYTHING IS EVERYWHERE

There is a useful parallel in physics. The first kind of thought we have described here—recycled imitative thought—is somewhat analogous to Isaac Newton's definition of a predictable universe. Newton was sitting under a tree, when he saw an apple hit the ground. He realized that there was something, an invisible force, which caused the apple to fall. His understanding was the basis of physical predictability. If you know the weight of the apple, the wind resistance, the height of the apple from the ground, you can predict with some accuracy the impact when the apple hits the ground. In just the same way, when there is a car accident, with damage to each of the cars, an insurance investigator will inspect the vehicles. You could say, "I was going very slowly, less than 30 miles an hour." But the investigator could say to you, "Based upon the degree to which the metal is bent, we can calculate that the car was going at 67 mph." Busted. We have gotten better and better at this, with the development of post-Newtonian science. We expect the universe to behave in a predictable way, and the universe mostly cooperates.

Most of the time, our own thoughts and the thoughts of everyone we know behave in this same way. Once you get to know someone pretty well, you can anticipate more or less how they will react and what they are going to say next, because our thoughts also behave in predictable ways. You can anticipate that one thought will create another thought, and that a certain stimulus will create a certain reaction. That is the science of predictability which Isaac Newton initiated.

During the last eighty years we have seen the development of a different kind of physics: quantum physics. It deals with the tiniest building blocks of matter: the subatomic particles that make up atoms, and then molecules, and then all the stuff with which we are familiar. Subatomic particles do not behave in the same way as the more physical world we are used to predicting. Under the Alps, in a suburb of Geneva in Switzerland, CERN, the European Organization for Nuclear Research, hosts the Large Hadron Collider (LHC), the largest particle accelerator in the world. It consists of a 27-kilometer ring of superconducting magnets with a number of accelerating structures to boost the energy of the particles along the way. In one Collider experiment, they shot a subatomic particle through a vacuum state down the particle accelerator. In the middle of this long tunnel was a lead wall, with two slits in it. You would imagine that the subatomic particle fired from one end of the tunnel would need to pass through one or the other of these two slits, before arriving at its destination at the other end. But in fact, their measurements (which have been duplicated many times since) indicated that the particle actually passed through both slits simultaneously. This means that in the middle of the tunnel it was behaving as a wave, although it behaved as a particle at its origin and at its destination. Werner Heisenberg, a German physicist, predicted these findings all the way back in the 1930s in his "uncertainty principle."

Subatomic physics shows us that the finest elements which make up physical things are both particles and waves at the same time. This means that a subatomic particle has a location in time and space when it needs to be measured, but is actually a wave located everywhere at the same time. Heisenberg predicted that the particulate appearance was caused in part by the need of a scientist to measure it. Without this need for a location in time and space, things become wavelike. This is known as the "observer effect."

Bruno Sciolla is one of our certified awakening coaches. He is also an associate professor at Lyon University in France, teaching quantum physics. After one of our training courses in Germany, Bruno and I both stayed on at the seminar center after the course was finished. We met in the sauna, and talked about quantum physics for close to five hours. (We were very, very wrinkled by the end.) I asked Bruno what had evolved in the understanding of the particle/wave nature of subatomic particles since Heisenberg's principle was first expressed in the 1930s. Bruno's response was, "We used to think that this wavelike nature was only true of subatomic particles. Now we understand that it's true of absolutely everything. All electrons, all protons and quarks and gluons, they all behave as particles when we try to measure them, but they are all wavelike otherwise. This means that actually everything is everywhere and everything exists at all times. Things only become solid with a location in time and space because of our needs to see them that way."

Newtonian physics and quantum physics both explore exactly the same physical world. One chooses to see things as predictable and solid, with a fixed location in time and space. The other recognizes that everything is emerging out of a unified field, flickering in its appearance of solidity, and then dissolving back again into the unified field. It is exactly the same physical universe, just looked at in two different ways.

How does this apply to our model of horizontal and vertical thoughts? Horizontal thoughts behave in a Newtonian way. They are predictable and repeating, largely because our habits of familiar perception need them to be that way. Vertical thoughts appear out of nowhere as the finest impulses, where previously there was nothing, just a unified field of emptiness, or formlessness. Vertical thoughts appear without anything previously causing them. They are "self-originating." They appear and bubble to the surface as a thought that has never been thought before. They become speech that has never been spoken before. They become actions that have never been taken before. They become songs that have never been sung before. They are the seeds of Radical Brilliance.

We can learn, through practice, to train ourselves to become more sensitive to these subtle events in consciousness which are the seeds of original brilliance. Just as quantum physics has evolved out of Newtonian physics, all that is needed to become Radically Brilliant is a curiosity and a willingness to pay attention to the finest building blocks of consciousness.

In the next chapter, we will understand how this kind of vigilance can be integrated into a way of life that makes brilliance not just a random accident, but the very fabric of why we are alive. Later we will learn very practical tools to harness the immense power at the finest levels of mental activity.

CHAPTER FOUR

THE BRILLIANCE CYCLE

We are going to go deeper now, by investigating the mechanisms through which we can become more comfortable with accessing original thought as it arises, as a fresh impulse out of pure consciousness.

This is not just a question of "sit down and do this technique for ten minutes a day." Radical Brilliance includes integrated mechanisms that involve not only a set of different practices for different phases, but also a deep understanding about why our brilliance gets blocked, and how we can restore it. Many of the habits we have inherited from religious and philosophical traditions and from our political, social, and educational systems actually interfere, in one way or another, with the free flow of original creative expression.

I have been coaching people to discover and express their "unique gift" for more than thirty years. During this time I have learned that the mechanism that allows for easy and repeating access to original thought is not one thing: it is a cycle that needs to be continuously repeated.

To explain this cycle, I am going to use the analogy of a clock face, which has 12 o'clock at the top, 3 o'clock on the right, 6 o'clock at the bottom, and 9 o'clock on the left. Obviously, this analogy conveniently assumes that there are an infinite number of points in between, so we can recognize a gradual and continuous shifting between each pole.

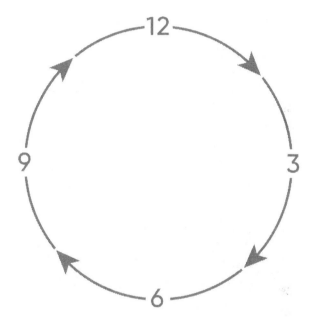

If we wanted to understand what makes for good human life, we would not say that well-being is only about breakfast. For sure, it is important to eat a good breakfast. But there are other elements needed as well, to be happy and healthy and successful. We would not say that a good human life is only about going to the bathroom. For sure, if you stopped going to the bathroom completely, you would quickly have serious health problems. But there is more to life than just the bathroom. A good human life involves friendship as well as solitude, vigorous exercise as well as sleep, intense focus as well as time to relax and rejuvenate. Living well is not about accentuating one thing, but about balance and the integration of opposites. A good human life is a cycle, where every phase is equally important. If you miss out on sleep, then you will also not fully enjoy your waking hours. If you are not actively engaged when awake, you will probably not sleep very well.

In the same way, the components that together make up the ability to access and express original creative thought involve every aspect of the cycle, not just one thing. As with waking and sleeping, we will discover that the elements in the Brilliance Cycle appear to be in opposition to each other, and to have completely conflicting values.

Now we will go through the different phases of the cycle and explain the major characteristics of each one.

12 O'CLOCK: AWAKENING

We will start at the top: at 12 o'clock. We talked about "Awakening" in the previous chapter: the ability to access and recognize "pure consciousness," the nature of awareness itself when it is not fixated on any external object. The most significant piece of our discussion was the inquiry about where the bubbles originate from at the bottom of the Coca-Cola glass. When a thought is not precipitated by a previously held thought, or belief, or statement, where does it come from?

Either you remain stuck in repeating recycled thoughts, regurgitated from what you have heard before, one giving rise to the other at the surface of the pond, or you learn to become familiar with the greater depths. You learn how to hover with attention at that place where silence and the first tremors of thought meet.

12 o'clock is that point in the cycle of being awake to this unmanifest pure consciousness. We can call it anything we want; it has been referred to by many names. It has been called "true nature," "pure consciousness," "source." In fact, perhaps the most significant characteristic of this phase of the cycle is that it is beyond words. It has no distinguishing characteristics at all. But for the sake of nomenclature we will call it "awakening."

If we want to understand this phase of the cycle, we have to turn to, and rely upon, mystical traditions, for this is where all the experiential research has been done. A moment of awakening is a moment where the attention shifts from the activity of thought and reactive feeling (and therefore also time, because we only experience future and past in thought) to that which is aware of thought. That which is aware of movement is still. That which is aware of noise is silent. That which is aware of boundaries and limitations is in itself boundary-less, infinite.

This recognition of the nature of consciousness itself, of the nature of awareness, has been accessed in every mystical tradition across all different cultures, all different geographical locations, and all different time periods. Every religious tradition finds its birth in this recognition of this "awakening."

Awakening Now is Not a Path to Enlightenment

There is a huge difference between the idea of being on a path— a journey toward an imagined future state of being awake — and turning the attention to that which is already awake in this moment now. Understandings derived from being on a path with a future goal are fundamentally different from those which come from a curiosity, here in this moment, about that which is already experiencing this very moment.

These are two totally different preoccupations, which easily get confused. What we are talking about as a moment of awakening is actually only possible when you have abandoned the preoccupation with a future state of "enlightenment." Ironically, that expectation becomes the greatest impediment to noticing what is already true in this moment. Our attention gets kidnapped by a preoccupation with a future state, or the imagined state of a revered other, and only a trickle of attention remains curious about the actuality of what is real now.

The recognition of your "true nature" can be thought of as a state of meditation. The true meaning of meditation comes from the Sanskrit word "*dhyana,*" which literally translates as "no mind," and refers to a state of consciousness where there is alert wakefulness without attention paid to thoughts which come and go. It shifts the attention from mental activity to the stillness in which that mental activity is occurring, like shifting the attention from the waves on the surface of the ocean to the wetness of the ocean itself.

This pure awareness is devoid of any distinguishing qualities that can be measured in time and space. It is neither male nor female, it has no age, it has no sound or vibration to it, no nationality, no belief system, and no preference. It is just aware.

Resting in pure awareness is absolutely irrelevant to the mental and emotional mechanisms that usually run our lives, which seek out pleasure (more stuff, more power, more security, more intimacy, more sexual or emotional stimulation, more of just about anything, stimulating the secretion of dopamine and noradrenaline in the brain) and which seek to avoid pain (less insecurity, less weakness, less loneliness, less unwanted physical and emotional experience, which stimulates a variety of pain-associated neuropeptides in the brain).

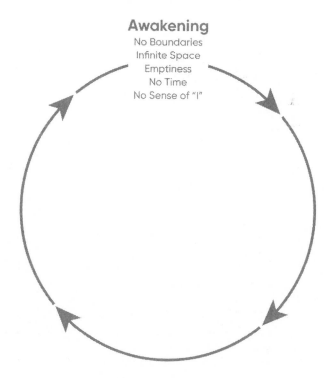

Awakening
No Boundaries
Infinite Space
Emptiness
No Time
No Sense of "I"

As the diagram illustrates, the 12 o'clock phase in the cycle has very specific attributes:

Flat

Silent

Still

Empty

No sense of "I"

No time

Effortless

Infinite

A conceptual description of a good Irish Whiskey could never ever be a substitute for a drop on the tongue: a real taste. So if these words left you with a nod and a wink and a "know what you mean," then we are on the same page. If you'd like a wee drop of Jameson's on your tongue, be my guest and join me here: radicalbrilliance.com/taste.

3 O'CLOCK: CREATIVE FLOW

Three o'clock is the phase of the cycle defined as "flow." Out of nothingness, out of infinite space and stillness, sprout original impulses that are not the result of premeditated thought and decision. Subjectively, "flow" feels like patiently waiting, and allowing impulses to arise on their own. These fine tremors begin at one second after midnight, and continuously grow in vibration and momentum as they move through the first part of the cycle. They reach a peak of creative frenzy at 3 o'clock.

Just as 12 o'clock was flat, silent, genderless, still and empty, so the first movement from 12 to 3 o'clock has almost limitless energy. Astrophysicists describe the Big Bang as an event where infinite energy arose out of nothing. The entire universe was initiated out of an explosion which occurred in no time and no space and no matter. All of the countless suns that we see in the sky as stars are just small sparks from that original explosion. The original event occurred out of nothing, and within nothing, without any raw materials to work with. This is a big clue as to how original creativity works in us too. The Big Bang is actually occurring within you, every time you hover with attention close to emptiness. Every time the attention enters into formlessness there is the potential of the Big Bang happening again, inside of consciousness, and generating another galaxy of Brilliance.

As well as having maximum energy, 3 o'clock is the most pleasurable phase of the cycle. It is the place of energy, of pleasure, of color, of laughter and of infinite imagination.

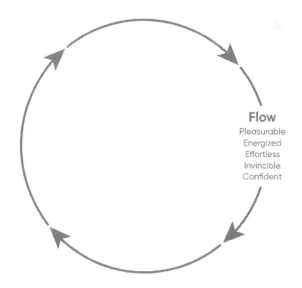

Flow
Pleasurable
Energized
Effortless
Invincible
Confident

Although it has close to infinite energy, it is also experienced as effortless. There is nothing that "you" have to do except relax and get out of the way. Nothing seems impossible. It is all arising on its own. William Blake is one of the most prolific and brilliant poets in the English language. But what remains of his work is only about one tenth of what he actually wrote. *The Collected Works of William Blake* is already several inches thick, but before he died he burned ninety percent of his output. We only have the ten percent that remains because he lived in great poverty and had to sell some of his work to be able to live. His wife Catherine would wake up in the middle of the night and find her husband bent over the table, his hand moving furiously. *The Book of Urizen* was written in this way. It is perfectly alliterated, perfectly rhyming, perfectly metered poetry, and was never edited. It flowed through him automatically; he simply had to surrender and allow it to come. Who wrote it, then? Aha, my point exactly.

When people speak of this phase there is very little sense of taking personal credit. "I didn't do anything, I just stepped out of the way and look what happened." If you wait patiently, it moves through you. One of my greatest teachers in learning how to be with this process has been my wife, Chameli. She travels around the world, teaching women the principles of feminine spiritual practice. She is an innovator in this field. She has been featured in several movies, given a TEDx talk, and is respected by all of her peers as a pioneer. But living close to her, I know that her greatest and most refined skill is actually resting: doing nothing at all. More than anyone I have ever known, she knows how to relax, to be still and wait, and not to push things. Sometimes she says to me, "I know something new is coming, I can feel it, I'm pregnant with it. I don't know what it is, but I know that it will emerge at the right time." Many other people would get impatient or panicky under such circumstances, and want to push the river a little bit. She waits. Finally, sometimes after many months, the time is right, and also without effort she writes a little blog post, or puts something on Facebook and a whole new tsunami of her work is suddenly happening on its own. Chameli knows how to relax and be danced, and how to not interfere with that process. It begins as a tickle. The art is not to scratch too quickly, but to wait and to allow it to grow on its own until it moves and becomes definite enough to turn into visible and audible expression.

In Kashmiri Shaivism they call this "*spanda.*" It is often translated in English as "tremoring." It means the first subtle vibration. First there is nothing — stillness — emptiness, and then there is the very first tremor. It originates, just like the Big Bang, out of nothing at all. This moment of original impulse has been described and substantiated plenty in ancient Tantric texts, like the *Spandakarika*. Our job here is to substantiate it from our own experience.

The tiniest tremor is infinitely ecstatic and blissful. The first tremor has the most energy you can imagine. Infinite energy. Most people get a taste of it in moments of sexual arousal. Imagine that feeling in your genitals taking over every cell of your body, your mind, and your emotions. That's *spanda*. The more embodied it gets, the more form it has, the less energy it has. A nuclear explosion is the collision of two subatomic particles. It is a collision happening at the most sub-microscopic level. An event infinitely small — too small to see — can blow up a city. In that tiniest meeting there is infinite energy, enough to create a bomb. We do not want to blow up any cities here, but we are interested in creating explosions of original authentic creativity. The tiniest level of matter creates the most energy. That is what is happening as we move from 12 to 3.

6 O'CLOCK: PRODUCTIVITY AND ACCOMPLISHMENT

Six o'clock is the opposite of 12. At 12 o'clock was stillness; at 6 o'clock is activity. At 12 o'clock there was no sense of a separate "I," there is no sense of anybody there. At 6 o'clock there is doing— there is a sense of responsibility. At 12 o'clock there is no time, at 6 o'clock there are deadlines and schedules and pressure. At 12 o'clock there are no boundaries, at 6 o'clock there are limits, contracts, rules to follow and restrictions to live within. At 12 o'clock there is oneness, at 6 o'clock there is the possibility of collaboration, which requires negotiation, agreements and contracts, and hence potential separation and conflict. Twelve o'clock is formless. Six o'clock is where everything comes fully into form.

At 12 there was no you. At 6 you are a man or a woman with a human body.

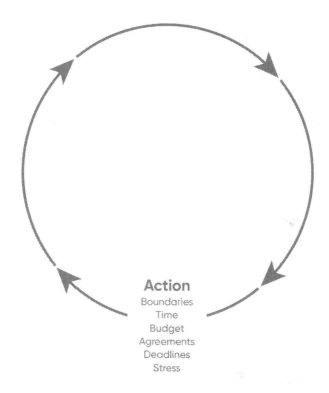

Action
Boundaries
Time
Budget
Agreements
Deadlines
Stress

Now we start to understand the cycle. There is silence, then there is the tiniest tremor, an almost inaudible melody, the melody becomes more and more pronounced, until at 3 o'clock it is fully flowing: you are playing the melody, the melody is fully actualized. Six o'clock is where you make the CD. You book the studio, you set the budget, you hire the session musicians, you have a contract with a music label, you have a producer, you are working with time and deadlines, you are making something happen. Six o'clock involves agreements, responsibility, doing what you said you would do, spending the money you said you would spend. Six is where things get done, and is all about boundaries and limits.

At 6 o'clock you come to discover why you are alive: you find the fulfillment of your sense of purpose and mission. In those moments when you navigate all the curve balls which life inevitably throws you, when you manage to keep all the plates spinning and balanced at the same time, you will experience, at least in snapshots, a deep sense of achievement, accomplishment, and success. Your small, human, and temporary life suddenly feels fully worth living.

But if you stay in a world of limits and boundaries, having to show up on time, and leave on time, honor all your agreements and get the job done, what happens? You will experience some degree of stress. You cannot operate at 6 o'clock without a well-formed sense of being a separate person, without adopting a clearly defined "I." If you stay there too long, there are going to be various degrees of stress. If you remain at 6 o'clock day after day after day, week after week after week, you will ultimately have a burnout. Even eight hours a day causes stress to accumulate.

9 O'CLOCK: LETTING GO AND DISSOLUTION

Nine o'clock is an essential part of the process, and cannot be overlooked. We can call it "Dissolution." Nine o'clock is about the return from contraction in form back toward formlessness. It is a kind of identity death. You cannot go straight from 6 to 12. Nine o'clock is about the dissolving of boundaries. Twelve to 6 was a movement from formlessness to form. Six to 12 is a return from form to formlessness. After being involved in activity, you stop and feel the effect of all those boundaries. If you work hard all week, pushing yourself, and then you stop to relax on a Saturday or Sunday morning, what is your subjective experience? How do you feel? You might say to yourself, "I've been working hard, I'm even going to stay up late and push to get all this done, and then I'm going to enjoy a nice relaxed happy weekend with my partner." So you stay up till two in the morning, you get everything finished, and then you go to sleep, planning on a wonderful honeymoon day when you wake up. What happens? You feel like shit. You had a beautiful day lined up, to go out for breakfast, to go for a nice walk, but instead you have a terrible fight.

As you start to move out of 6, this part of the cycle starts as inherently painful, and unpleasant. Burnout feels horrible, when you have pushed yourself hard enough that you are exhausted. Even if you manage to sleep at night, you wake up in the morning with no energy. Everything feels overwhelming.

But eventually, as you continue to move out of stress and into rejuvenation, the feelings of exhaustion turn into a softening, a deep sigh of relief. Now you discover the true gift of 9: which is a sense of innocence, trust, humility, and relaxation. It is where all our learning happens. It is the part of the cycle where we remember to surrender to a force greater than our small and limited mind.

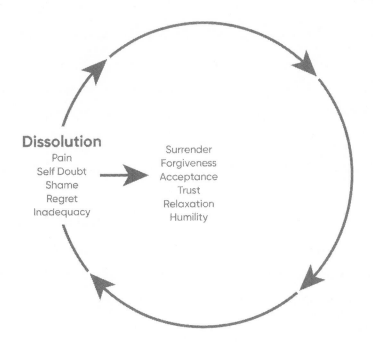

In the next chapter we will discover how we can get stuck at any phase of this cycle, and how we shut down the Brilliance that is natural to us. But first, let me tell you about one of the most significant meetings of my life, which has been very formative in the development of this model.

MEETING LEONARD COHEN

One of the greatest blessings of my life was spending time with Leonard Cohen. In many ways, this book is about him. He was, and is, the poster boy for Radical Brilliance, in all of its phases. In his own way he lived each and every phase of the cycle fully in his own life.

Originally, I wanted to interview Leonard for my 2005 book *The Translucent Revolution*. It had a chapter on "Translucent Creativity," and his 2002 album, *Ten New Songs,* seemed about as perfect an example of what I wanted to talk about as could be found.

Sometimes you get an album that has one very catchy song. You buy the CD, and it's just fine, but there is just one song that you keep playing over and over. But with this album, every single song is *The One*. I don't think there has ever been a better CD produced in the whole of the history of humanity. Even in Renaissance Italy, I don't think they made as good a CD as this!

So I reached out to his manager, Kelly Lynch, to request an interview. We went backwards and forwards for months and months. He was on retreat, then he was busy, then he was writing, then it was Hanukkah. Always a new reason. Then she just stopped responding at all. I was close to giving up when I got an email from a woman called Kateri. She told me that Kelly was no longer representing Leonard, that she was his new assistant, and that she would be delighted to help me arrange an interview. Wow! This was great news. We also went backwards and forwards but this was a very different experience. She would answer my email at two in the morning, then early on a Sunday. She got back to me so quickly sometimes that our emails became like a live conversation. To be honest, the tone of our exchange bordered on the flirtatious. There, I've said it. Not proud, but it's true. I flirted with Leonard Cohen's assistant. Finally, we arranged a date. I flew to LAX, rented a car, and drove to the address I had been given in the Wilshire District. This was a rundown part of town, not an area frequented by the rich and famous. The house in question was a small duplex: one apartment upstairs, and another downstairs.

Leonard greeted me at the door with the wry grin that has always been his unique trademark. He was profuse in his offerings of refreshment, and equally generous in his willingness to answer each and every one of my questions. We sat in his tiny kitchen, where the furniture was well used and quite possibly had been purchased from a garage sale. We sipped tea, and talked about everything for hours.

Finally we came around to the topic of *Ten New Songs*. I explained to him why I had wanted to make this album the central topic of my chapter for the book.

"Leonard, this album is amazing," I said to him.

"Yeah, yeah," he replied, dismissively.

"No, but really, Leonard," I protested, "you've got to admit it, this is like the peak of the peak of the peak."

"Nah." He waved me aside with a gesture and another wry grin.

We went back and forth like this for half an hour. I was militant. I insisted with religious fervor that *Ten New Songs* was something close to scriptural. I compared it to the Upanishads, one of those rare moments when something comes through from the "other side" and lights up our world.

Finally, after about half an hour, Leonard Cohen acquiesced. "I guess you're right," he said. "Something really did come through on that album."

His language is really important. *Something came through.* It was not a doing or a striving. He had hesitated to take personal credit during our conversation because he knew that ownership of the album was not really his to claim. It had come *through* him, not from him.

This is what is happens in the phase between 12 o'clock and 3 o'clock. It is as though the phone rings one day. A voice you do not recognize on the other end asks, "Could you take a message?"

"Okay," you say, fumbling for a pen. "Hold on, what is the message?"

Then the voice dictates the message, and you write it down word for word. It is the most beautiful poem anyone has ever written. Every word perfect. Later your roommate finds what you have written.

"Wow!" you hear. "You are an extraordinary poet! A genius!"

"No, no,"you protest. "I just took a message."

That is how it goes. This is the state of flow. Flow comes naturally, out of spaciousness, when there is nobody there to take any credit.

Leonard went on to describe in vivid detail the process through which that album came to be. He was living at the Mt. Baldy Zen Center, as a monk, getting up at 4:30 in the morning to practice Zazen with the other monks. He lived in a tiny room with almost no possessions, just a small notebook and a pen. In other words, lots and lots of time at 12 o'clock.

He told me that the lyrics and the melody that became that album came to him in tiny tremors and snapshots over a period of two years, spent meditating many hours every day. He just wrote them down, as a dutiful scribe, when they appeared. Twelve to 3 o'clock.

> *I swept the marble chambers,*
> *But you sent me down below.*
> *You kept me from believing*
> *Until you let me know:*
> *That I am not the one who loves*
> *It's love that seizes me.*
> *When hatred with his package comes,*
> *You forbid delivery.*

Later, he told me, he came to the recognition that he was not born to be a monk. He spoke to Kyozan Joshu Sasaki, his teacher (more than 100 years old at the time), and made arrangements to leave the monastery and return to his house in Los Angeles. It was there, tiny notebook in hand, that he began to take those subtle impulses that had come to him in meditation and to turn them into *Ten New Songs*. It took him another two years in the small studio at the back of his home to give those impulses clearly defined sound and rhythm and form. He recorded and rerecorded with relentless precision. Backup singers, technology, software and hardware to purchase and learn, a deal with Sony to sign. All 6 o'clock. And he did it all himself. He was the sound engineer as well as the artist.

Both before and after that album Leonard knew more than his fair share of depression, self-doubt, and despair, as well as the sweet surrender, trust, and humility waiting on the other side. All of his albums are permeated with these feelings.

> *I make my plans*
> *Like I always do*
> *But when I look back*
> *I was there for you.*
> *I walk the streets*
> *Like I used to do*
> *And I freeze with fear*
> *But I'm there for you.*

There is a delightful ending to the story. After we were done with our afternoon of conversation (one of the most important days of my life), he showed me around the tiny apartment. It didn't take very long. He opened the door to his office, where I saw one of those plastic-top tables with folding legs, with many cardboard boxes stacked on top. "Oh," I said. "So this is the office. Where does Kateri work?"

"Kateri …," said Leonard. Another wry grin. "Let me introduce you to Kateri." Remembering the slightly flirtatious tone of my sometimes late-night exchanges with Kateri, I flushed for a moment with embarrassment. Leonard led me into the kitchen. He opened a kitchen cabinet high on the wall, next to the sink. There, on the top shelf was a statue of a young Native American Indian woman. "This is Kateri." I glanced at Leonard for a moment, and then looked at the floor. The realization sank in slowly. I had been flirting late at night with none other than Leonard himself. He chuckled at my discomfort, and then explained to me that Kelly Lynch, his previous manager, had defrauded him while he was in the monastery and taken all his assets, more than $12 million. He had no money available to pay for an assistant. So he invented Kateri, as a front, and sent out emails from her name.

CHAPTER FIVE
GETTING STUCK

Since this map "came to me," I have observed this cycle more and more in myself, as well as encouraged my coaching clients to do the same. I realize that it is a very rare for the cycle to flow freely in a healthy way. In the same way, Chinese medicine claims that energy flows in meridians, but rarely does a Chinese doctor take your pulse and say all the energy is flowing freely in all the meridians. That would be a state of perfect health. The very nature of the body means that some kind of excess or depletion of energy is somewhere in the system. There are many theoretical maps that describe how the body would function in a state of perfect health, but it is next to impossible to find someone whose body is operating at such peak potential. The very nature of being alive involves imbalance. We are all of us out of perfect health in some way or another.

In the same way, I have come to understand that I have not yet seen anybody who is perfectly flowing through all the phases, moving freely from one to another. The difference between human beings is not whether they are blocked or whether they are flowing, but how they are blocked in the cycle.

We get blocked in several ways. First, we may become addicted to one phase. Second, we judge its opposite. Third, we aspire to the next phase while simultaneously resisting it, which can lead to the fourth and final block, the very common habit of "looping."

Let's explore more deeply these four ways of blocking brilliance, and then see how they can be recognized at each point in the cycle. Once we thoroughly understand how and why we get blocked, and the price we pay for it, we can develop an elegant and useful understanding of an almost infinite variety of practices and disciplines, and see how they fit somewhere in the map.

ADDICTION

One reason we get stuck in any place in the cycle is because it is always possible to go deeper. There is always the feeling that you have not yet fully explored it. The strong temptation is to stay longer in that place, rather than moving on through the cycle.

At 12 o'clock you could always relax more deeply into an infinite, silent, still meditative state. There is infinitely more of infinity available.

At 3 o'clock the creative process is never finished or complete. There are always more songs to be written, always more things to create. Always another project to initiate.

At 6 o'clock the to-do list never runs out. In fact completing any particular task often becomes the foundation to add three more things to the bottom of the list.

At 9 o'clock we are never fully done with working on ourselves. There will always be more things to release, more ways to improve ourself.

At each and every phase of the cycle you move on: not because you are done, but because you recognize that a balanced life requires you to live in all of these phases. Otherwise you can get stuck in any one point in the cycle indefinitely, and just continue looping there.

We move on to create a life of balance, not because we are complete at any particular point.

JUDGMENT

The second way we get stuck is through judgment. Wherever we are most caught up in the cycle, the opposite point will seem most foreign to us, and we will frequently have judgment of people identified there. We will see in a moment how this works at every phase.

ASPIRATION / RESISTANCE

The third way we get stuck arises from the mixture of both desire for and resistance to moving into the next phase. This is the disposition of "I know I *should* move on to ... but I'm not quite ready yet." For example, someone stuck in 6, addicted to their "to-do" list, checking things off in boxes, knows they *should* rest, says they *want to* rest, but resting keeps getting postponed into the future. When you're stuck in one phase, the next phase in the cycle is something you aspire toward (it is not against your values) but you have difficulty moving on. You want it and resist it at the same time.

LOOPING

This gives rise to the very common habit of "looping." We start to move on through the cycle, which is the natural way to stay in balance, but before we get very far we retrace our steps and repeat the same phase of the cycle over and over again. Dealing with looping is an extremely common phenomenon in coaching Radical Brilliance. It is the primary way that people get stuck.

The good thing about any map is that it offers a way to understand our experience, but we need to be careful that the process itself does not become dogmatic. The best way to make a map is first to study the territory and then create the map. Don't make the map and then try to make the territory fit into it: that is how we create dogma. If you create a map and ignore the territory, you may wind up walking into a lake.

So let's learn to recognize each of these ways of getting blocked: addiction, judgment, aspiration/resistance, and looping. At each phase of the cycle, please don't take my word for anything, check it against your own experience and ask yourself if this is true. Once we understand the nature of blockage and addiction, we can discover conscious practices all the way around the cycle, as a way to free up the emanation of brilliance.

STUCK IN AWAKENING

Addiction to Awakening

It comes as a shock to some people to think that you could get addicted to the spiritual phase of the cycle. Seeking oneness seems so ultimate, so epic. Here 's what addiction to awakening looks like: someone who goes on numerous retreats and pilgrimages, may have a spiritual teacher, and then barely manages to tolerate the more worldly stuff in between. There is a philosophical and pragmatic preference for formlessness over form. As Buddhism has spread from the Orient to the West over the last few decades, we have seen a huge popularity for Buddha statues. Today they are even sold at Cost Plus and Walmart. This kind of statue, which has spread like confetti throughout the spiritual subculture, shows someone preferring formlessness to form: he has his eyes closed and his body is still. There are very few statues that show a figure dancing or fully alive. The iconography puts a higher value on inactivity over activity. Because of the extreme masculine influence over spirituality, there has also been a glorification of not feeling, non-involvement, and detachment.

This is a problem for a radically brilliant life because when the first tremor of creativity arises, it is squashed by an ideological preference for formlessness. *Don't touch thought ... thought is the enemy ... favor thoughtlessness. Return to the mantra. Return to witnessing.* If that kind of an attitude is applied generally toward any kind of a stirring in consciousness, there goes your flow, right out the window. Any little sprouting that starts to happen is squashed by the preference for emptiness.

From a young age, every time I started to meditate, and there would be a settling into a more calm and spacious consciousness, there would follow a melody, or an idea, or the beginning of the poem. But I had been conditioned, continuously over years, to ignore all mental activity, and return the attention to the watcher, the witness, to silence. For years and years, I just thought I was a really bad meditator. The more settled and expansive I became, the more fireworks went off in my brain. Since then, I have discovered that many of my clients, colleagues, and friends have the same experience. When they sit to meditate, as soon as settling starts to happen, it initiates a process of creativity. Denying those impulses causes us to remain stuck at 12 o'clock.

Judgment of Productivity

When you feel addicted to Awakening, there will simultaneously be judgment of the opposite side of the cycle: 6 o'clock. An Awakening addict looks down on very active people as Type A personalities, obsessive-compulsive, running round in circles. "You are just a human *doing* machine, you need to learn to be a human *being* ... (like me!)." If you get a preference for one part of the cycle, you will develop a dislike of the opposite. People who love to retreat from the world for extended periods generally don't like action, deadlines, and feeling constrained. It looks too stressful.

Aspiration / Resistance to Flow

People who are addicted to Awakening often speak about feeling they have an elusive gift to give, and develop an interest in learning about "life purpose." There is an ambition to discover and unleash this unique gift to the world, but it always gets postponed in favor of another meditation retreat. This leads to looping between 12 and 3: moving continuously back and forth between meditative spiritual practice, then a little trickle of creativity, which quickly fades out and goes nowhere. Because the finest tremor is not honored or cultured, there is a return back to the meditation cushion, again and again, hoping for another new impulse to take hold.

STUCK IN FLOW

Addiction to Flow States

You can also get stuck at 3 o'clock: in flow states. Flow is blissful. The arising, the quivering, the tremor of the first impulse of energy out of formlessness is inherently pleasurable. It is the nature of pure happiness. It is like sex that has been set free from the constraints of the genitalia, and now has a hall pass to become orgasmic throughout the whole body.

This is also the realm of "the next shiny glittery thing." Many people who are categorized as suffering from ADHD are caught in compulsive flow. They are unable to stay with any new impulse long enough to see it into form. It is the personality type that wants to keep creating. I must confess to being a prime example of this kind of personality. At any one time I'm usually writing several books at once, as well as creating online courses, working with multiple clients, not to mention attending to multiple half-completed building projects around the house. The greatest fear is running out of interesting things to do, but it can become an addiction. It is the buzz of novelty.

Judgment of Dissolution

A Flow addict usually also has judgment of the Dissolution phase. Compulsively creative people don't like to feel helpless, hopeless, or low energy. They look down with impatience at self-doubt, introspection, or humility. When a 3 o'clock addict starts to feel emotional pain, or inadequate, their impulse is to initiate another creative act. You start new projects to avoid feeling pain, to avoid feeling contraction.

Aspiration / Resistance to Productivity

Getting stuck in Flow states also sets up a block to moving on to productivity at 6. When you get addicted to flow and initiating new things, you aspire to see them to completion, but at the same time you don't want to get trapped in time, in projects, and getting pinned down. This is the predicament of all creative artists, whether musicians, painters or novelists. Novelists hate deadlines. In publishing houses, there is frequently a struggle between the author and the editor. The writer is always late, the editor sends frustrated emails that go unanswered. (How do I know this? Go figure...) Have you ever been to a painter's studio? Do you see a stack of neatly catalogued completed paintings, and only one current painting project, and all the brushes and paints neatly organized? Probably not. Most artists' studios are filled with stacks of half completed projects.

Leonardo da Vinci is celebrated as one of the most renowned painters in all of history— after all, he painted the Mona Lisa and the Last Supper. How many paintings do you think he finished during his forty-six year career? The answer is twenty-seven. Almost all of those were commissioned: he had to finish them to get paid. There are endless notebooks filled with ideas and sketches— here he is inventing a helicopter, there a parachute, then this, then that. On his deathbed his last words were, "I have offended God and humanity because my work did not reach sufficient quality." He felt incomplete. Leonardo is a poster boy for addiction to flow. He is often referred to as a "Renaissance man." His energy was constantly moving in multiple different directions at the same time. The mind of a genius can get caught in endless initiating. Steve Jobs was the same—he loved to initiate but relied on others to bring things to completion. Some of the most creative people in the history of humanity were addicted to flow, in judgment of dissolution, and aspiring to, but at the same time resisting, the move into productivity, to see projects to completion.

At 3 o'clock, someone caught in an endless creative flow aspires to get the paintings into a gallery, to bring the product to market, to actualize their dreams, but the reality somehow always gets postponed. They want to do it, but they also have resistance. The resistance is not because they judge it; in fact they aspire toward it. Stuck in flow, they can only admire as heroic the people who have mastery over the next phase in the cycle, rather than the one where they are currently caught.

Looping 3 to 6

This is a highly creative person who loves to initiate new projects. He or she will occasionally get excited about bringing something to completion, set up a marketing plan, and even entering into collaboration with others to bring something to completion: she may hire a designer, build a website, design packaging, even create contracts to bring it all home. But before any of this can be fully realized, so that it fully benefits other people, there is a looping back into creating something new or tweaking what has been created, so nothing ever gets completed.

STUCK IN PRODUCTIVITY

Addiction to Productivity

You can also get addicted to 6 o'clock: details, action, and completion. You get addicted to checking off boxes and completing things. This is the compulsive inability to go to bed at night until you have completed everything on your list. Getting addicted to productivity and achievement means that you run on a sense of responsibility, of impending doom if you don't successfully operate within boundaries. Where would you be likely to find people who are addicted to 6? Where do they hang out? Not in monasteries or meditation centers: those are the awakening addicts. You won't find them in artist studios: those are flow addicts. People addicted to productivity are to be found in offices, in banks, in corporations, managing output in factories. As soon as you get a job where your responsibility is to make sure that the product or the project gets completed with all of its components in place, you are in the world of production. The corporate world employs people to perform within budgets and deadlines. "*Where's the report? I want it on my desk by 11 a.m.*" That is imposing the boundaries of 6.

You can get addicted to the endorphin rush of completing something. Your entire life becomes about accomplishment, and often also about making money, tidying up... dotting i's and crossing t's. Everyone has experienced that. I don't like completing a book, I much prefer talking about it in its inception. But I realize I have to, unless I just want to be a wannabe writer. I also know the feeling of elation when I type the last period, and hit send. There is a tremendous rush of endorphins. We can get addicted to that, too.

Judgment of Awakening

When you get addicted to productivity, you have judgment of awakening states. This is why spirituality, meditation, and spaciousness are dismissed with a wave by very practical people. It has taken a mountain of metrics from the mindfulness community to convince corporations to even begin to look at meditation. You have to prove that it's going to increase productivity, reduce absenteeism, and help the bottom line. Google has spent millions installing meditation rooms and other means to support well-being at their campus in Mountain View, California. They have an entire area set up in the building with special meditation chairs, light and sound technology, the latest and the best of everything. All sorely underutilized, as the Googler who showed me around explained. But it makes sense. Google is full of people trying to get things done on deadline. Time spent in emptiness when you are addicted to deadlines just seems like time wasted.

Aspiration / Resistance to Dissolution

When you are stuck in 6, it creates an aspiration to rest and unwind, but also the burdensome sense of, *I just need to get this finished first.* So the only way a true productivity addict will finally move through into letting go is through a burnout or a breakdown. In large corporations, burnout is a huge problem. There is always another box to check off. You move a little bit on toward 9, when you have to, but then instead of following the cycle through to 12 and back into fresh impulses at 3, you loop from 6 to 7 to 6 to 7 repeatedly. When people feel they are going to burn out, they instead medicate or manufacture energy artificially through power drinks, or even cocaine. The more we keep looping, the more the stress builds up, until we simply cannot push ourselves any more. The addiction to productivity often means that you keep adding unnecessary extra activities to the to-do list, simply because of the addiction to a feeling of being under pressure, as well as an addiction to the high of checking off another box. It is an addiction to the urgency of having something to complete within limits.

Do you currently have or have you previously had a to-do list? You will notice this more if it is not super well-organized, not in software, but on multiple bits of paper. You write notes to yourself frequently, so you end up with reminders everywhere. You start to build up a terror of all the things that have been left undone. You wake up in the morning with an impending sense of doom. It feels like you have 500,000 things to do and they are all on scraps of paper scattered all over your environment. Once consolidated onto one list, there may actually only be five things that urgently need to be done, easily accomplished in a few hours. The actual list is short, but you created a huge panic around it. That sense of panic, of impending doom, becomes a self-fulfilling prophecy. The terror of not getting things done ironically causes you to add unnecessary items to the list. One of the benefits of having a coach is to go through these lists and mark each item: delete it, delegate it, postpone it, or do it today. Otherwise, the fear of the list perpetuates the list for a productivity addict.

Looping 6 to 9

The most frequent occurrence of looping I see is between 6 and 9 o'clock. You have been super busy working long hours on a project. Finally it's complete, and it's time to rest. You plan to take the day off, go out for a leisurely brunch with your family, take a long hike, and unwind. In reality, you only get started on that plan before one of two things happens. First, the phone rings with an emergency work crisis that it seems only you can solve. Why? You didn't switch off your phone, or delegate someone else to take your calls, because of your addiction to the feeling of emergency. Naturally, you bite the bait. You go back into work on the weekend. Alternatively, which is even more common, you get midway into a time of rest and relaxation, and then it is you who comes up with a new emergency all on your own. You decide to rebuild the back deck instead of resting, or to reorganize the closet. Looping means that you never really move on from 6 fully into 9, to decompress and unwind and feel yourself, and so you never move on into 12, through into 3, and back in the 6 again, with renewed inspiration. You spend your life looping between activity, a little bit of rest, more activity, a little bit of rest, until you lose all joy and energy and descend into burnout.

When you are stuck in one phase, the next phase in the cycle is not exactly against your values, it's more something you aspire toward but have difficulty moving on into. You want it and resist it at the same time. Active people aspire to rest and to take care of themselves, and admire people who know how to do that. But the work of taking care of yourself is always postponed until the next list of to-dos get done.

STUCK IN LETTING GO

Addiction to Dissolving

We get stuck in the dissolution phase when we develop a fascination with the mechanics of the process of letting go. We develop a morbid obsession with our wounded-ness, with how we got wounded, why we got wounded, under what circumstances we get triggered again. We develop an active interest in psychological processing. The endless world of self-improvement — working on yourself, deep bodywork, past life therapy, new diets to combat food sensitivities, you name it — becomes a way of life on its own.

In the dissolution phase, you can get caught in a backwater of continuously trying to improve yourself before you are ready to unleash your innate brilliance. You can get so stuck in trying to improve yourself, heal yourself, that it becomes your entire way of life. You forget why you started in the first place. Your entire life is spent in the toilet analyzing what you just dumped in the bowl, and how it got into your body. You forget to flush.

Judgment of Flow States

Getting stuck in working on yourself means that you now have judgment and distaste for very creative, high-energy people. When you get caught in self-improvement, in working on yourself, you get addicted to the idea that *"I am broken, there is something wrong with me, and therefore I have no gift. Nor, for that matter, does anyone else, once I glimpse their human flaws."* The idea of having anything to give seems ridiculous. When you are really caught up in your own process, the idea that you have anything to give just seems to be disgusting, horrible egotism. Creativity becomes abhorrent to you. That is why the self-improvement industry does not generate a lot of fresh new impulses. Everybody is busy working on themselves, preparing to give a gift ... later.

Aspiration / Resistance to Awakening

If you are stuck in the state of dissolving, deep meditative states and theories about self-actualization and enlightenment become the Shangri La you aspire to, but also seem to be out of reach. People so interested in self-improvement that it becomes a way of life frequently aspire to a goal of arrival ... later ... in the future ... after more workshops and therapy and healing. Some people code name this "Enlightenment," or self-actualization, or getting clear, or an endless catalog of other names. It is always just around the corner, yet unattainable.

Looping from 9 to 12

This creates another kind of looping: round and round between 9 and 12. People stuck in 9 like to do extreme things to get themselves out of their minds, out of suffering, to evolve to the next stage. This could be hallucinogins like Ayahuasca or LSD, intense weekend seminars like EST or the Hofmann Process, or spending time in the presence of a charismatic spiritual teacher with a name like Sri Boobooji. Generally it works for a short period of time, and leads to a feeling of peace, dropping of defenses, and of optimism, until the habit of looping kicks back in and finds some new defects to work on.

GETTING STUCK IS NOT THE SAME AS HAVING STRENGTHS

Getting stuck in a particular phase of the cycle is not the same as simply having a personality type where that phase is your strength. Someone is stuck only if they have a pathological or unhealthy inability to inhabit other parts of the cycle as well. For example, some people are naturally creative. That is the greatest contribution they have to make to a team. Such a person will shine much more when they are in their creative phase than when they're passing through 6, 9, or 12. But that is a very different thing than getting stuck in a phase of the cycle to your detriment, so that life no longer works well.

Once you recognize that your primary strength may be in one particular area of the cycle, I have summarized some tips that will apply to you.

Tips for 12 o'clockers

You will know that you are strongest at 12 o'clock if:
- you enjoy meditation and retreat more than the rest the day,
- you make sure you always get plenty of rest,
- when there's nothing pressing on you to do from the outside, you are more than happy to relax and do nothing.

So make sure that you:

- Find a way to be sensitive and to pay attention if something wants to express itself through you

- Remember you will have a predilection toward wanting to go back into awakening meditative states. Find a way so things can bubble up and come to expression through you with minimum effort.

- Be careful about your judgments of people who are strong in productivity at 6 o'clock because their values and strengths are the opposite of yours. You may have a habit of dismissing such people as compulsively overachieving, anal-retentive, hyper, type-A personalities. You need to collaborate with these people in order to create a balanced team.

- Establish the discipline of regularly exercising 12 to 3 practices. For example, if you like meditation or going on retreats, make it a discipline to have a notebook with you where you write, or a sketchpad or a musical instrument. Discipline yourself to create a little bit every day.

- Don't push yourself too hard to excel at 6 o'clock. It may be so antithetical to you that you are better off teaming up with other people who do that well.

Tips for 3 o'clockers

You know that this is your primary gift and your comfort area if:

- Your greatest pleasure in life is initiating new things.

- When you sit to practice meditation, or just to rest, it doesn't take long before new ideas to start bubbling furiously on their own.

- You have many new projects in various stages of development at any one time.
- You like to have multiple projects going on.
- People compliment you for being creative.

So make sure that you:

- Discipline yourself to move from 3 o'clock through to 6 o'clock. You will find lots of ideas about how to do this in the "Practices" section on our website. When you try to bring a project to completion you may feel like an ADD child, who can't sit still and focus on one thing for very long. Press forward in short blasts of a few minutes, then relax and reward yourself.

- Be careful of your judgments and antithesis toward 9 o'clockers. You may find yourself looking down on and feeling impatient with people who are very introspective, shy, who feel inadequate, or not quite ready yet. You wonder why they don't just channel that energy into something creative.

- Because 9 is the opposite of 3 you are best off collaborating with people who are strong at 9. This means that it's probably a good idea to talk with a psychotherapist or coach from time to time, to explore things that you may instinctively bury under the carpet in your eagerness to keep creating.

Tips for 6 o'clockers

You will know you are strong in 6 o'clock if:

- People can always count on you to keep your word, and to get things done.
- You are a good organizer.
- You primarily take pleasure in checking off boxes.
- You are tidy, well-organized, and punctual.

So make sure that you:

- Discipline yourself to stop regularly, even if you haven't completed everything on your list. Create a discipline of rest and relaxation, whether that means stopping to have a cup of tea, or taking a walk, or a regular practice of meditation, yoga, or Tai Chi. Remember, all of those things will seem like they are getting in the way of getting things done, but if you can schedule them in a neat and orderly way, and make doing nothing into another "to-do," it will keep you moving through the cycle.
- Be aware of your judgments and distaste for spiritually oriented people. People who spent a lot of time resting, staring at trees, or in meditation will appear to you to be lazy, and wasting life. You may mock them for staring at their navel for too long.
- As someone comfortable at 6 o'clock, you keep all the wheels turning, but it is your nemesis at 12 o'clock who maintains connection with the source of energy, bigger than our individuated doing.

Tips for 9 o'clockers.

You will know you are strongest at 9 o'clock if:

- You have a finely attuned sensitivity to your own weaknesses.
- You are very aware that you could have done things better.
- You know when you've made a mistake.
- The primary pleasure in life is working on yourself, having new insights about your psyche and shadow.
- You may view the very purpose of your life as being to heal your childhood, and wash yourself clean of trauma from the past.
- You have a seemingly endless fascination with new therapeutic methods to work on yourself, and improve yourself.

So make sure that you:

- Recognize that there is no end to self-improvement, and therefore know when it's time to "flush." Remember the refrain to Leonard Cohen's "Anthem": *Ring the bells, that still can ring, forget your perfect offering ...*
- Accept the validity of your frequently occurring thoughts, "I am not good enough," "I am a failure," and then deliberately and consciously hand these thoughts over to something bigger and more intelligent: whether it's a teacher, a community, or some intuition of divinity.
- Be aware of your judgment of 3 o'clockers. People who write books, create art, furiously share their gifts with the world may appear to you to be arrogant, or half-baked upstarts.

You are going to often judge someone as not qualified to do what they're doing, because as far as you're concerned, there is always more preparation and work on yourself to be done.

Let's summarize everything we have covered here in one nifty little table. Very attractive to the 6 o'clockers, but it was also fun to create at 3.

phase	o'clock	strong in	aspires toward	judges	been there / done that totally easy!	primary practice to move on through
meditative	12	letting go of the personal perspective	life purpose, mission, contribution	hyper active, Type A personality	working on yourself, preparing, psycho-therapy	pay attention to finest tremor
creative	3	initiating	completion, marketing, reaching people	holding back, inadequacy, not ready yet	connceting to source	ground and stabilize, bring one project to completion
active	6	getting things done	stopping, rest, rejuvena-tion	sharing at navel, shangri la, chanting OM	knowing what to do	make a discipline of stop and rest
reflective	9	seeing your own shadow	enlighten-ment, dissolving, oneness	half baked, premature, unqualified	taking impulsive action	let go, give up on yourself, hand over to a higher power

CHAPTER SIX
THE SMALL PRINT

So far we have described the different phases of the cycle, how we can get stuck, and how this inhibits the expression of brilliance. But remember that age-old phrase "The devil is in the details"? I have taught this way of understanding and working with brilliance to thousands of people now, in seminars and professional training, and through dialogue together we have been able to refine our understanding of how this works in practice.

What follows are some of the most useful and important questions which people have asked me about the map. You may not want or need to read all of this chapter in detail: when you see a question that piques your interest, stop and linger there for a few minutes. In the next chapter we will explore the guidelines for practices and disciplines which can allow anyone to move freely through the cycle.

AWARENESS IS THE KEY

Q: I first learned about this cycle from you about a year ago in a seminar. Quite honestly, I haven't done many of the practices you taught us. But just since I heard about this cycle, I have noticed my creative energy has been flowing much more. How is that possible?

Lots of people say this. Many years ago, when I was a very young man just out of university, I attended a seminar with the teacher Paul Lowe. He could be quite brutal at times, pointing out to people where they were stuck or unconscious. One woman was having trouble with her boyfriend. Very cool and calm, Paul proceeded to point out to her all of the ways that she was controlling, manipulative, and dishonest. She was devastated, completely exposed in front of everybody.

"There is certainly some truth to what you say," she gulped. "So now what should I do?"

"You don't have to do anything," replied Paul with a penetrating gaze. "Awareness is ninety-seven percent of the work."

I have remembered that phrase through all these years. *Awareness is ninety-seven percent of the work.* Simply understanding the different phases of the cycle, noticing how they play out in your life, frees up creative energy. You don't have to do anything more than that. Through this understanding you can easily recognize at what phase you are in the cycle, where you may have got addicted, and therefore resistant to moving on. The awareness on its own loosens things up.

The Cycle Goes Only One Way

Q: What happens if we try to go through the cycle in the other direction or skip over a step?

It's important to understand that the cycle moves in a clockwise direction. For example if you're up against deadlines, restrictions, and budgets — working in 6 — you cannot stop and try to go back into flow. The flow has no real creative force behind it. You end up with writer's block. You need to go through the de-stressing of 9, then some kind of taste—at least —in the direction of 12, before real fresh impulses will come again in 3.

You have to be willing to keep moving forward through the cycle. You can't go back. Shifting back into action after just a little bit of letting go also doesn't work. The action has no inspiration, it is just mechanical. If you try to go back into dissolution after a moment of awakening, you end up recreating psychological problems that have already disappeared. It becomes an endless loop of self-improvement. If you try to dip back into awakening from flow, you get frustrated. Many people tell me they don't feel they deserve the rest, without having exhausted some impulse. We have to be willing to follow the cycle through in a clockwise direction, visiting each phase of the cycle regularly.

ADDICTION AND JUDGMENT ARE BEDFELLOWS

Q: You talked earlier about how addiction to any phase always coexists with judgment. Why is that true?

The entire Brilliance Cycle is created through dynamic polarities. The values and qualities of any one point on the cycle are the direct opposite of the other side. Therefore, when you develop a preference for a particular phase of the cycle, you will inevitably create a judgment or dislike of the opposite phase of the cycle.

For example, 3 and 9 are opposites. Flow is intensely pleasurable: the brain is producing massive amounts of dopamine, very similar to what happens when you use cocaine or during sexual arousal. It is the addiction to novelty. Dissolving, on the other hand, is initially painful, but quickly relaxes into humility and restful states of rejuvenation. At 3, you have almost limitless amounts of energy, and at 9 you feel depleted and needing rest. At 3 you feel you can do anything, you feel invincible. At 9 you feel inadequate, and you learn to rely upon a higher power. Every quality and definition we can give to 3 o'clock would be the exact opposite of what is true at 9.

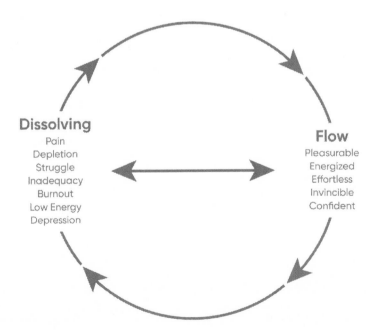

Equally there is the same polarity between 12 and 6. Awakening is the place of mystical experience and meditation. There are no boundaries: limitless, empty, conscious without content, unborn, and free. Productivity is all about boundaries, deadlines, budgets, agreements. In 12 o'clock there is no sense of doership, no "I," things are just happening on their own. At 6 o'clock there is responsibility, everything boils down to a sense of a central "me." At 12 o'clock nothing is happening, it is still. Six is all about action.

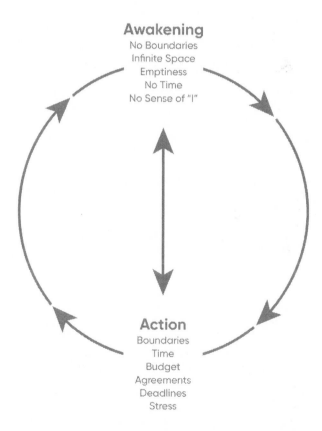

The entire cycle is created by this polarity between opposites. Equally, once we get an understanding of what it is like to be at a midpoint, the same applies. For example, 1:30 could be characterized as having some of the qualities of 12 and some of the qualities of 3. There is still a feeling of spaciousness, limitlessness, and no boundaries, but there are very also fine impulses of creativity arising, not yet fully formed. The opposite would be 7:30. There is still the contraction of action, deadlines, and boundaries, but it is falling apart, waning, and dying, and melting into rest, surrender, and forgiveness.

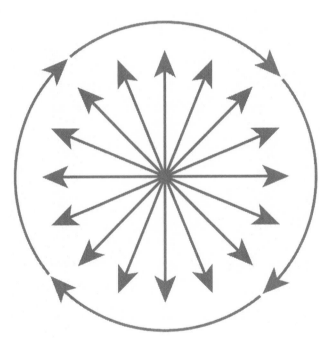

If we linger at any of the infinite points around the cycle, we will discover that whatever is true about that point, exactly the opposite is true on the other side of the circle. We do not need to try to merge these different qualities, or to think that because one is right, the other must be wrong. The important thing is to realize that they all equally exist as important aspects of brilliance, and we need to be able to visit all of the points regularly.

THERE ARE INFINITE POINTS ON THE CIRCLE

You have compared this cycle to a clock, and you have defined four points on the clock. Do we stay in 12 for a while and then go directly to 3, or are there other points in between?

Just like on a clock or a compass, there are actually an infinite number of points in between. If you think about a clock, the hour hand is only *exactly* at 12 o'clock for an infinitesimally small period of time. The hands are always moving. So it would be more accurate to say that you are not really "at 12," but "moving through 12." It is a continuous movement. Understanding that there are an infinite number of stations along the way makes it much easier to understand exactly where you are.

For example, you might find yourself with a very faint sense of a story that wants to be told through you. Maybe little fragments are coming in dreams, or sometimes just when you are staring vacantly into the horizon. But they easily fade away into the distance and get forgotten. Sounds like these moments might be characteristic of 1:15.

In the same way, I remember when I visited Leonard Cohen he was pretty much done with a new album, *Dear Heather*. The songs were recorded, and it was close to time for final mixes, cover art, and distribution. But he told me that every now and then something still wouldn't feel quite right, so he would go back into the studio and record that part again. That sounds like 5:15. Most of the creative energy has spent itself, and you have mostly moved on into action, But there are still a few dying embers of creativity flickering and flaring.

I once worked with a client, Stefan, when he was completing a big research project funded by the German government. He had come to the point of feeling that he was in the wrong place at the wrong time. Although the project had gone well, he had really lost most of his enthusiasm. He was still getting up and going to work each day, he was still dotting the i's, and crossing the t's, but he was much more interested in talking with me about a process of soul-searching. He suspected he was wasting his life, as though his ladder was leaning against the wrong wall. Stefan was somewhere around 8:15. He could still get somewhat motivated to check off boxes, but he was mostly done with it, and he felt much more drawn to a process of self-examination.

When I first worked with Ursula, she was coming out of several years of recovering from addiction. She had been part of Alcoholics Anonymous for many years. She had been working with a therapist. She had done the Hoffman process and many other psychological journeys. But she had recently come to the place of giving up, feeling she was unfixable. She only had to hear one introductory talk with me about Awakening Coaching, and she immediately registered to take the coaching training. She was really done with despair, with working on herself, and ready to explore her intuition of something bigger, beyond the mind. Ursula was at about 10:45 when we met. She could still get engaged in conversations about shame, inadequacy, and regret, but it was starting to feel like a broken record.

HOW DO I CHOOSE A PRACTICE?

Q: Once I understand the cycle, and how we get stuck, how do I know what practice to do?

Actually, you are probably the least qualified person on the planet to decide what practice you should do! Because everyone so easily gets caught in addiction to a particular phase of the cycle, and therefore into judgment and resistance to other parts of the cycle, it is very difficult for anyone to have an objective view of what is the best practice. That is the great benefit of collaboration and coaching: someone outside of your mind can advise you on how to best practice with your mind.

It has been a fascinating task for me, to look at different practices from different kinds of traditions and backgrounds and to see how they all fit somewhere in the cycle. Of course, because the cycle is built on polarities, a practice that would be helpful at one phase of the cycle will be exactly the worst thing to do at the opposite phase of the cycle.

For example, if you are stuck somewhere between 12 and 3, it is helpful to adopt practices that allow you to pay more attention to the finest impulses happening in your mind. When you hear a faint melody playing in your head, you need practices to become more sensitive. You might carry a recorder around where you can capture what you just heard. If you are a writer, like me, and you get stuck between 12 and 3, you need a way to honor and record new ideas as they sprout. If you are stuck somewhere between 6 and 9, however, where your mind is in overdrive, constantly convinced there is another emergency which requires urgent action, you need practices that help you let go, and allow you to let thought pass through, without having to pay it any attention. These practices are opposites.

In the same way, if you get stuck somewhere between 3 and 6, you are going to need to adopt a task management system, make a business plan, divide it into small discrete segments, check off boxes, get an accountability partner to make sure that you don't break your word. On the other hand, if you get caught between 9 and 12, you may need just the opposite kind of practice: support in letting go, recognizing the futility of individual action, and handing everything back, realizing the insignificance of your small personal efforts relative to the grand forces that give us all life.

How Long does the Cycle take to Complete?

Q: Ideally, over what time period should you pass through the cycle?

That's a great question. Actually, you are passing through the cycle in smaller ways and bigger ways all the time. There are cycles within cycles.

When you wake in the morning, you don't really know where you have been during the night. There are a few memories of dreams, but mostly it was dreamless sleep. The body was deeply at rest, and the mind went back into an infinite empty state. Although it is unconscious, we go into 12 every night. So the day starts with revisiting 12, but now in a more conscious way. It is a great time to sit silently in meditation. Around dawn is the best time for creative ideas, entering into the 3 phase. Everything around you is waking up, your energy is at a high level after sleeping, and you will be at your clearest. After breakfast, the middle part of the day is devoted to 6: getting things done and keeping your word. As the light fades in the evening, you start to fatigue. This is a good time for self-reflection, for recognizing and owning your mistakes; it is the 9 phase. And then, as the evening follows, you unwind back into the darkness of 12 again.

The cycle also plays itself out during the week. For many people Sunday is a time of doing nothing, the 12 phase. Sunday night or Monday morning is a good time to reflect upon what you want to create during the week; it is the 3 o'clock phase. The middle of the week can be more active, getting things accomplished. On Friday night or Saturday morning the energy dips, and you can learn to anticipate feeling more irritable and down on yourself. This is the 9 phase. And so you come all the way back to 12 again.

The cycle also plays itself out during a year, corresponding to the different seasons. Winter is a time of pulling in, a time of darkness, and an ideal time to do a meditation retreat. Just as the first blossoms appear on the trees, and the birdsong returns, spring is a good time to devote more attention to new sprouting of creativity. From late spring until early fall is a good period to get things done: build the house, record the CD, bring the product to market. The days are longest and you have the most energy. As the leaves drop from the trees in the fall, the days get shorter and often more rainy, it's a good time to welcome the 9 o'clock phase. You may feel a natural sense of melancholy or defeat. It is a great time to accept the limitations of your humanity.

Finally the cycle also plays itself out, in any timeframe, over the life of a creative project. Depending on the size of the project, the time spent in each phase may be shorter or longer. You might start by going on a retreat or on vacation, relaxing really deeply, letting go. If I go on vacation, the first two or three days I sleep and sleep and sleep. Then I go for a walk on the beach and I start to have ideas. They start flowing, just coming on their own. You start to record them, you make notes. In the next phase you hire a web designer, you create a budget, you make a plan and execute it. For many people, when they finish a project, it is common to have a period of creative depression: burnout. You have to pass through that, let go, and then find new energy again in 12.

SPACIOUSNESS IS PART OF A BIGGER CYCLE.

Q: Many different traditions cultures, and teachings have recognized life as a path, a journey toward a state of arrival, which is been called enlightenment, or liberation. How does this map fit into that kind of model?

One of the most useful and revolutionary effects of the cycle has been to help people to put spirituality and experiences of spaciousness into a different context. We have all of us been influenced, from many different traditions, by the kind of spiritual map you are describing. It is the idea that we are moving forward on a spiritual path, trapped in the ego, but slowly evolving and growing, and one day, in this lifetime or another, we will get to an enlightened state and then it's all over. If that makes sense to you, who am I to tell you different? I can just be honest with you and say that I don't see it like that anymore, and that many of the people I have coached and taught as students have felt a great sense of relief once they stopped seeing it that way as well. The Brilliance Cycle allows us to recognize that moments of deep relaxation into stillness are part of a bigger cycle. We don't actually need to stay permanently in expansive states of consciousness.

If you never connect with the infinite dimension of the mind, you cut yourself off from the real source of inspiration and sanity. But if you decide that you never want to leave more expansive states of consciousness, then you never visit 6, and nothing ever gets done. The map of the Brilliance Cycle gives you a very different way of understanding how awakening fits into the bigger context of a brilliant life. As a coach, I support people to be brilliant. I've coached people to complete movies, books, to bring products to launch. I coach people to take an idea and to make it real. That is my area of mastery, in my own life as well is in coaching. Other coaches, teachers, and mentors can support you in other ways.

Being here on this planet is a little bit like going to Disneyland. You pay the price of admission, and then there are hundreds of rides available for you to go on. Some of them are very slow, with music that goes "tinkle tinkle tinkle." Some of them are very fast, with a big "wheeeeee," and then an "aaaaaahhhhh!" and then a "splo-oooosh." Some of the rides are very scary. Some are funny. Some are in the dark, some are full of bright lights. You can take any ride you like. There is no "ride police" checking on which one you choose. You can take the same ride over and over and over again, if that's what you want. So no two people will ever have exactly the same experience of a day at Disneyland. Everyone chooses their own unique combination of rides.

Human life is just like that. There are no rules. If you like the idea of sitting in a cave with your eyes closed, contemplating OM, go right ahead. No rules. If you enjoy the idea of experiencing the "victim ride," you are welcome to that also. Making lots of money? Out-of-this-world sexual adventures? Political power? Being mean and evil? Saintly and righteous? There are no rules. Enjoy the ride you choose, and then let everyone else enjoy their ride too. But if you feel stuck in your seat, wherever you are, understanding the cycle can help.

BECOME A GARDENER

Q: How can I tell the difference between original thought and recycled thought?

I have been eating vegetables for almost sixty years now. Last year, for the first time in my life, I experimented with growing them myself. This was a new and very timid adventure for me. I bought the seeds, read the instructions on the back of the packet at least ten times, and then, with the trepidation suitable for your first-ever parachute jump, I went out into the garden, made a little line in the soil, and sprinkled my seeds into the furrow. I brushed the soil back over to cover them up. Then I prayed fervently. Several times a day, I went back to the garden anxiously waiting for progress. It took every flicker of self-control I could muster to stop myself from digging them up to see how they were getting on. Finally, after ten agonizing days … a miracle. Tiny, tiny, shoots of green started to poke their way through the soil in search of sunlight.

All glory, glory, glory, hallelujah.

For days and weeks I watered them, I sang to them, I shaded them against too much sun, and then I climbed and pruned trees to ensure my vegetables had enough sun. After a few weeks, I invited Chameli to join me in the vegetable garden to marvel at the miracle together. She knew full well just how important this was to me. She cooed at the sight of the two little ears of the zucchini plant. She laughed with delight at the small tomato plant. And then she took a step backwards and planted her foot firmly on a row of carrots. I screamed, at the top of my lungs, just as one might do witnessing mass infant genocide. Of course, she immediately removed her foot, apologized profusely, and offered up various forms of lifelong atonement. I know that she had no conscious or unconscious intention to murder my babies. She stepped on the carrots that day because they were very small and ... wait for it ... here comes the punchline ... they looked almost exactly like weeds. Unless you had, like me, made this vegetable garden the very center of your universe for weeks on end, it would be quite difficult, to the undiscerning eye, to notice the difference between those tiny green carrot leaves and an ordinary garden weed that grows everywhere.

It is just the same with creative flow. There are so many random, crazy, chaotic, and absolutely totally and completely irrelevant thoughts bouncing around in our heads each and every moment. They are mostly distractions from the creative process: small shoots to be weeded, not watered. Just a few of them, if you know where to look, are actually original creative impulses. How on earth are you going to tell the difference between a thought which is a weed and an impulse originating directly from the mind of God? The answer is by becoming, like I did, interested in gardening. You need to spend time in the garden, playing in the soil, getting familiar with what's going on at that very fine level. Then, and only then, you know what to weed out and what to nurture.

YOU NEVER ARRIVE

Q: I've been practicing meditation for many years. When I spend time at 12 o'clock, as you call it, I always feel like it could go deeper, that I haven't really arrived yet. Although you say there is no such thing as enlightenment, I do have a strong intuition of an ultimate state of liberation that I have not yet attained.

What you are describing is true at every phase of the cycle. This is an incredibly important insight we can have, to free up creative brilliance. Wherever you happen to find yourself in the cycle, you will always have the sense you could go deeper, and hence you want to stay there longer. There is no point of arrival anywhere, although we have been persuaded — by all kinds of influences — to believe there is. At 12 we have the belief that *if I just meditated a little more, I would tip over the edge and become one with infinity, and the personal ego, and all its attendant nastiness, would disappear forever.* As far as I'm concerned, that is a myth, a fairy story. The infinite nature of pure consciousness is always here, to be tapped into and visited, but there is always infinitely more of infinity, however deep you go.

The same thing happens at 3. Creative people will always feel that they are not yet finished. I know this from my own experience. At some point you just have to publish the book, imperfect as it is. If you keep waiting for more creative impulses to help you make it better, you wait forever. The music is never perfect. The painting is never ultimately beautiful. We spent time at 3, in the creative flow, and then at some point it's time to move on, even though you are never really done.

At 6 you experience the same thing with your to-do list. Very productive people have the sense that *if I could just devote a little more time, I would finally empty my list, and achieve some kind of state of perfect order, where everything is done.* But life is not like that. You check off one thing, and three more things appear. The to-do list is getting emptied and refilled continuously, as long as you are involved in life. There is also no point of arrival.

Finally, perhaps most important, you are never done with working on yourself and healing yourself at 9. When I was a child, my father had several friends who were deeply involved in psychoanalysis. They saw a shrink for one hour every day. I kid you not. I went off to university, and after I graduated I traveled to India, and then to live in Italy. In my early twenties I went back to stay with my father in London, and he had a dinner party in my honor. I met all these same friends again, who were now all a little grayer, more wrinkled, and balding. I asked one of his friends, "Are you still involved in psychoanalysis?"

"Oh no," she said, "I stopped that a few years ago."

"Oh, did it finally work?" I asked her. "Did you get completely healed?"

"No," she replied, slightly embarrassed. "I ran out of money."

It is like that, you see. You are never going to completely heal your childhood trauma once and for all, and completely rid yourself of all neurosis. Instead you realize that 9 o'clock is a healthy place to visit for a while, but sooner or later you give up on perfecting yourself, and turn your attention to something bigger than the small "me."

SHAME AND REGRET AS TEACHERS

Q: I find it hard to accept what you say, that shame and regret are also a healthy part of the cycle. I think shame is a toxic emotion.

Nine is not only about releasing. Nine is also the position in the cycle where we experience shame. Shame gets a bad rap today, as do regret, remorse, atonement, and inadequacy. Shame is often considered to be a toxic emotion. Getting addicted to shame, when you feel it for no reason, but simply as a pervasive habit, is unhealthy. But under the right circumstances, I have learned that shame is a healthy and intelligent thing to feel. Sometimes.

The feeling of being "lesser than," or not enough, can be crippling if you compare yourself to other people. But if you compare yourself to the big force that gives you life — we don't know what it is — then feeling "lesser than" is quite smart. It is like somebody on a train trying to run up the length of the train to get there faster, and then relaxing and realizing that "whatever is driving this train is going to get me where I want to go so much faster than me trying to run. I might as well just sit in my seat and be carried."

Every day I feel a little ashamed of myself about something: if I forget to put out the garbage, if I break my word to my wife. Running a coaching school presented me with almost daily opportunities for feeling shame. There were so many small details; I was always forgetting something. Someone didn't get the certificate, a replay from a call was not posted correctly. Shame is a useful thing to feel, at the right time, under the right circumstances.

Feeling ashamed is what allows you to learn and to do better. You don't feel any shame at 3 o'clock. You feel inspired, positive, optimistic. There is no shame at 12 o'clock: there is no longer any sense of anyone doing anything to feel ashamed about. Shame begins to become a possibility down at 6 o'clock, where there are deadlines and agreements, budget and the need to take action, to take a stand and make decisions. This area is ripe for opportunities for shame. You have a 50/50 chance when you make decisions to either feel good about it or to feel like you screwed up. Shame, regret, and failure are extremely likely consequences of engaging at 6 o'clock. I would suggest that they are really good things to feel.

If you really want to get from 6 back home to 12, passing through shame, to the appropriate degree, is the easiest route. The fastest way to return to spaciousness is to feel the undeniable truth of your own inadequacy. Viewed in this way, feeling inadequate, or "lesser than," is an intelligent response. You are lesser than the mysterious force that gives you life.

We can re-contextualize these kinds of feelings. When you recognize that you are in the dissolution phase, then you can see that feelings of regret, failure and shame are shortcuts to letting go of your identity and coming back to formlessness. When you are in 9, these feelings of failure will often arise. It is the process of letting go. It took me a long time in my life to learn to thoroughly celebrate these feelings.

YOU HAVE TO PLUG IT IN

Q: Why do we need 12? Can't people just be creative anyway?

Have you ever bought a blender? We have a very nice one at our house, made by Vitamix. When you buy a new one, you bring it home, you get it out of the box, and you assemble it. It has a jug that needs to be set on top of the motor base. Maybe you already tried a smoothie in your local health food store. You know how good it tasted. So you decide, "I'm going to make a smoothie."

You put in some coconut water, banana, blueberry, spinach, avocado, pineapple, protein powder. You put on the lid. You wait. But when you try to pour it out, all of the ingredients are still solid. Strange. Then you realize that there are some blades in the bottom. Maybe they are supposed to go around and around? So you dig your hand down through the pineapple, and the banana, and you start to turn the blade by hand. You still don't have a smoothie. You try to turn the blades even faster, but it makes almost no difference. What you have to do with that blender, in order to get a good smoothie?

You have to plug it in. Blenders don't blend unless you get power from somewhere else. The same is true with computers, washing machines, vacuums—they are all useless unless you connect them to a source of energy.

You are also useless, unless you are plugged in. You can't do anything, as a separate entity, when you are disconnected from the source that gives you life. That is why there has to be 12 in the cycle.

Without 12, you are limited to turning the blender blade with your hand. Without 12, there is no originality, no spontaneity, no humor, no brilliance, nothing.

UNDERSTANDING TRAUMA

Q: You describe the 9 phase as a time of letting go of stress that has built up during the day or the week. But what about deeper trauma we have accumulated over a much longer time period?

We could define trauma as any kind of event that is overwhelming, whether suddenly or slowly, to the point that you can't discharge it, so it gets trapped in your system. A car accident is traumatic, but so is working too long in your IT company without adequate breaks. In both cases we build up stress more quickly than we can dissipate it. Trauma can come from a sudden sharp blow, but also through prolonged wear and tear.

The facing and the releasing of trauma is central to 9. When we talk about practice, you will see how important this is. Any method that releases trauma is potentially helpful at 9.

You get stuck in 9 when you forget to flush. Flushing means that instead of following through until you feel completely processed, at some point you give up. You say to yourself, "I am unfixable. This human form is permanently and irrevocably imperfect. It is cracked." You could do primal therapy. But if you keep doing therapy with the aim of getting rid of every primal wound, you are going to stay at 9 o'clock forever. You could do the work of Byron Katie, but if you keep doing those four questions endlessly, until there is nothing left, you will just keep doing Byron Katie's work for the rest of your life, and never get on with living. You could do Rolfing, but if your aim is to have a completely tension-free body, you will spend your whole life getting bodywork and never accomplishing anything else. It's the same with any self-improvement scheme. We can never reach a final point of perfection. At some point we simply choose to give up and hand ourselves back to a source we do not understand. Otherwise we never actually move on into our gift. There has to be a point when you say enough, and you flush. "I may not be mended completely, but I am mended enough to be of service to the force that gives me life." That is the moment when you move through the cycle to 12. You let go of the effort to improve yourself.

THE DOUBLE BIND

Q: I heard you say yesterday that the 6 o'clock phase will inevitably result in a feeling of failure, shame, and regret. That sounds a little pessimistic. Aren't there people who achieve great things in life at 6 o'clock, and then feel really satisfied with what they have accomplished?

Definitely there is satisfaction from getting things done at 6 and bringing a project to completion. It is a pleasurable experience because the sense of completion releases endorphins in the brain. But please let me explain to you why I made that comment about the inevitability of those feelings.

One of the greatest thinkers of the 20th century, along with Alan Watts, George Gurdjieff, and Albert Einstein, was a genius named Gregory Bateson. He was a radically, radically, brilliant man. In his book *Steps to an Ecology of Mind,* he describes a phenomenon known as the "double bind." It goes something like this. When you immerse yourself fully in participating in life, what we here are calling 6 o'clock, you will have to meet all the things we have discussed: deadlines, agreements, budgets; but also, much more than any other phase of the cycle, 6 o'clock involves choosing: making decisions for which you will later be held accountable. Sooner or later, such responsibility will lead you to impossible choices, which Bateson aptly calls the "double bind."

The classic example of this happened to my namesake Arjuna, 5000 years ago in the Kurushetra battle, and led to his immortalized conversation with Krishna in the *Bhagavad-Gita.* Arjuna faced an impossible dilemma. He was called upon to fight in a war between the forces of *Dharma* and *Adharma,* loosely translated as the good guys vs. the bad guys. He was called upon to uphold the values which sustain life in a state of order. But there was a hitch. On the opposing army were many of his relatives, including his great-uncle Bhima, who had more or less raised him since childhood. This was an impossible choice, for which there was no obvious solution. Either fight, which would probably mean killing the people he most loved, or surrender the fight, which, because of his status as a *Kshatrya* warrior, would be the ultimate ignobility. Faced with this double bind, he collapsed in a state of panic and depression, which provided the perfect opportunity for Krishna to guide him beyond the dilemma into a truth that transcended, and at the same time included, both sides of the paradox.

More or less the same thing was true thousands of years later for Hamlet, who was also faced with an impossible choice. Hamlet meets his father's ghost, who tells Hamlet he had been murdered by his brother, and commands Hamlet to avenge his death. Hamlet was also faced with an impossible choice. Should he take action, as the ghost instructed him, and restore justice, or is it possible that this ghost was just a figment of his own troubled mind, and to be ignored? This dilemma is summed up in one of the most famous passages in the English language:

> *To be, or not to be –that is the question:*
> *Whether 'tis nobler in the mind to suffer*
> *The slings and arrows of outrageous fortune*
> *Or to take arms against a sea of troubles*
> *And by opposing end them.*

Almost everybody faces this kind of double bind at some point. Bateson's view is that this is how we grow and evolve as human beings. A man finds himself in a loveless marriage, fraught with bitterness and conflict, with two young children. If he plucks up his courage to leave the marriage, he potentially gives his little ones the lifelong scar of feeling abandoned by their father, their protector. If he stays in the marriage, he faces giving his children a model of conflict, and brewing violence. No way out. No way to not make a mistake. No way to avoid regret, shame, and a feeling of failure.

Another man I worked with was faced with his unique flavor of double bind. He had inherited the family business, which was now losing money. Should he let go of half of his employees, many of whom had worked for the family their whole lives, or should he keep them on and risk bankruptcy, letting down his shareholders?

Bateson's idea was that when faced with a double bind like this, one of two things will happen. You may collapse under the weight of *"damned if I do and damned if I don't,"* which puts you into a schizoid, fragmented state; you become split into different parts of yourself that are in conflict with each other. The alternative is that you grow and evolve as a human being by transcending the duality, and accessing a part of yourself that transcends and includes both sides of the split. Essentially you move through 9 to 12.

This is why feelings of shame, remorse, guilt, and inadequacy are not just merely the result hanging out at 6. They are, sooner or later, inevitable. When faced with a double bind, whichever choice you make is going to cause harm that you will then feel responsible for, and even guilty about. There is no way around it. In sitting with these feelings of "*I messed up, I'm a failure, I hurt people, I am not good enough,*" and accepting that they have their own wisdom, sooner or later you relax your grip on the idea of being the one in charge, and you continue around the cycle by handing your life back to the force that gives you life.

Leonard Cohen once said to me: "We think that we are here to gloriously fulfill our given mission. But then, as we mature a little, we discover that the point of being here is to fail, but to learn not to take it personally."

KINDS OF CREATIVITY

Q: You are presenting a kind of a formula, and a method for how to be brilliant. I feel like there are tons of creative people who don't necessarily access infinite consciousness in the way you're describing, and who don't utilize practices in this way.

Yes, you definitely right. If we look at the whole smorgasbord of art, literature, entrepreneurship, technology, architecture, the model I am presenting to you here only applies to a certain kind of creativity. There are several reasons I am aware of for this.

First of all, not every kind of creativity would qualify for what I am here calling "brilliant." Sometimes creativity is just the vocalization and expression of emotional pain, anguish, and confusion. It may be popular, and make money, but it doesn't necessarily bring into this earthly realm a flavor of "the beyond," or advance the evolution of humanity.

Secondly, many people transmit brilliance whether they like it or not, as though they've been randomly selected to carry a certain message or frequency, and there's nothing the "I" can do about. This is particularly obvious with child prodigies. For example recently, I first heard the song *Scars to Your Beautiful* by Alessia Cara. It is completely brilliant. I seriously doubt that she followed any of what I'm suggesting here. There are reasons far beyond our own understanding for why some people bring in this kind of brilliance from an early age.

The Brilliance Cycle is a way to understand how *you* can make brilliance more predictable. It has been built around my experience of teaching and coaching people. If you dig a little bit, everybody has a gift to give. Everybody has their innate brilliance. But for most people, it gets covered over by habits that inhibit that gift being given. The Brilliance Cycle is a set of disciplines to make brilliance less of a random accident, and more of a probability.

CHAPTER SEVEN
BRILLIANT PRACTICES

If you have stayed with me this far, we now have a shared understanding of the different components that contribute to a brilliant life, and how one phase naturally leads into another if we don't interfere with the process. We have also created together a shared and fairly sophisticated understanding of several ways that the cycle gets blocked. Now comes the really useful part: how to exercise gentle disciplines (I prefer the word "practice") to unblock the cycle.

What I mean by "practice" is any conscious intervention that means you are no longer operating on conditioned habit, addiction, or fear. These are conscious deliberate choices to be more present, more creative, more intelligent, more humorous, and hence more brilliant. In this way, taking a walk every day is a practice. Meditation is a practice. Doing yoga or Chi Kung is a practice. Saying five things you appreciate or that you are grateful for is a practice. Taking supplements is a practice. Having sex at least once a week as a decision rather than just feeing horny is a practice. Saying "I'm sorry" is a practice.

In this chapter we are going to explore practices in all four groups. We will discover the kinds of practices that move us from 12 to 3, then those that move us from 3 to 6, then from 6 to 9, and finally from 9 to 12. For each group, I will give you one practice with very detailed instructions that you can try immediately. I will also give you a web link to 26 others in each group, to give you an idea of the breadth available. You will see that I have a pretty wide definition of what I mean by practice.

Before we go on, there are a few simple but important insights we need to share about the nature of practice.

INSIGHT #1
YOU ARE MOVING THROUGH THE CYCLE ANYWAY

Even if you do nothing, you will eventually move through the cycle anyway. For example, if you hang out at 3 as a painter, a musician, a writer, or an inventor, sooner or later a painting will get finished and sold, a CD will get completed, a book will get published, or a product will emerge (if not, see Stuck in 3, above). If there are a lot of beliefs and resistance, it may take a frustratingly long time. The same is true everywhere in the cycle: sooner or later you will move on. When resistance is present, you will move more slowly than is natural. With conscious practice, you can learn to move on more easily. Instead of waiting for instinct to carry you to the next stage, you make a conscious decision to move on just slightly before you would do so anyway. This is the essential difference between a life of art, humor, and free choice, and a life of unconscious automation.

INSIGHT #2
YOU ARE NOT THE BEST JUDGE

As I mentioned earlier, out of the more or less 7 billion people on our planet today, you are quite possibly the least suitable person alive to recognize which practices will be most useful for you, how often you should do them, and for how long.

You cannot use the conditioned mind to make adjustments to the conditioning of the mind. We get blocked in our brilliance because of addiction, resistance, and judgments. These very habits which block the cycle will also enthusiastically volunteer decisions about which practices will be best. Disastrous. This is where peer support, mentoring, or coaching saves the day.

INSIGHT #3
ONE PERSON'S MEDICINE IS ANOTHER PERSON'S POISON

There is virtually no practice imaginable that would be universally good for everyone at all times. This is why practices need to be tailor-made and personal. For example, someone stuck at 12 will think, because of their addiction, that the solution to any problem is just to keep meditating, more and more, longer and longer. In fact, the best practice to move on from 12 is to pay more attention and respect to the subtle finest tremors of creative expression: to nurture them, feed them, and honor what they have to say. On the other hand, for someone stuck in 6, who just cannot turn their mind off when it is firing on all cylinders with new, urgent things to do, exactly the opposite practice would be useful. Then it is best to disengage from thoughts, to pay them no heed, and to shift the attention to the sensations in the body.

INSIGHT #4
YOU CANNOT TRAIN IN ALL OF THEM WHILE READING THIS BOOK

The last point about practice may sound a little bit like a commercial plug. My apologies. This right here is a book you are reading. I have packed as much useful content as I can between its covers, but it would be unrealistic to try to train you in every practice in rigorous depth as we go, without making the book thousands of pages long, and also very confusing. I would like for you to get a deep and broad understanding of the nature of practice, and how each practice fits into the cycle. If you want more tailor-made training in the right practices to use for you, I have created numerous resources to help guide you. We have a Global Brilliance Practice Community which includes regular live webinars where you can talk to me. I teach weekend seminars and longer retreats. You can also participate in one-on-one coaching, either with me or one of the many coaches I have trained. More information about all of these resources are available at radicalbrilliance.com.

We can start to explore practices anywhere in the cycle. I think the most useful jumping-in point is around 11:30. Here is an effective practice to move you into 12: the realm of awakening to your true nature.

PRACTICES TO MOVE INTO 12

These practices are mostly designed to redirect attention away from the *content* of thought, and the stories created by reactive feelings and events, toward the underlying unified field of consciousness: which we experience subjectively as silence, expansiveness, peace, and timelessness.

The richest resource for these kinds of practices is any mystical tradition or teaching which focuses on awakening, meditation, and moments of enlightenment. For better or worse, I have spent about forty-six of my sixty years on this planet absorbed in exploring this part of the cycle.

As an example, there exists a little-known text called the *Vigyan Bhairav Tantra*. In Western culture, the word "tantra" has become synonymous with sexuality, but in fact it literally means "weave," and refers to any effective method, technique, or practice. The *Vigyan Bhairav Tantra* tells the mythical story of a conversation between Parvati and her husband Shiva, in which she asks him, *"How may I know this mystery and intrigue more deeply? I get easily caught up in images created in the mind. Please lead me into the wholeness beyond all these parts."* (From the excellent translation by Lorin Roche.) Parvati is asking Shiva for instruction upon how to go beyond the mind, and experience pure consciousness. The *Vigyan Bhairav Tantra* is probably the most useful compendium of tools that work to get the job done in returning to spaciousness.

SAMPLE PRACTICE TO MOVE INTO 12

Here is a very simple method liberally borrowed from the Dzogchen tradition in Tibetan Buddhism. It is referred to there as "pointing out instruction." A very similar approach was favored by Ramana Maharshi, who is unparalleled in his influence on the wave of tasting awakening that has happened in recent decades. I have used this particular method with tens of thousands of people over the last twenty-five years, and I have trained more than 2000 people to use this method very effectively with others as coaches. I have written the steps out for you here, but there is also a guided audio version of it available for you as a gift at radicalbrilliance.com/taste.

Step 1. Simply notice the sounds, the colors and movements and shapes, and the body sensations in this moment. You could label a few of them: *car horn ... tension in belly ... corner of table ...etc.* Take two minutes for this.

Now simply acknowledge the unavoidable truth that these things are being experienced: *I hear the car horn ... I feel the tension in the belly ... I see the corner of the table ... etc.* Take two minutes.

Step 2. Now simply ask yourself a very fundamental question about what is already occurring. Remember, this is not about changing any condition at all, but simply about becoming curious about the condition that is already here. The question to ask is:

Who is experiencing this moment?

To break it down, this means:

Who is hearing the sounds?
Who is feeling the sensation in the body?
Who is seeing the color and the texture and the movement in the shape?

It could also include:

Who is aware of this thought, or this emotion?

4. Rinse and Repeat. When you ask any one of these simple questions, there are really only two possible things that can happen. Either you come up with an answer, like *my brain ... my eyes ... I am ... my inner child ... a pink flamingo called Josephine that lives inside my pituitary gland...* Or, there is no clear or obvious answer.

The practice is very simple. If you get any answer at all as to who or what is experiencing this moment, you can then ask yourself: *is that a sound ... is that an image ... is that a body sensation ... is that a thought or emotion?*

Check it out for yourself. Any answer you come up with will be one of these things. Then you can simply ask again:

Who is experiencing this?

If you continue in this way for 5 or 10 minutes, the attention will naturally shift from its usual obsession with the objects of experience to that which is experiencing, which is consciousness, awareness. It is actually nameless, formless, and mysterious.

Please do feel welcome to download the audio version of this, which will allow you to relax and be guided, instead of guiding yourself.

PRACTICES TO MOVE FROM 12 TO 3

Practices in this phase of the cycle emphasize paying attention to, nurturing, and then giving expression to the finest impulses of creative energy as they arise on their own out of stillness. There is a strong element of wait and allow to this phase. The impulses arise on their own when "you" step out of the way. So there is also a strong element of trust needed: trust that if you do nothing, and take your hands off the steering wheel, creativity will happen naturally on its own, despite you, not because of you.

These practices entail encouraging these impulses, celebrating them, sharing them and giving them room to breathe. We want to find the sweet spot in this phase of the cycle between repression and pushing. Repression would mean believing that thought is bad, and that instead of following it, you should return to a mantra or an expansive meditative state. Pushing would mean an attitude of impatience, wanting these impulses to become stronger more quickly.

This phase of the cycle is usually the one where people need the most support and attention in a coaching relationship. I spend a disproportionate amount of time helping people to settle in and to get comfortable in this phase of the cycle.

Practices in this phase involve bringing together two different components: tickle and capture. "Tickle" means to stimulate the finest tremor of the creative impulse, and to bring it alive. "Capture" means ways to record that creative impulse when it is still very fine, in such a way as to retain its original flavor and subtlety. I have identified dozens of means of doing each of these. I usually offer my coaching clients a smorgasbord of at least seven types of tickling, and seven types of capturing, which gives everyone 49 opportunities for experimenting to find just the right combination that works.

SAMPLE PRACTICE TO MOVE FROM 12 TO 3 FEEL PLEASURE IN THE BODY

Original impulses of creative energy do not begin in conceptual thinking or symbolic logic. They start as undefined, unformed impulses of energy. You can access this as sexual energy in the genitals, or just as pleasure anywhere in your body. Let your attention rest with pockets of pleasure, and allow them to expand and grow into shoots of radical brilliance.

Sit with your eyes closed. Breathe into your belly, and let out a gentle sigh on the out-breath. Now, with each in-breath, seek out pockets of pleasure. These could be in the genitals, or anywhere in the body. Focus the in-breath into the center of the pleasure, and with the out-breath allow this pleasurable energy to spread and dissipate into other the rest of the body. Continue in this way for several minutes, and allow the pockets of pleasure to become stronger. Then find a way to give that pleasure expression on the out-breath, first with a sigh, then it might turn into a melody, an image, or an idea.

You can find a list of 26 other practices to move from Awakening to Flow, with descriptions, here: radicalbrilliance.com/12to3

PRACTICES TO MOVE FROM 3 TO 6

Practices in this part of the cycle are mostly to do with overcoming procrastination, short attention span, and the inability to trust yourself to keep your word. Using different components, practices in this area focus on how to make a realistic plan, break it down into small doable parts, utilize peer support, and finally to get things done in a way that brings a project to completion. They allow you to take a strong creative impulse, an idea that is already humming at 3, and to ground it in something that becomes visible, tangible, and that can be shared with other people.

The movement from 3 to 6 begins with an intention and ends with accomplishment.

You can do many of the previous 12 and 3 practices on your own. You don't need other people to sit on a meditation cushion with you, or to be sensitive to what is happening within your own consciousness. Practices between 3 and 6, on the other hand, really benefit from having other people involved. Collaboration, mentoring, and feedback all help. This is the area where coaching can make the biggest difference.

Once again, there is the danger in this phase of the cycle of a practice being too weak or too strong. Weak practices between 3 and 6 would be setting objectives and goals which are so easy to accomplish that they feel meaningless. For example, if you committed today to put a stamp on a letter, and put the letter in the mailbox, you could probably easily be successful, but it would not feel like much of a triumph. On the other hand, if we make commitments and plans that are too big, we end up not completing them within the timeframe we set, and then we feel a sense of failure. That can become a rut: not getting things done today as planned makes it even more likely that you will not get them done tomorrow. The ideal balance is to have a plan each day that you can realistically execute by the end of the day, and at the same time feel that you have achieved something significant. For many people, this would mean setting up achievable goals that take two or three hours to complete when you have an eight-hour day available. (Much of your day will also be spent in handling things that were unexpected).

When we explore this set of practices, we frequently refer to whether they are "directly aligned with your mission and purpose." Of course, not everybody has a strong sense of what their mission and purpose is. Getting clarity about this is a big part of what can happen with a good coach.

Sample Practice to Move from 3 to 6: List 5 Things

This is probably the simplest and most powerful practice in this phase of the cycle. In the morning, after you have finished your 3 o'clock creative practices, write down five things to accomplish today. There needs to be a balance. Some of these may be things you have to do to avert catastrophe: like filing your income tax on time, gassing up the car, or going to the dentist when you have a cavity. A lot of life is about maintenance. I would wish for you that at least one of these items falls in the category of taking care of yourself, like receiving a massage, taking a walk with a friend, or researching something you find interesting.

At least two of the five should be connected to your sense of life purpose: they should directly move forward the gift you have to give to the world. For me, this would mean two of my items might include writing or editing a chapter for a book, doing an interview, conducting a seminar for an online course, or coaching a client. A well-lived life would include at least two such items, and hopefully more.

At the end of the day, after you finish working but before you go to sleep, look back at the list and check off how many you completed.

If you initiate only one practice for this phase of the cycle, this should be the one.

You can find a list of 26 other practices to move from Flow to Productivity, with descriptions, here: radicalbrilliance.com/3to6

PRACTICES TO MOVE FROM 6 TO 9

Practices in this part of the cycle ensure that you regularly move on from the busy-ness of 6, and don't get stuck there so long that you end up in a burnout. Practice is particularly helpful at this phase of the cycle because 9 is so unattractive to most people. Instinctively we don't want to feel inadequate, like a failure, or powerless. Practices in this phase of the cycle are most effective when they help you to disengage from the story, or the need to do anything about it, and simply allow you to feel what you feel and then let it go.

Particularly in the United States, but also increasingly in the rest of the world, we live in a "hustle" culture. That is how the West was won. Each man and woman for themselves: work hard, and achieve the American Dream. Without nationalized healthcare or higher education, with relatively sparse unemployment benefits, without adequate pregnancy leave for women, America is a culture where you need to learn to hustle. If you get sick or depressed, your American Dream quickly becomes the American nightmare. In such a culture where everyone is rushing to get ahead and focused on their own achievements, the 6 phase of the cycle quickly

eclipses every other phase. America prioritizes performance, afflu-
ence, achievement, getting things done, and productivity, and for
the last several decades the rest of the world has followed suit.

In the not-too-distant past we still saw remnants of cultures that
put much greater focus on the 6 to 9 phase: Catholicism, Judaism,
Puritanism, and even totalitarian political regimes. These ideologies
can put an unhealthy emphasis on sin. *I made terrible mistakes, I
need to be punished, I need to make atonement.* These ideologies are
unpopular in our culture today because we are in withdrawal from
an overdose of the values which, for many of us, our parents or
grandparents grew up on.

Practices between 6 to 9 encourage self-reflection: dwelling upon
where you might have missed something, where you might be unconscious, where you might have hurt someone or let someone
down, so you can learn and grow and evolve. This phase is about
feeling the limitations of your humanity, your inadequacy relative
to the bigger force that gives us all life. It allows you to recognize
your limits and then to forgive yourself.

Just as in the other phases, these practices are all about maintaining balance. Weak practices in this phase mean that you do not feel
deeply enough. You might apologize by casually saying, *"I'm sorry,
I made a mistake, my bad,"* but those words can just be superficial
social niceties. Then there is no real learning. If the practice is too
much it becomes a form of self-flagellation, *"I'm a terrible person,*

I just hate myself, I need to be punished. I want to die now." The sweet balance between these two is when you can deeply feel the consequences of making mistakes, hurting people, inconveniencing people, but you have enough distance to be able to learn and forgive yourself and set new intentions for the future. It is best to do these practices at the end of the day when the sun is setting or at the end of the week.

SAMPLE PRACTICE FROM 6 TO 9
WHAT DID I DISCOVER TODAY?

One superb coach taught me this simple but powerful practice. I do it every evening, writing in my journal.

First, ask yourself these questions. Take a few minutes to journal:
What did I discover about myself today?
What did I notice?
What did I learn?

You might even like to add the question:
Where did I make a mistake today?

The second part of the practice is to write answers to these questions for a few minutes:
What do I intend to do differently in the future?
How would I like to create different outcomes?
What support do I need to be able to do that?

Here is is a real-life example that is true for me in the very moment that I write this for you in this book:

What did I discover about myself today?

I got distracted half way through the day, and lost focus.

I spent time not really getting anything done, but also not really deeply resting or enjoying myself. I was spinning my wheels for a while.

I learned that once I get tired past a certain point, not only do I lose the ability to focus but I also lose the ability to make good choices.

The mistake that I made was not checking in with myself frequently enough to know when it was time to stop and change gears.

What do I intend to do differently tomorrow?

My intention for tomorrow and the days that follow is to set a timer to go off after one hour of focused activity. Then, my intention is to check in with myself and see if I need a change of pace or a walk or rest before going on.

You can find a list of 26 other practices to move from Productivity to Dissolution, with descriptions, here: radicalbrilliance.com/6to9

Practices to Move from 9 to 12

Practices in this phase of the cycle are all about letting go: letting go of the needs to be somebody, to fix yourself, or to improve in any way. Practices here emphasize self-acceptance, relaxation, but there is also a strong element of feeling and trusting an intelligence greater than your own mind. In this phase of the cycle, practices encourage you to let go of focusing on yourself and to shift the attention to what remains when you let go of yourself. It is like a dewdrop when it melts into and becomes the ocean.

Just like in the other phases, practices here can be too much or too little. If they are too little, they give only a weak taste of a consciousness bigger than your own mind, which quickly gets captured by the mind as another "experience," and so becomes part of the toolbox of self-improvement. Practices in this phase of the cycle are too much when they bypass individuality too quickly, and so cause us to gloss over the important lessons that we can learn and the mistakes we can avoid making again. This is sometimes called "spiritual bypassing," when we use the recognition of 12 as silent, still, and perfect to imagine that the individual identity is also silent, still and infallible.

Any practice which takes you from thought to being awareness itself, from emotions to being love itself, from being the body to being formlessness, is a 9 to 12 practice.

We already explored a sample practice in this phase earlier in the chapter. It was the question "who is experiencing this moment?"

You can find a list of 26 other practices to move from Dissolution to Awakening, with descriptions, here: radicalbrilliance.com/9to12

CHAPTER EIGHT

YOUR BRILLIANT BRAIN

We are going to dive together now into the challenging and (very tentative) science of Radical Brilliance. I am not a scientist, but fortunately I was able to speak to some of the greatest cutting-edge experts in this field, and you will meet some of them here.

Fairly early on in this investigation I discovered something interesting. Those who have explored neuroscience the most deeply are the ones who emphasize most emphatically how little we really know about the brain. On the other hand, people untrained in neuroscience often come to more solid conclusions.

One brain expert compared this arena of study to an office occupying an entire floor of a high-rise building. All of the blinds on this floor are drawn. Inside, the lights are on but it is only possible to see faint shadows and outlines moving behind the blinds. Occasionally, you might decipher a lot of activity in one corner. Or you might see people moving behind many windows at the same time, apparently operating in rhythm with each other. At other times, the whole office goes very quiet. Once in a while you might notice particular kinds of trash being discarded from that floor. Sometimes the waste pipes actually show particular kinds of refuse. Now, based on these scant clues, try to determine what kind of business is being run there, and how much money they are making. Of course, it is possible to hazard some wild guesses, but any conclusion would be more in the realm of conjecture than solid conclusion. Brain science is something like this.

One way of measuring brain activity is to look at the electrical field, which is constantly changing. Dr. Fred Travis is the director of the Center for Brain Consciousness and Cognition at the Maharishi University of Management in Iowa. He has spent decades researching the EEG of higher states of consciousness. According to Davis, "This electrical field is the sum of all the results of the individual neurons talking to each other: it's called 'slow graded potential.' There are 100 billion neurons in the brain. We are not getting information on what each neuron is doing, but rather seeing changes in groups of neurons. The different frequencies we can measure indicate what kind of activities are going on. For example, when the brain is repairing itself, we see very slow frequencies, called Delta, of around one cycle per second. On the other hand, when someone is following internal mental processing, thinking about ideas, we see Theta brain wave activity, of 5 to 8 cycles per second. But EEG gives us very limited 3D spatial resolution. We are collecting information from a 2 cm area on the cortical surface across the scalp." As he points out, that leaves us guessing what is happening deeper inside.

Another way to explore the brain is to measure blood flow, through functional Magnetic Resonance Imaging (fMRI). This allows us to see which parts of the brain are getting more blood at any time, and are therefore more active.. Measuring the blood flow in this way gives us an insight into different networks in the brain, where different areas "light up" together to perform certain functions. For example, the "default mode network" is commonly associated with being awake but not focused on anything in particular, like daydreaming or mind-wandering. The "default task network," on the other hand, is associated with different brain regions working together to perform a focused task. But of course it is difficult to perform an fMRI scan when the subject is engaged in any kind of activity that involves physical movement, particularly of the head

Another way to get an insight into brain function is through an understanding of neurotransmitters, such as serotonin, dopamine, and noradrenaline. Some of the most innovative work on the brain chemistry of more integrated states of consciousness is being done by Daniel Schmachtenberger and an impressive team of scientists at the Neurohacker Collective. Schmachtenberger told me, "It's hard to get real-time brain chemistry. Researchers can get downstream effects of brain chemistry in the blood, saliva, and urine, but that is always one step away from what is happening in the cerebral spinal fluid, which is one step away from what is happening in the chemistry in the synapses, which also only gives some indication of what is stored in the presynaptic neurons. So the ability to study brain chemistry real-time is fairly low."

There is, however, a very convenient way to "reverse engineer" the brain chemistry, which is what Schmachtenberger and his colleagues have been exploring. He explains, "We can postulate brain chemistry more accurately because now we can induce experiences quite reliably through chemistry that are very similar to the experiences people report naturally in states of higher functioning. This allows us to make very plausible hypotheses." In other words, if they give someone an organic or synthesized substance which they know increases serotonin secretion, or inhibits its uptake, and carefully note that subjective experience, it is reasonable to assume that when people have that same subjective experience on their own, they are producing the same kind of brain chemistry naturally. This is probably the most reliable way to conjecture what is happening in the brain chemistry at different phases of the Brilliance Cycle.

Before we continue to explore some of these informed conjectures about brain study, there are a few more limits to put on the table. This book is about higher functioning: more integrated and evolved states of brain functioning than are considered "normal." But this kind of "brilliance" very rarely gets researched or funded. Most of the research done on the brain, and indeed on the rest of the body, is the study of pathology and its alleviation. Current science is more interested in states of disease and how to heal them than states of more integrated functioning.

And then there is the possibility of vested interest. Here is Schmachtenberger again: "One of the beautiful things about science—not necessarily the way it is practiced, but as a philosophic system—is that science is about radical earnestness: not wanting reality to be a certain way, but being profoundly interested, curious, earnest, about what is true, and then going about setting up an experiment. If your idea of what you thought it was is not right, you can say, 'Wonderful, I'm glad I found out I was wrong, so what actually is true?' The enemy of science is bias. Who funds scientific research? Who does the research? Who has the energy to do it? Often it is someone whose ego wants to be the one who makes a discovery, and then they want it to continue to be true, even in the face of new stuff coming out. Or someone funding research wants to then be able to produce technology; they are looking for a return on investment. The practice of science ends up having bias all over the place. The philosophy of science is about this profoundly earnest, unbiased inquiry into the nature of reality, which requires noticing your bias, and checking it continuously. It is actually a very deep spiritual discipline, but it is as hard to practice as Zen: to notice bias and to drop it continuously and inquire deeper."

With all of these caveats and limitations on the table, let's explore now some of the most interesting conjectures that these brilliant scientists have shared with me about what is happening in the brain during the different phases of the Brilliance Cycle.

TWELVE: AWAKENING

Here is an ad hoc summary of what scientists have conjectured about the brain during moments of awakening. Bear in mind that this is a very under-researched field, and be ready for frequent revisions and updates as this arena is explored in more depth. Dr. Andrew Newberg is one of the most prominent researchers in the emerging field of "neurotheology." The experience of infinity characteristic of awakening "relates to what is going on in our parietal lobes, which are how we help to determine our sense of self and our sense of space and time," he says. "I refer to this as the 'orientation area.' It helps us to construct our sense of self and how it spatially and temporally relates to the world around us. During intense moments of awakening, we see a decrease of activity in this part of the brain. Hence, we see a loss of the sense of an individuated self, and the sense of spacial dimensions lessens. This is also associated with a decreased sense of boundaries, and hence a sense of unity."

The frontal lobes, on the other hand, normally increase in activity when we are concentrating on something, trying to solve a problem. In moments of awakening, we see a drop of this activity.

Dr. Jeffery Martin is the founder of the Transformative Technology Lab at Sophia University in Palo Alto, and the Center for the Study of Non-Symbolic Consciousness. He speaks of a "dialing down" of the default mode network, which he describes as "many regions of the brain interconnected in neural sub-networks interacting to give us a sense of time and space, spatial orientation, and a sense of self." This is what is responsible for what he calls "symbolic logic," by which he means thinking about yourself and reality in abstract terms. *Who am I, what do I want to be?* All of this kind of activity—

associated with the default mode network as well as the prefrontal cortex— decreases in moments of awakening.

In terms of EEG, Travis makes an important distinction between Alpha-1, associated with higher frontal blood flow, and Alpha-2, associated with decreased blood flow. "Alpha-2 is known to be an idling state: that part of the brain is not shut down but in the background, ready to be used." During experiences of awakening, the frontal part of the brain goes into an Alpha-2 idling state, which he associates with wakefulness without focused activity. In addition, Gamma EEG activity in selective brain areas is associated with heightened alertness.

In terms of brain chemistry, all of the scientists I interviewed saw a strong relationship between awakening and increased serotonin secretion and decreased serotonin uptake, which is associated with reduced depression and anxiety. At the same time, the neural hormones and neurotransmitters associated with stress, like noradrenaline, epinephrine, and cortisol, all decrease.

Most interesting of all, several scientists suggested that what happens in the brain during awakening, particularly with more sustained experience of awakening over a longer period of time, is the emergence of new kinds of brain chemistry with which traditional science is unfamiliar. Schmachtenberger says, "The serotonin receptors can become susceptible to other forms of nontraditional tryptamines that are endogenously produced. These are not part of the normal states of consciousness or brain chemistry." Travis seems to agree. "Awakening consciousness has different brain chemistry than either waking, dreaming, or sleeping. The *raphe nuclei*, some of the most important serotonin-producing sites in the brain, are more active, while the *loci coerulei*, responsible for noradrenaline, are at their slowest state. But instead of the Delta associated with deep sleep, we now see Alpha activity, so the brain is not repairing itself, but is also not actively engaged. It is giving the brain a whole new experience of unbounded awareness outside of time and space."

Finally, all of the scientists I interviewed observed the correlation between awakening and coherence between different brain regions: between the left and right hemispheres, but also between other parts of the brain including the occipital lobes, the parietal lobes, the temporal lobe, and the basal ganglia.

THREE: CREATIVE FLOW

As we move around from 12 to 3, researchers suggest that we still see the secretion of serotonin, but now with increased secretion of dopamine, subjectively moving us from contentment to excitement. Travis explains that there are two major dopamine systems. One is the pleasure circuit, which accounts for the intense bliss people feel in the first impulses of creativity, soon after 12. At this point the receptors are very sensitive, so even a small secretion of dopamine will cause very intense pleasure. By the time we move around to 3, the brain may be secreting more dopamine, but the receptor sites are less sensitive, and so the subjective experience of bliss may be less.

The second dopamine circuit has to do with motor activity: it smooths out repetitive motor tasks. This is associated with the *basal ganglia* deep in the brain. Research in just the last years tells us that the *basal ganglia* is also involved in monitoring smoothness of cognitive thought. This cocktail of continued serotonin secretion, now with the addition of dopamine, is what allows this phase of the cycle to be experienced as effortless, devoid of individuated doing (serotonin), together with a smooth flow of motor activity as well as creativity (dopamine).

Schmachtenberger explains that dopamine is also associated with regulating pattern analysis: "If the level is too high, you get schizophrenia and false patternicity. If it is too low, then you have a lack of awareness of meaningful connections and patterns. The increase in dopamine in the creative phase allows us to recognize novel patterns and thus to initiate creative ideas and to innovate."

Travis explains that the idea of "action in silence" is another way to understand creative flow. "We still see higher coherence in Alpha-1," he says, "at the same time as the faster frequencies of Beta and Gamma, which are needed to take attention to sequence, attention, and curiosity about what comes next." Travis explains that the frontal lobes are still not engaged. "You are not following executive, step-by-step predations, instead your activity is coming from feeling. Scientists have looked at jazz musicians in the neural imaging scanner, and found increased activity deeper in the brain, in the *insula*. This part of the brain takes bodily sensations and coordinates them with social feelings. So when a jazz musician says, 'I'm really feeling it,' it is literally that, it is not a cognitive process, but coming from feeling. The visual cortex, the auditory cortex, and kinesthetic cortex get increased blood flow during artistic flow states."

Schmachtenberger explains that understanding 3 o'clock has a lot to do with automated learning. "Our conscious mind has a relatively small bandwidth, and a relatively slow input/output ratio. The number of bits of conscious processing is relatively fixed. Unconscious processing, on the other hand, can integrate much more information. So when our brain senses that we're doing the same thing more than a few times, it automatically tries to free up working memory to be adaptive to new situations that could arise. This process of automating learning determines how quickly we can take some new learning and make it a new automatic default behavior, so it becomes effortless flow."

Dr. Newberg told me almost exactly the same thing about creative flow states: "These processes have been trained within you. You're not going to pick up the guitar for the first time and play like Eric Clapton. But if Eric Clapton plays it enough, he's able to get into that kind of flow state because it's the very essence of how he is able to play— his frontal lobe activity goes away and it just happens for him."

SIX: ACCOMPLISHMENT

As we move downward in the cycle from 12 at the top to 6 at the bottom, so we also feel more embodied. At 12 there is no form, and therefore also no sense of gender. Subjective reports tell us that you experience yourself to be neither male nor female, you feel identified with the infinite. As you identify more as an embodied human being, you also feel more identified with masculine or feminine energy. So as we move from 3 to 6, we can notice a more masculine and feminine style of getting things done, each of which could be accessed by men as well as women.

The more masculine style of achievement is driven by the secretion of testosterone into the bloodstream, which is associated with goal orientation, getting the job done, and the tendency to push through and go it alone. The more feminine style, associated with the secretion of oxytocin and estrogen, is associated with trust and collaboration with other people as a team.

Travis comments: "Under stress, typically men become less verbal and more action-oriented, with a lot of passion, drive, and energy. When women are under stress, interpersonal connection become more important. Women have more input fibers than men, so a sound is louder to a woman than it is to a man. Women typically have smaller retina cells, which are more sensitive to detail and color. Men have larger retina cells, more sensitive to movement. So the shift from 3 to 6 will be quite different depending on whether you are more identified with a masculine or feminine style of getting things done."

Travis tells us that in terms of brainwave activity, at 6 o'clock we see higher Gamma EEG. While Alpha-1 and -2 is more commonly seen over large brain areas, Gamma is selective. It is found in localized areas depending upon what you are doing. Gamma waves can get very high with focused activity: from 30 to as high as 120 cycles per second. In states of high functioning or accomplishment, we also see higher coherence, with different brain areas functioning together. However, the coherence is no longer across the whole brain, but in isolated parts of the brain, operating together coherently.

In terms of brain chemistry, getting things done within deadlines is associated with increased secretion of noradrenaline. Under challenge, the brainstem activates noradrenaline in the back part of the brain. We are able to see colors more distinctly, hear sounds more sharply. At the same time, noradrenaline increases information flow through the executive prefrontal cortex.

As we move from 3 to 6, we are adding structure to flow. The sympathetic nervous system, more associated with the fight-or-flight response and the exercise of will, becomes dominant over the parasympathetic nervous system. All of this is associated with the secretion of noradrenaline and epinephrine in the brain, and cortisol and adrenaline in the body. Schmachtenberger points out that this is also associated with a different perception of time. "In states of awakening, we experience time as eternity. In creative flow, we experience time as now. But in states of focus and accomplishment, we experience time as sequential. Time is limited. So the brain shifts to allow us to experience causation, consequence, duration, and chronology." None of those seemed as real in previous phases of the cycle.

Schmachtenberger continues: "Operating successfully at 6 o'clock requires 'design by constraint,' the exercise of impulse control. It requires us to put off pleasure as well as action motivated by feeling states, including messages from the body such as hunger, fatigue, or restlessness, in order to get the job done. This kind of impulse control is associated with decreased perfusion in the Reticular Activating System. When the RA system is very active, it filters your awareness for relevancy and productivity. Dopamine may still be present, but now the secretion is associated with discrete hits based on phases of accomplishment. Dopamine secretion gets postponed, and secreted only when a milestone is reached.

NINE: DISSOLUTION

As we discussed previously, the longer you stay at 6 o'clock, the longer you find yourself faced with impossible choices, which we called a "double bind." Schmachtenberger explains: "We stay in 6 o'clock, running on noradrenaline for as long as we can, but finally this buildup of stress fires the *amygdala*, the alarm system in the brain. Subjectively, this means there are no more creative ideas, we feel mentally and physically exhausted. This phase of breakdown is characterized by decreased energy systems in the body, specifically decreased ATP output. In this breakdown phase soon after 6, studies show blood sugar instability, and many other factors related to decreased cellular energy production (in the brain as well as other organs), increased ACTH, and increased cortisol-to-DHEA ratio. These are also the symptoms of the different phases associated with adrenal burnout. Subjectively, we also experience insufficient memory consolidation, symptomatic of the buildup of insufficient deep sleep. The body and the brain are out of balance."

Once the results of this kind of intense focused activity build up too much, the brain and body can quickly and suddenly flip from sympathetic to parasympathetic dominance. At 6 o'clock you repress messages from the body, tuning out aching, the need to go to the bathroom or to go to sleep. When it kicks over, we experience what is known as "parasympathetic flooding." Now the messages (often of complaint!) from the body, emotions, and intuition come flooding back, with a vengeance.

Some of the best work on this rebalancing from sympathetic to parasympathetic dominance has been done at HeartMath Research Institute, in Santa Cruz, California. HeartMath Inc. CEO Deborah Rozman tells me, "People often push aside a voice inside themselves that has been telling them what is the healthy thing to do. Then the mind gives up, because there's nothing more it can do. It cannot solve the problem, and it knows it. There is a surrender of the mind.

When there is no place else to go, people finally go to their heart for answers. Some call it the still small voice. We have to be quiet enough to listen. We start to connect with the intuitive guidance of the heart, the intelligence of the heart. It's always there, but we may have ignored it or pushed it aside out of ambition, or another kind of drive."

The key metric HeartMath uses to measure the interaction of the parasympathetic and sympathetic nervous system is the "Heart Rate Variability Pattern." The heart rate actually varies with every heartbeat and plotting the heart rate variation over time reveals a Pattern. Frustration, anxiety, anger and other stressful emotions create a chaotic HRV Pattern. Genuine feelings of love, care, gratitude and other warm-hearted emotions create a smooth and ordered HRV Pattern generating a coherent waveform. HeartMath has created an HRV sensor and smartphone app called the Inner Balance™ that helps you self-regulate your sympathetic and parasympathetic nervous system and shift into a state of inner balance and positive feeling. By seeing your HRV Pattern displayed in the app on your phone, with extraordinary real time accuracy and sensitivity, you can, within minutes learn to create more coherence in your HRV pattern consciously.

This study of the intelligence of the heart has increasing validation in modern science. The vagus nerve, which connects the brain to the heart and the gut, is one of the primary pathways of parasympathetic activation in the brain. Travis explains that scientists used to think that this was all about the brain telling the heart and the gut what to do, "but now," he says, "we are finding that 95% of the traffic is coming the other way: the intelligence of the gut is communicating to the brain. The digestive system has just as many brain chemicals in it as the brain itself. The 'enteric' nervous system in the gut has more cells than are in the spinal cord."

As we move around from 6 to 9, the scientists I interviewed referenced an increase in the natural secretion of the neurotransmitter GABA in the brain, which causes us to subjectively feel safe, innocent, and allows us to relax enough for repair to happen in the brain and nervous system. The longer we stay at 9, feeling safe, cozy, and resting, the more opportunity our body has to accumulate serotonin in the pre-synaptic nuclei, which prepares us for the movement from 9 to 12, and new moments of awakening.

THE CYCLE AS A SPIRAL

Travis emphasizes, "I hope you can bring out in your book the importance of what moments of awakening do to rewire the brain. It's not just that these glimpses of limitless consciousness happen and then disappear, they are continuously happening. The more frequently we visit awakening states of consciousness, [the more] our actions cease to be determined by the individual level of learning and experience and desires, and become driven by the needs of the whole world. So the phases of the cycle unfold in sequence, but everything is also there simultaneously supporting the next step."

Schmachtenberger explains that one of the unique things about human genetics compared to other primates is our radical neural plasticity: the capacity to be soft-wired based on our environment rather than genetically hard-wired. "This means we are highly adaptive to changing environmental stimuli. We are also able to rewire the way that our brain works according to changing circumstances. This relates not only to how we process nutrients, how we process pathogens and toxins, but also how we process information." Consequently, the more we move through the cycle on a regular basis, we are not only cycling through a repeating set of conditions in the brain, we are also rewiring the brain as we move through the cycle. This kind of evolutionary neural plasticity turns the cycle into a spiral of evolutionary brilliance.

PART TWO

THE TERRITORY

In other words, all of my books are lies. They are simply maps of a territory, shadows of a reality, gray symbols dragging their bellies across the dead page, suffocated signs full of muffled sound and faded glory, signifying absolutely nothing. And it is the nothing, the Mystery, the Emptiness alone that needs to be realized: not known but felt, not thought but breathed, not an object but an atmosphere, not a lesson but a life.

– Ken Wilber, in his foreword to
***Thought as Passion* (2000) by Frank Visser**

I called the first part of this book "The Map," to present you with a somewhat theoretical overview of how these different phases work together to create brilliance.

But, as my buddy Ken Wilber is fond of reminding us, the map is not the territory.

In the summertime I love to go camping, often with one or both of my sons. Before we leave for our trip, we gather together to look at the geographical survey map — basically a bunch of squiggly lines indicating elevation, with some little round circles here and there to mark lakes.

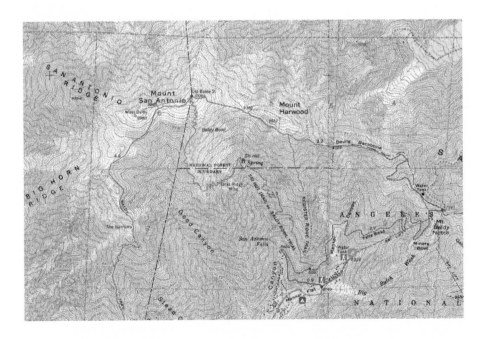

It is absolutely essential that we study the map so we have some sense of where we are going, how long the hike is going to take us, and how exhausting it will be. If we were to miss out the map-studying stage, we would just be wandering around aimlessly in the wilderness. We might get lost, we might even die out there.

But then comes a very different experience, which involves getting into the car, with our backpacks loaded up, driving along a long, long, long, long dirt road to a remote parking lot, and starting to hike. Now we are no longer sitting in a warm room, sipping on cocoa, looking at a piece of paper spread out on the dining room table. Now we are dealing with mosquito repellent, damp socks and hiking boots, changes in temperature as the sun rises in the morning. Now it is all about water, and snacks, and blisters, and sunscreen.

The experience of the territory is very different from the map. Both are needed for a real adventure.

CHAPTER NINE
BRILLIANT ROUTINE

Now we will get down to the nitty-gritty of how to live the transmission of brilliance as a way of life. Once you recognize, understand, and respect the Brilliance Cycle, how will this play itself out in the decisions you make about how you live each day? If you can set time aside to maximize each part of the cycle in your day, you will also maximize the chances of being brilliant.

In this chapter I list many components that you could choose to integrate into your daily routine to make your life more brilliant, a smorgasbord of elements you could add to your day. I will also include some suggestions for components to integrate into your week, and into your year. At the end of this chapter, I will show you the routine I use when I'm working on a book or online course: when I want to maximize the possibility of brilliance.

It is extremely unlikely, verging on impossible, that you will want or be able to integrate all of these components into your life. Even if you are able to integrate just a few of them, it will have a powerful effect on your brilliance. It is also important to experiment and to see what works for you and what does not. The components I am listing have been derived from my own life, my coaching clients and students, and the hundreds of brilliant people I have interviewed.

But not everybody does everything. It is up to you to find out what fits your particular life circumstances, personality type, and body type. For example, if you have young children, or if you commute to an eight-hour day at an office, you will of course be much more restricted than if you have a fairly open schedule.

I have listed these elements in descending order of importance. If you only have time for one thing, do #1. Two things: do #1 and #2, and so on. The items at the end of the list are for dangerously fanatic die-hard zealots, like me.

ELEMENTS OF A BRILLIANT ROUTINE, IN DESCENDING ORDER OF IMPORTANCE

#1 Sit Silently Wearing a Blindfold Every Day

I recommend to all of my coaching clients to sit silently, wearing a blindfold in the morning, after sleeping, for a minimum of 20 minutes and sometimes for as long as an hour. That is really the only instruction that I give: sit with your spine straight, set the timer, put on the blindfold, and wait to see what happens. I prefer not to use the word "meditation," as it so often suggests doing something, and some kind of a goal of a specific result. More about this in Chapter 17 on sitting.

Later we will enhance this by drinking a 16-ounce glass of water first thing in the morning, with half a lemon, a pinch of sea salt, a pinch of xylitol, and about 2 fluid ounces of aloe vera juice. This makes sure that you are adequately hydrated before you start the sitting. You can also take two Qualia Step One (explained in Chapter 14) , which makes your meditation much deeper.

#2 Track and Capture Impulses Every Day

As soon as possible after you take off the blindfold, and certainly before you get into the busy-ness of the day, spend at least 10 minutes capturing the impulses that arise naturally in stillness. If you're a musician, this might mean humming or playing a melody. If you're a writer, it means jotting down some ideas. If you run a company, this might be writing notes on a new marketing idea, or even a new product. Many of these kinds of practices were covered already in chapter 7.

#3 Enjoy Light Exercise and Movement

Make sure that every day you move energy through the body. The objective of this morning routine is simply to warm up and stretch the muscles, and to get energy circulating through your whole body. This does not need to be a vigorous workout, it is simply a way to antidote stagnation and a sedentary lifestyle. I like to shake this up a little bit, and do different things on different days. Also, I have noticed that different coaching clients respond best to different kinds of light exercise.

Some of your choices can include: a 10-minute walk around dawn or even a bicycle ride; dancing to music; Chi Kung or Tai Chi exercises, or even making love. I have certainly noticed that some forms of exercise are much more suited to women's bodies, and others are more suited to men's, because of the significant hormonal differences. As a man, I use a simple warm-up routine that is used before any kind of Chi Kung practice. You can find it on the Radical Brilliance website here: radicalbrilliance.com/chi-kung-warm-up. Many women tell me they feel much better with dancing to music for ten minutes. You need to feel for yourself the best kind of movement, and the best order to sequence these elements. Some people prefer to do some movement after the sitting and before the creative expression. Others prefer to record creative impulses directly after the silent sitting.

#4 Use Supplements that Feed your Brain

When I coach people to amplify their natural brilliance, their most common complaints are of fogginess, sleepiness, and a distracted overactive mind. Of course, there are many factors which influence our state of consciousness in this way, but one important factor has to do with brain chemistry. If I suggest using supplements, some people object, saying, "I don't want to become dependent on expensive pills from bottles. It should be possible to get all my nutrition from food." Theoretically, this is true. But the depletion of minerals from the topsoil, toxins accumulated from the environment as well as prescription drugs, and many other factors contribute to a situation where even a healthy organic diet, bought at your local health food store, may still leave you with deficiencies and toxicity that create fogginess. In chapter 14, I will list for you the most important supplements you might consider using, in descending order of importance. In chapter 15, we will consider some of the supplements that are still considered illegal in most parts of the world.

#5 Reconsider Your Sleep Patterns

Another very frequent factor that comes up in coaching has to do with habits of sleep. Over the last decades, many of my clients have been working in technology, often in Silicon Valley. Many tell me that they habitually go to bed after midnight, and wake up with an alarm clock at seven in the morning. This frequently leads to the need for a strong caffeine fix in order to make it to work on time. Skimping on food throughout the day means that the heaviest meal may not happen until after eight at night, which leads to yet another night of going to bed late, with the additional burden on the body of digesting a heavy meal. All of this is followed with a complaint of feeling foggy and exhausted, and wanting to know what to do about it. In order to maximize your chances of living radical brilliance, it will almost certainly be necessary to reconsider your sleeping habits: what time you go to bed, how long you sleep, when you wake up and whether you use an alarm clock or wake up naturally, and any additional naps during the day. We will cover all of this in the next chapter about sleep.

#6 Set Clear Intentions and Find a Way to Manage Tasks

Another important element that interferes with the flow of brilliance for many people in today's busy world is the feeling of having too much to do. Writing the book, making the CD, developing the new product or website or social initiative gets postponed to "when I get time." People frequently explain this to me with a mixture of shame and frustration. The key is to set small, easily accomplished goals each day that only take a few minutes each. I suggest setting five goals each day, two of which should be directly and unambiguously connected to the greatest gift you have to give to the world. We covered some of this already in chapter 7 about practices, and we will visit it again in chapter 21 about coaching.

#7 Take Frequent Breaks

During the middle part of the day, I advise people not to stay in a focused, productive mode for longer than one hour without taking some form of a pleasurable and rewarding break. This could include a five-minute walk, dancing to some music, eating a superfood snack that replenishes brain chemicals quickly, or even allowing yourself a few minutes of distraction on social media. If, like me, you work at home and your spouse does as well, you might enjoy a few minutes of "making out" together to refresh your energy. More about all these kinds of pleasurable and refreshing breaks in several of the chapters to follow.

#8 Schedule a Daily Nervous Breakdown

As we discussed earlier, our culture since 1945 has emphasized accomplishment and achievement above all the other phases of the Brilliance Cycle. Hence, feelings of inadequacy, regret, failure, or even guilt and shame have been given a universally bad rap. The problem with trying to avoid these kinds of sometimes painful feelings is that they are also the best portals into self-reflection, learning, and humility, all of which are important ingredients to connecting back to a source beyond your own mind. If you try to block these feelings through staying busy, alcohol, recreational drugs, or the multitude of other forms of distraction that are popular today, they will build up and eventually demand to be listened to anyway. So instead of waiting and postponing until you are faced with a real burnout or breakdown, I suggest that you schedule a mini-breakdown into each and every day. Take some time at the end of the day, ideally as the sun goes down, to reflect upon your mistakes, things you regret, and even things you feel ashamed about, where you know you have violated your own values and integrity. You might journal about this, or practice any of the other 6 to 9 tools described in chapter 7. Make sure that you also set intentions during this time, and work with a mentor or coach so you don't become isolated with these difficult feelings.

#9 Rethink your Habits about Diet and Eating

There is one word to sum up the habits we have got into as a culture around food and eating: SAD. It is an acronym for the Standard American Diet. The way that we grow, harvest, distribute, and consume food has changed dramatically since the Industrial Revolution. The consumption of white sugar, wheat, and a multitude of preservatives created through chemical synthesis calls us to frequently consume "food -like substances" which any of our ancestors for countless generations back would not recognize. Along with this, the advent of electricity in our homes, little more than 100 years ago, has completely changed the times that we eat food. In chapter 13 I will explain why eating most of your food at breakfast and lunch, and having an early supper of little more than soup, will almost certainly increase brilliance. We will also review a checklist of the foods best to eat, as well as the foods best to avoid to keep consciousness clear.

10 Create Brilliant Friendships

We are social beings, evolved out of tribal cultures. Most of us get stimulated and inspired and become more brilliant when we are in relationship with other people. But just as not every thought is a brilliant and creative thought, so not every social interaction is in the service of you becoming the most brilliant version of yourself. This may not be possible every day, but certainly during the week it is important to schedule time with friends and role models who stimulate the best in you. We will explore more of this in chapter 19: Brilliant Friendships.

#11 Regard Sex as Creative Medicine

I am not anticipating too much pushback from you on this one. There is a rich history in many traditions of exploring the possibilities of sexual arousal not just for procreation or even for pleasure, but as a way to light up powerful energies, and then to spread them into other parts of the body. Using sexual energy as a catalyst in this way is not only tremendously beneficial for health and longevity, but it is also an almost essential ingredient to staying brilliant and creative. If you are lucky enough to have a delicious and willing partner, make sure that you set time aside at least once a week to use sex as a deliberate practice. Daily is even better. I am currently trying to talk my wife into considering hourly. If you are single, it is still possible to stimulate sexual energy in this way. More about brilliant sex in chapter 12.

SAMPLE DAILY ROUTINE FOR MAXIMUM BRILLIANCE

- 4:30   Wake up naturally without an alarm.
- 4:35   Drink 16 ounces of lemon water with salt, xylitol, aloe vera and probiotics.
- 5:10   Take Qualia Step One.
        Put on blindfold and sit for 25 to 40 minutes.
- 5:50   15 minutes of nonstop creative expression, using any medium.
- 6:10   40 minutes Chi Kung. Adjust the time and type of exercise to suit.
- 6:50   Walk and dictate blog post or article into a mini recorder.
- 7:30   Prepare cooked breakfast.
        Take Qualia Step Two and supplements.
        Eat breakfast.
        Write a list of 5 promises to accomplish during the day.
- 8:00   Clean up, tidy up, shower, get dressed, tell wife how much I adore her.
- 9:00   Fire up computer, check email, social media, and review meeting schedule.
        Get stuff done, take a pleasurable break every hour or so.
        Take naps immediately when feeling sleepy.
- 12:30 Large cooked lunch of vegetables and protein.
- 1:30   30-minute (max) nap with a timer.

- 2:00   Get more stuff done.
- 5:00   Start decompression process.
  Unwind, reflect on day, lessons learned.
  Good time to meet a friend, take a walk, have a tea.
- 6:00   Light supper of soup and sweet potato or kidgeree.
- 6:30   Spend time with wife or reading. Minimum or no electronics.
  Walk round the block.
- 8:00   Get into bed. Fall asleep before 9 pm

THINGS TO DO EVERY WEEK

- Schedule a sex date once a week.
- Get coached once a week.
- Go to the gym, or serious exercise three times a week.
- Take a "12 o'clock day" (no computer, work, or tasks) once a week.
- Invite a role model out to lunch or for a Skype interview once a week.
- Spend time with brilliant friends who inspire you several times a week.
- Set intentions for the week on Sunday night or Monday morning.

THINGS TO DO EVERY YEAR

- Take a one-week Silent Retreat once a year in the winter. At the end of the retreat, write your intentions for the year.
- Take a creation vacation of 2 to 5 days four times a year.

CHAPTER TEN
BRILLIANT SLEEP

Fortunately for us, a huge amount of research has been done in the last few decades, which broadens and deepens our understanding of the importance of sleep. During the manic drive for success of the 1980s and '90s, many people were looking for ways to get more done with less sleep, all in the interest of perceived productivity. But more recently, books like *The Secret World of Sleep* by Penelope Lewis and *The Sleep Revolution* by Arianna Huffington have convincingly made the case that good, deep, nourishing sleep that starts and ends early is the essential foundation for creativity, happiness, and productivity. I highly recommend both books—they will convince you to become a sleep zealot.

Many things happen to the body and the psyche during sleep, many more than we could possibly cover in this short chapter. The liver is the primary organ refreshed and replenished at night, although it is also important for digestive function, physical healing and balancing of brain chemistry. The liver produces glutathione, particularly at night, which protects the brain from free radical damage. Inadequate glutathione production, often the long-term result of taking fever suppressants in childhood, has been widely associated in studies with symptoms of ADHD. In other words, glutathione is an essential brain chemical for staying focused … and brilliant. Low glutathione levels also inhibit the growth of the myelin sheath, which insulates your nerves and protects the brain from overstimulation. Many studies have shown that one of the primary effects of sleep deprivation, including going to bed too late at night, inhibits glutathione production.

AN HOUR OF SLEEP BEFORE MIDNIGHT…

You probably heard from your grandparents when you were little that "an hour of sleep before midnight is worth two after midnight." Although modern research is divided about this, there is plenty to support this view in traditional medicine, which was coincidentally all developed before we got so out of balance with natural rhythms. Although our lifestyles have changed dramatically in the last hundred years, it takes much longer for the neurology and biochemistry to also change.

For example, Chinese Medicine, with 5000 years of experimentation and documentation, proposes that each part of the body has a time of the day when it is most dominant, and most likely to be repaired and restored. Master Chunyi Lin was born in China into a family where healing with "Chi" (vital energy) goes back seven generations. He moved to Minnesota in the 1990s, and founded Spring Forest Qigong. He explains, "Our bodies and our energy function by following the movement of the sun and the moon. We have different 'meridians,' or energy pathways, in the body, each associated with a different organ."

"In the evening we have to go to bed before 10 o'clock, 9 o'clock is even better," Master Lin explained to me. "Why? You need to be in the deepest part of the sleep cycle by the time the liver meridian is active between 1 a.m. and 3 a.m. That is when your liver will repair itself: 70% of the toxins inside your body come out through the liver. From 3 a.m. to 5 a.m. the lung meridian is dominant, 30% of the toxins inside the body comes out through the breathing system. If you are too late for this whole section of time to be in deepest sleep, you will not be able to detoxify your body properly. Equally the ideal time to get up is before 6 a.m.: that is the time the large intestines meridian is active. If you are awake and active at that time, you are able get the garbage dumped out of your system."

Here are the different times when different organs are most active.

- 7-9 p.m. is the time of Circulation, where nutrients are carried to the cells. It is a good time to read and to be passive.
- 9-11 p.m. is the time of the Triple Heater, when balance is restored and enzymes are replenished. This is an important time to be asleep.
- 11 p.m. to 1 a.m. is the time of the Gall Bladder. "Yang" energy is restored as the Gall Bladder repairs itself, which gives us the capacity to be active during the day. Again, important to be asleep.
- 1-3 a.m. is the time of the Liver, and when we should be in deepest sleep.

- 3-5 a.m. is the time of the Lungs: we cleanse and repair the entire respiratory system. Good to be asleep, in a cool, well-ventilated room.

- 5-7 a.m. is the time of the Colon. A great time for meditation, for washing the body and the hair, and for combing the hair and stimulating the scalp. Also the ideal time for a bowel movement.

- 7-9 a.m. is the time of the Stomach. Best time to eat a well-balanced meal, and also to take most of the supplements you choose to use.

As with Chinese Medicine, the ancient Indian science of Ayurveda promotes "early to bed, and early to rise." Mary Jo Cravatta started her career as a chiropractor, but trained in Ayurvedic medicine more than thirty years ago. She was one of the first Western doctors to train in India, and to bring Ayurveda to the West. Ayurveda was developed more than 5000 years ago in the Indus Valley in Northern India. She explains that in the ancient Ayurvedic texts, the hours before 10 are recognized as a natural unwinding time, for all of nature. "Around 10 o'clock," she explains, "a more active time starts again. You need to be asleep before that happens; otherwise, if you are still awake, it will become more difficult to go to sleep. You may feel increased fire and creativity after 10, but then you will not want to fall asleep again for several more hours. That fire time of increased energy is not for you to be awake. It is for you to be asleep, so that organs in your body can have deep rest. Those hours between 10 and midnight are worth so much more than the hours afterwards so the liver can restore itself later in the night. It is not just a cleansing organ, it creates a lot of different chemicals and hormones in the body. It processes fat metabolism. The time before midnight is also important for healing emotions. During the day, we are too busy to process things. We allow our whole inner being to process as we sleep.

"Waking up before sunrise is also very, very important. It is known as *Brahma muhurta,* and sometimes referred to as the 'ambrosial hour.' We go into a slower time, a very special energy that allows you to get rolling for the day. There is more air movement in the environment, a little breezier, the temperature is a little cooler. We can take advantage of this movement by being awake during that time. If you wait until afterwards, you will be a little more sluggish throughout the whole day. To wake up during this time, when you have also had enough sleep, is another reason to be in bed by 9 and asleep by 10. Then you are refreshed, you can think clearer. There is a spaciousness around that time that allows you to expand more into your full potential. It is the perfect time of day to sit and meditate, because of that expansive quality."

Both traditions emphasize the benefits to health, longevity, and mental clarity by being awake before the dawn, and hence asleep before 10 p.m.

LIFE BY CANDLELIGHT

In our own cultural traditions, we only have to skip back over a few generations to a time about 100 years ago when most residential houses did not yet have electricity. Although the incandescent light bulb was invented by Thomas Edison in 1878, electric light was not widely available for residential use in America or Europe until the 1920s, less than 100 years ago, and even later in other developing countries.

Have you ever tried to live only by candlelight for a few days, during a blackout, on a camping trip, or when visiting an undeveloped country? As you may know, it is very difficult to cook, to eat, and to clean up after dark. All of your major cooking and eating has to happen before the sun goes down. After dark, your belly is full, dishes are washed, and all you have is a candle or a hurricane lamp to illuminate the pages of your book. It does not take long before your eyelids start to droop, and you crawl, in the darkness, to the magnetic rest between the sheets.

If your ancestors were Swedish, during the summer months this could potentially all have happened quite late. But further south, and in the winter, life before electricity could have forced your great-grandparents to be fed with their supper by 5 p.m., and heading off to bed by 7 or 8 in the evening. There is a limit to how long the human body will sleep, so it is also likely that great-grandpa and grandma were awake again before the dawn, feeling cold but also hungry, and ready to start their day. With twelve hours already since their last meal, they would have eaten a large, cooked breakfast soon after the sun rose, and hence they would have been hungry again by the time the sun was at its peak in the sky at midday.

This is the hard-wiring of your DNA. Your biological inclinations are built out of raw components from countless generations who were obliged to live in harmony with the circadian rhythms and with the changes of the seasons. Only relatively recently, within the last two or three generations, we have gained the freedom, but also the curse, of being able to override these natural rhythms.

REINVENTING CARL

Carl was a banker, working in New York, when he asked me to coach him. He was working for a hedge fund, managing a very large portfolio designed to create immediate short-term increases, so as to lure corporations to trust their retirement funds to his firm. His mandate was to try to avoid any investment going short, even for a day, as it would lead his clients to get the jitters and potentially to look elsewhere. He had been operating as a "day trader" in this way for more than ten years. He could do it in his sleep. Buy low at the start of the day, wait it out, sell high at closing. Carl's dream was to start his own fund, focusing on environmentally and social responsible companies, with a more long-term vision. His heroine was investment advisor and author Amy Domini. He told me he had asked to cut back his hours, so he potentially had two or three hours a day of his own time to work on his real dream. But ... like so many of the people I have worked with living in New York, Tokyo, London, and Sydney, Carl felt too foggy and unfocused to do anything new or innovative.

Right in the first session I asked him the same questions I ask every new client:

What time do you go to bed?
What time do you wake up?
Do you need an alarm?
When is your biggest meal of the day?

And Carl gave me the same answers, more or less, as every other fast-paced, sophisticated, big city dwelling, seven-figure-income-earning over-achiever. He was going to bed after midnight, sometimes at 2 or 3 a.m. He woke every day with not one but three alarms spread throughout his penthouse apartment. He started the day with an espresso, or two, or three, drank Red Bulls throughout the morning, and ate nothing more solid till a working late lunch, often just a sandwich consumed at his desk or standing up while talking on the phone. The only real meal of the day was huge, eaten in one of New York's many five-star restaurants, downed with alcohol and a rich dessert often as late as 10 p.m. It was not surprising that he got home after midnight every night.

I had to ask Carl to give me the benefit of the doubt for four weeks. I knew he would hate me, kick and scream, threaten to fire me, and demand a refund. He did all of those things. Weekly. I asked him to keep a simple log of what time he turned off the light at night, and simply to make it ten minutes earlier every night. I did not address his wake-up time, only bed-time. After a week, I also asked him to start eating a cooked breakfast, and a sit-down lunch. And finally, after another week I asked him to stop eating after dark, just as an experiment, and also to not use electronics in the evening. Negotiating all this was harder than getting my teenage kids to clean their rooms, which I remember was my other struggle at the time. I also asked Carl to keep a little journal of his progress with all this, using a 3" by 5" notebook and a pencil (no electronics in the evening, remember) where he also recorded his energy level on a scale from 1 to 5. Every time Carl relapsed, which he did frequently, I did not scold him, I just asked him to review how bedtime, meal time and sleep time affected his energy and clarity.

The first week his bedtime went from 2 a.m. to 1.a.m. The next week, from 1 a.m. to midnight. Week three: midnight to 11 p.m. And then, luckily for both of us, on week 4 he took a 5-day mini-vacation, slept 14 hours one night, and for the first time in his adult life went to bed at 9 p.m. It was after that vacation that Carl got his clarity back. He could think straight again. And most important, he was soon able to wake up naturally before the alarm went off, before the dawn. And yes, since you ask, and corny as it may sound, he *did* start his socially responsible fund, he *did* quit the bank, and yes, he did move to New Hampshire. He probably also married his high school sweetheart and now has a golden retriever. Roll the credits with the violin music.

THE FORMULA

Bankers, film producers, software engineers, rock musicians, from L.A to New York to Frankfurt to Tokyo have all hated me. For a while. I have heard every possible argument: *There is no halfway decent restaurant in New York that even serves people before 9 p.m. I am different from you, I am a night owl. I will lose all my friends. Everyone in my office works till after 8 p.m., it's the culture. I can't take a long lunch break, they will fire me.* And all that is before we even broach the topic of the afternoon nap. I ask these high achievers to simply treat it as a scientific experiment, and to record the results. They can always go back to their old lifestyle later. But it works, more or less every damn time.

These six factors have proven, close to invariably, to lead to much greater clarity and the ability to have new and original ideas: to become more brilliant:

- Go to bed ten minutes earlier every night, till you are waking up naturally, without an alarm, before the dawn.
- Eat a cooked breakfast, ideally involving three eggs.
- Eat a large lunch of cooked vegetables and protein, or salad.
- Don't eat anything after the sun goes down, but if you have to, keep it to soup.
- Avoid or minimize electronics after dark.
- Record your progress with these things, and correlate them with your energy level and mental clarity each day.

THE TALK

I also encourage my corporate clients to set up an appointment with HR to have "the talk." It tends to generate about as much anxiety in my clients as a gay teenager preparing to come out to his or her evangelical parents, a pastor and his wife in the Midwest. It requires enrolling the HR department, or supervisor, or even the CEO in our wacko experiment. It goes something like this. "I love this company. I want to give my best. I don't just want to show up brain dead and repeat automatic tasks. I'd like to make a difference. I want to contribute. So I have hired this coach. He is very tall, looks like a stick insect, and sounds like John Cleese. Very strange man. Anyway, this coach has asked me to change some things in my life to be able to have better ideas. So I'd like to ask if you could accommodate me for a month, and to see if it makes a difference to my performance."

"OK," says the HR person, cautiously. "Go on."

"Well," my client gulps, now glancing nervously at the door, "I'd like to be able to take an hour for lunch every day so I can eat properly."

"All right, what else?"

"And although I can be here at 9 a.m. or even earlier, I need to leave by 6, so I can have my soup and go to bed with alacrity."

"Excuse me?" says HR person. "I did not catch that. You want to go to bed with who? We have strict policies about this, you know."

"No, I want to go to bed early."

"Okay. Was there something else?"

More nervous fidgeting. "Yes, I can't take work home any more. Just for a month. As an experiment. So we can see the result. My coach says no electronics after dark. He is very firm on this one."

And, just like the pastor and his wife, the people whose judgments we have feared often exceed our expectations and embrace us for our true potential more than their ideology. I have asked many people to try this conversation, and we have received no rejections so far. In fact, after the one-month experiment, their productivity and innovation has often improved so much that one of my clients was asked to train other employees in the same approach to sleep.

MILK AND COOKIES TIME

The last element that rounds off the sleep cocktail is to take one or more short naps during the day. (Another HR conversation to rehearse in the mirror.) This will be easier if you spend your day in your playroom at home all day, like I do, playing with toys, but it has also proven to not be impossible in a corporate setting.

There are two important keys to effective napping. One is to limit it to no more than 30 minutes, and often 20 will do just fine. If you nap longer than that, you start to enter deeper theta sleep, and then you remain groggy afterwards. The second key is to take your nap as soon as possible after you first notice symptoms of fogginess. Taking a nap within minutes of losing focus may only require a few minutes before you feel sharp again. Waiting longer will require activating stress hormones to push you through, and then also require much more time to unwind and drop into sleep.

The painter Salvador Dali used to nap during the day sitting upright in a chair, holding a bunch of keys. On the floor next to his chair, directly under the keys, was a metal plate. He would start to drift off, enter an Alpha-2 state conducive to enhanced creativity and refreshing his focus, but as he started to drift deeper he would lose consciousness, drop the keys on the plate, and wake up refreshed. It is to this technique that we must be grateful for watches melting over desert landscapes, ships with butterfly wings, and elephants with trombone heads.

GETTING OFF TO SLEEP

One last word on the sleep topic is what to do when you make your bedtime ten minutes earlier each night, but then you cannot get off to sleep. Reducing bedtime by only ten minutes a day, or even less, will partly take care of this. But here are some other tips:

- Take a hot bath (as hot as you can tolerate) before bed. Add mineral salts.
- Breathe deeply into the belly after you turn out the light, resting your hand on the lower belly so it is pushed up an inch or more with each deep breath. Continue till you fall asleep.

- Try reducing the temperature of the room, and the heaviness of the blanket or quilt. You could even think about trying a ChiliPad™, which reduces your body temperature with a cooling pad. Research shows that we sleep deeper and get more cell repair and rejuvenation with lower temperatures.

- Try these five yoga postures for 15 minutes right before sleep: radicalbrilliance.com/sleepasanas

- Once a week, or even less frequently, try using Gabatrol. This will allow you to induce a much longer catch-up sleep on the weekend. Before you do this, listen to Brian Johnson, the inventor, talk about how to do this here: radicalbrilliance.com/gabatrol

- Read a book before bed, rather than watching YouTube videos or TV shows on your computer. Make it a real book, rather than an e-reader. *[Oh, sorry, let me explain, for our younger readers. A "book" is a rectangular object, usually 6 inches by 9 inches, often with a colorful picture on the front. It is made of multiple sheets of "paper," bound on one side. It is possible to open the edge opposite the bound one, and hence to read the words on the "page." This used to be quite popular with previous generations.]* The movement of the eyes back and forward from left to right, without the electromagnetic emission from an iPad or other e-reader, will cause seratonin secretion in the brain, which, when in a supine position, is a precursor to melatonin production, and hence to deep, restful, sound, nourishing, warm, safe, yummy, delicious, well-earned sleep.

CHAPTER ELEVEN
BRILLIANT VACATIONS

More or less everybody looks forward to going on vacation. It is a time to relax, to get exercise, to catch up on sleep, to see amazing new places, to have terrific fun with the people you love, and prepare to live longer. I thoroughly recommend that you take a good one-week vacation four times a year, or as often as you can.

Of course, vacations seldom produce the outline of a best-selling novel, or the seeds of a new symphony. I am going to explain to you here how to take a "creation vacation," which will almost invariably result in a torrent of shiny new brilliant ideas.

On the surface, a creation vacation might look very much like every other ordinary humdrum vacation. You are still going to be traveling somewhere, quite possibly on a plane. You will still need accommodation, you will still be eating food in restaurants. What makes a creation vacation so completely different is not so much its outward appearance, but the intention, and hence the result. A creation vacation is a concentrated time to go more deeply into the cultivation of brilliance. It belongs within the bigger cycle of your year or project, but a creation vacation also has its own cycle within itself.

Before we go on, let's quickly review what a "normal" vacation usually looks like, and why it does not always lead to brilliance. People often go on vacation when they already feel exhausted, stressed, and overwhelmed: in need of a break. In other words, people wait to go on vacation until they are not feeling good. The body is running on a backlog of adrenaline and cortisol, and probably depleted of the feel-good brain chemicals like serotonin and GABA.

A Google search will quickly tell you that the most frequent problem people face going on vacation is fighting. Here is how the story goes. There is a last-minute scurry to get all of your work completed, which probably involves burning out even more than you were already. You need to get a sitter for the cat, put the mail on hold, research and purchase airline tickets and accommodation, find a new swimsuit and suntan lotion, and a host of other tasks. If you travel to your destination, this may require you to get up earlier than usual to make it to the airport, and quite possibly then getting dehydrated on the plane. By the time you arrive, you are probably also jet-lagged. Now we can add to the backlog of months of built-up stress the more immediate stress from dehydration and sleep deprivation. You wake up on the first morning faced with a glistening beach, fresh mangos and pineapples, an endless list of enticing excursions, and ... feeling like something the cat threw up.

So what do you do, faced with this ridiculous paradox of a gorgeous external environment, and a horrible internal one? *"I know it's only noon, but what the hell, we're on vacation, aren't we? Besides, my part-*

ner just stormed off in a huff. Yep, I think I'll have myself a little drink. Ha, I needed that. Pour me another one, would you? Nah, make it a double." Ethanol alcohol acts on the receptor sites of the neurotransmitters GABA, glutamate, and dopamine. The effect on the first two results in the physiological effects of drinking, such as slowing down movement and speech. But it is alcohol's effect on dopamine sites in the brain's reward center that produces loss of inhibition, confused thinking, and poor decision-making. Very often, that is what leads to the next drink. The lack of inhibition often creates a fight.

Besides alcohol, it is very popular to indulge in fast, dangerous sports while on vacation: like waterskiing, parachute jumping, ziplining, kite- surfing and bungee-jumping. The danger and novelty of all these activities also give a dopamine rush to the brain. [Quick personal note, in case you're getting the impression that I'm a total party pooper: I LOVE fun vacations in beautiful places. And I take them as often as I can.] A conventional vacation will give you a certain kind of rest and rejuvenation, but it's not usually setting up the perfect circumstances for the deeper dive required to inspire brilliance.

So here is a different kind of vacation, not as a substitute for two weeks of fun in the sun, but as an addition.

You can take the creation vacation alone, or with one or more friends. I take most of my creation vacations alone, because the whole cycle comes very easily to me now, and I don't need a lot of discipline or peer support to enforce it. If you can follow the instructions in this chapter, you will probably also do just fine. But if you are very concerned about getting distracted or losing focus, you could arrange to go on a creation vacation with a friend (or friends) who has a similar agenda. On the other hand, don't try to do this as a family reunion, or with a group of people who want to go drinking, partying, or sightseeing. It is only worth even thinking about doing this with other people if you are sure they have the same motive as you. I am very lucky, because my wife is also extremely dedicated to being the best version of herself, and to giving herself as a gift through her work, so it is very easy for us to do this together, and to support each other.

LEADING FROM A DEEPER SOURCE

Amy Elizabeth Fox is the founder of Mobius Executive Leadership, a coaching and training company based in Boston, Mass., with offices in Amsterdam, Geneva, and London. She and her support team of 250 help high-performing leaders of Fortune 500 companies discover new experiences, insights, and daily practices that can change their mindset and unleash their full potential. Many of her senior experts are professors at Harvard, but her team also includes facilitators, coaches, mediators, as well as expressive artists, musicians, dancers, and theater performers. In 2007 she formed a partnership with global management giant McKinsey & Company. Mobius served the Obama campaign as its leadership provider. Additionally, each year the company donates more than a million dollars in pro bono services to worthy non-profit organizations. Trust me, I could fill pages listing the many spinning plates that Amy balances. She is running a big, big, big ship.

But at the core of all this activity is the central importance Amy places on taking care of Amy. "I have three different kinds of vacation," she told me. "I spend about eight weeks a year in a classic restorative vacation: in a beautiful setting, unplugging, spending time by the pool, in the spa, and going out to lovely restaurants, music, theater, and art with friends. Secondly, I spend twenty to thirty days a year going somewhere more retreat-like, and focusing on healing from my own lifetime of difficulty, through various practices. The third kind of vacation I call 'timeless time,' which is the deepest period of restoration. Timeless time cultivates such a profound quality of stillness and dissolving that new ideas can come from a deeper source.

"With each of these vacations, it takes me a few days to slow down. I have to change pace, stop the flow of my thoughts from the regurgitating familiar thinking, the focusing on the things I already know, before I can drop into something that is quieter, more still, and more accessible. This state is more of an abiding, a receptivity that makes me available for direction, for guidance, for the spark of a brand-new idea that is not coming from my own imagination or vision. While all three types of vacation are restorative, with timeless time, I especially recognize that receptivity as a gift. I'm being given a gift of a new way of looking, a new possibility or a new priority that emerges naturally out of that stillness. It is very clear that this is not coming from the noise of my consciousness. You need to be very intentional that accessing this stillness is what you are doing, and to distinguish it from a recreational vacation."

HOW TO PLAN THE CREATION VACATION

If you are going to take timeless time for yourself, I have found that the wintertime, between the beginning of the year and the start of spring, is best. That is a natural season to withdraw from the world and go on retreat.

It is very important to choose the right spot for a creation vacation to work. It requires being quite selective and checking your facts in advance. In order to stimulate the right kind of brain chemicals for brilliance, you are going to need a place that has the unusual mixture of being beautiful, quiet, and stimulating all at the same time. If that sounds impossible, it might be easier to understand what it is that you are not looking for.

- Don't try this kind of vacation in a place that emphasizes lots of socializing, like Club Méditerranée, or the party scene in Ibiza. Being around a lot of people all the time will not allow you to drop deep enough into the source of brilliance.
- Don't go to a place that is too quiet and reclusive, unless your creative juices are already flowing well in advance of the trip. You need some stimulation in order to move from 12 to 3.
- Similarly, don't go to a place that is too stark and austere, like a Monastery or Zen center. You run the risk of getting stuck in 12 that way.

Says Amy: "I go to the same three or four hotels around the world, where I know the staff very well. For one thing, they sincerely respect when I'm in periods of silence and don't want to be disturbed. But also, each place feels like coming home. There is a welcoming embrace and familiar touch to being there that creates a field of warmth and generativity in which brilliance becomes more likely. I also choose to stay in places that have beautiful natural environments: ocean, forest – any place where I can really source from the natural beauty of the world."

Like Amy, I, too, have locales that have worked out brilliantly for me. I have made a list of a few. Remember, these are just random examples to inspire you. There are plenty more where these came from. You can find the list here: radicalbrilliance.com/vacation-spots. Please bear in mind that these locations are just suggestions to put you in the mood. Once you get the idea, you understand that the world is overflowing with great places to do this kind of vacation.

WHAT TO BRING

Here is a quick checklist of things to remember to bring with you, which is not exactly the usual vacation packing list:

- Voice recorder
- Notebooks
- Pencils and pens
- Felt tip pens
- Watercolors
- Musical instrument

- Bathing suit
- HeartMath inner balance sensor
- Qualia
- Gabatrol
- Probiotics
- Any and all supplements that work well for you
- Laptop computer
- Blindfold for sitting practice
- Phone with a timer

How Long To Go For

The minimum even worth considering would be a long weekend: meaning you arrive at your destination before dinner on Friday, and don't go home until the end of Sunday. But you would really need to consider that a mini creation vacation. The real brilliance juices kick in more around five days to a week, and two weeks would be ideal. Anything less than a weekend you could simply call a 12 o'clock day, and don't worry so much about invoking brilliance.

The Phases of the Creation Vacation

The creation vacation passes through most of the phases of the Brilliance Cycle that you are now familiar with. You are almost certainly going to enter into the cycle at your destination somewhere in the 6 to 9 phase. For all the reasons I mentioned at the beginning of the chapter, you are not only dealing with accumulated stress and tension built up from your daily routine, but you are also dealing with the effects of travel. Anticipate feeling irritable and out of sorts for the first couple of days.

On the first evening you arrive, get settled in, and lay out all your creative supplies to be easily accessible. Eat a good meal the first night, but don't drink alcohol. Draw a hot bath or take a hot tub and be in bed by around 9 p.m. You might then consider taking a higher dose of Gabatrol, but make sure that you first visit this page, and watch the video: radicalbrilliance.com/gabatrol. Then go to bed. You may have an exceptionally long sleep the first night, perhaps as much as 12 hours.

On your first morning, let yourself sleep as late as you can, and then do some stretching. If you are lucky enough to be by the ocean, go for a swim. Eat a good breakfast or brunch. Remember, don't get distracted by sightseeing or big excursions, and minimize meet and greet with other guests. Stay off social media and web-surfing.

Then explore the practices listed in chapter 7 for moving between 9 and 12. This means that during the first day you can get into a rhythm of sleep, meditate, stretch, eat, soak, nap ... repeat. And wait. During a one-week creation vacation, you will stay in this phase of deep rest at least for most of the first day. Even on a weekend, it will occupy the first half of Saturday.

Once you start to feel rested, you will fall into deeper moments of awakening, and you can start to explore moving from 12 to 3. This is the bulk of the vacation. For a one-week creation vacation, this would take up all of days two, three, four, and five. On a weekend, it will start in the middle of Saturday. As you get caught up on sleep, the replenishment of GABA in your brain leads to a natural feeling of well-being, and the capacity to drop deeper in. Cultivate feelings of well-being in your body. The middle part of the vacation is spent in a combination of tickling and capturing practices, with frequent pleasurable short reward breaks. You don't really need to follow a fixed regimen; you can consider this to be something like a playful kindergarten for adults.

You just relax, resting and waiting for impulses to rise. You could do this in meditation, soaking in a hot tub, lying on the beach in the sun, playing in the ocean, playing in a swimming pool, getting massages, or ... you fill in the blank. Find as many ways as you can to experience deep rest and relaxation, and then as you start to notice pleasure, energy, and lightness in the body, pay attention and let it expand and grow. You simply start to become more attentive to the little sprouts of ideas and creativity that are wanting to push their way through. This will happen quite naturally, if you are not too social.

Then you can capture this aroused creative energy by taking a walk with the voice recorder, using pen and paper, a video camera, paints, crayons, musical instruments, or any other way of giving it expression.

Every time you move from tickle to capture and find that you have completed something, however small, give yourself frequent pleasurable breaks. So if I complete part of a chapter of a book, I follow it up by sitting in a café facing the beach, staring at the horizon for a while and sipping something nice that has a little umbrella and a cherry. Or I might walk somewhere beautiful. Or, if I am on creation vacation with my wife, we might retreat together to the bedroom for a while. Whenever you take a break, look for the most a pleasurable activity available to you, in the area where you are staying. But go easy on alcohol, socializing, and overstimulation.

You end the vacation in the 3 to 6 phase. For a one-week retreat, this would be the last day. On a weekend, it is just the last afternoon. You are not yet actually doing anything, just setting strong intentions for when you get home. You can plan how you will implement the impulses you captured, and playfully create a list of things to do when you get home. This is also a good time to make plans for how you will take care of yourself after vacation. You might like to make commitments to yourself to meditate regularly, to go to the gym several times a week, to practice yoga, and anything else that works for you.

The creation vacation is a wonderful way to initiate a project. I have found that, whenever I take one, it is the best investment of time of the whole year. It is how this book came into being, by taking time alone to allow these small sprouts to grow into a plant.

I would suggest that before you read any further, make some plans: think about when and where you can take at least a weekend, or preferably a week to experiment with a vacation like this. I send all of my serious coaching clients off on a creation vacation: doctor's orders! After you try it once, you may find, like me, that a regular old vacation, complete with alcohol, sightseeing, shopping, and dancing late into the night, no longer looks quite so attractive, and you may get to enjoy a creation vacation so much more.

CHAPTER TWELVE
BRILLIANT SEX

Just like good food, music, and dancing, people all over the world, from all different cultures and beliefs, love to make love. It is one of the things where we all find our common ground. You can have sex for many reasons: to make babies, to release tension and stress, for physical pleasure, or to express love for the person you feel closest to. People also use sexual energy to improve health and longevity. In this chapter we will learn specifically how we can use sexual stimulation in a very enjoyable way to cultivate creative brilliance.

In some ways, we could say that sexual energy actually is creative brilliant energy, but experienced in the genital area. So they are not two things: it is one energy that can be channeled in different directions. In many ways, your relationship to your sexual energy will be very similar to your relationship to your creative energy. If one is blocked, the other will likely be blocked as well. And if one is flowing, they are probably both flowing. Hence, knowing how to practice consciously with sexual arousal is a powerful and effective practice for enlivening brilliance.

Dr. Saida Désilets is one of the foremost living teachers of women's sexuality, trained in both tantric and Taoist practices.

"Everyone inevitably thinks of sexual energy as just in the genitals, and in the physical act of sex," she says. "Sexual energy is aliveness, which informs the whole body and is not just in the genitals. Sexual tension is exactly the same as creative tension, and creative tension is what is needed to bring genius into the world."

Barnet Bain agrees: "When we have sex, we experience our aliveness, our inner vitality that underlies our physicality. We are most connected with what is most real. The veils between the dimensions are very thin in sex. When I am connected to that aliveness, it allows me to fire up the resources of my birthright. It allows me to become more of who I am, to re-stoke the furnace."

In fact, sexual energy follows very much the same cycle as we have described earlier in this book. From 12 to 3 is the phase of flirting: feeling and then tickling the faintest subtle impulses of attraction. As with the Brilliance Cycle, these subtle impulses of faintly perceived sexual energy can be ignored, sublimated, or suppressed, or they can be acted upon. As we move from 3 to 6, it begins with foreplay: kissing, touching, and caressing. As the energy builds, just like with the Brilliance Cycle, it becomes more focused and goal-oriented. The more we move around the cycle to 6, the closer we come to a moment of peak orgasm, and release. From 6 to 9 is the period of post-coital resting, and the clichéd reflective question, "How was it for you, babe?" For a man, the energy drops at this phase of the sexual cycle, and he may fall asleep. It is also frequently a time when people reflect upon their sexual performance. From 9 to 12 is a period of sexual rejuvenation. It may involve not thinking or desiring sex for a little while, so that a new wave of arousal can build.

Not Unisex

Almost all of the other practices referred to in this book will be very much the same for both men and women. But when it comes to the conscious cultivation of sexual energy, obviously there are different body parts, hormones, and subjective experiences involved. At 12, the spaciousness and silence is neither masculine nor feminine. The fine creative impulses that arise between 12 and 3 are also exactly the same for men and women, not gender-specific. Sex is a powerful way to bring us down into the body, and as we move down into 6, into embodiment and action, everything becomes very different in the expression of masculine and feminine energy. Therefore we are going to examine sexual practices separately for the male and female body.

Fortunately, the art and science of cultivating and transforming sexual energy has been well explored and documented for thousands of years. There are two primary traditions which we can rely upon for practical and time-tested advice. One is the Tantric tradition, mostly associated with Kashmiri Shaivism. The other is the Taoist practices that date back thousands of years in China.

We will explore the basic principles of the practices here in this chapter. If you want to go deeper, the Bible of cultivation for men is *The Multi-Orgasmic Man* by Mantak Chia and Douglas Abrams Avara. It has everything an aspiring radically brilliant dude needs to know. The best resource for women is the work of Saida Désilets. And the best book for couples is *The Multi-Orgasmic Couple*, by Mantak Chia and his wife Maneewan. I have assembled all of these resources for you here: radicalbrilliance. com/sexual-practices. For the truly zealous, our online Brilliance Practice Community provides instruction in these practices from qualified teachers.

SEXUAL CULTIVATION FOR MEN

The Multi-Orgasmic Man emphasizes that practice starts for a man by learning to separate orgasm from ejaculation. Whenever I say that, men frown, and ask me to repeat myself. We have gotten used to mixing these two things together, thinking that peak states of arousal will always involve the loss of semen. But it is not true; you can experience powerful orgasms without ejaculating, and in fact you can experience orgasms not just in your genitals, but in other parts of your body as well. Don't believe me? The only way to find out for sure is through practice.

The first stage of practice is breath. Chia describes how to use intention to focus the breath down into the pelvis, to wake up the energy there, and to learn to spread this warmed-up energy through the body. Most of us do not breathe fully, and we are often not even aware of it.

The second stage is to strengthen the PC muscle, which is located between the scrotum and the anus. This is sometimes referred to as Kegel Exercise. Making this muscle stronger allows you to control and prolong ejaculation, and to spread energy into other parts of the body.

The main practice which Mantak Chia teaches is called "the big draw." It is actually quite simple. You can expect good results in just a few weeks. Once you have familiarized yourself with the basics of breathing and muscle control, you do this simple practice every day. You can sit cross-legged or in a chair, without pants or underwear. Stimulate your penis with your hand until you get an erection: yes, that's right, just like they told you not to do in Sunday school. Once you feel aroused, just at the very beginning of the hot sexual energy building at the head of your penis, you practice using your breath and intention to draw the energy down the shaft of the penis to the area of the perineum. Most men find they can accomplish this in a few days. Then you continue using the in-breath in short sharp sips to pull the aroused energy from the perineum up through the spine. After a few days, you will be able to feel that alive arousal in your belly, then in your solar plexus, then moving up to the heart area. Once you get good at it, you will be able to draw the energy all the way up into the base of the skull and, when you curl your tongue back to the roof of your mouth, the aroused energy then cascades down the front of the body.

CHAPTER TWELVE: BRILLIANT SEX | 181

This allows you to create what is known as the "microcosmic orbit," a flow of aroused energy, which was previously associated with the head of the penis, moving up the spine and down the front of the body. The more you practice, the more you will be able to accumulate this aroused energy in different parts of the body, and hence you can start to experience an orgasm of the heart, or the belly.

You will also gain control and choice about when you want to ejaculate. The Taoist practices do not say that you should never ejaculate; that could cause blockage and even lead to prostate problems. They say that you should develop control and choice about how often you ejaculate. Once you get good at this, which Mantak Chia anticipates only takes about 21 days, you can bring your practice to your partner if you are in a relationship.

Important note: what I have written here is hopefully just enough to inspire you to want to learn the practices. If you actually want to experience the benefits fully, it is important to read Mantak Chia's book, and even to get some instruction from a qualified teacher.

SEXUAL CULTIVATION FOR WOMEN

For thousands of years, men have instructed women on what they should do with their bodies, with their sexual energy, and with their lives. Enough of that already. Ladies, I am not going to be arrogant enough to tell you how to cultivate your sexual energy. I live inside a man's body, and I have no idea how it is for you. For that, we will return to Dr. Saida Désilets. "All my training is to get women into a profound state of relaxed arousal. I believe that a woman's genius is interconnected with who she is as a sexual and sensual being; they are inseparable. Research shows that in relaxed arousal the centers of the brain associated with creativity, confidence, self-esteem, and transcendent states become more active."

Dr. Désilets states that this state of relaxed arousal is stimulated in several ways, the most powerful of which she calls the *Erotic Field Meditation*. "I am uber-creative," she says. "I have created a lot in my life, and I worked a lot with my sexual energy. Before cultivating this practice it was like having twelve horses pulling in all directions: I was going nowhere fast. Now it is like they are all lined up. Just the slightest intent and Boom! We are off. The difference? Understanding my own vitality, and life force, and aliveness. The *Erotic Field Meditation* is a new orientation for a woman, the notion that her erotic energy, which informs her entire life, which brings aliveness to her, is everywhere. She is a field of conscious erotic energy.

"Because of social mandates, and early conditioning, women are separated from their pelvic floor. Many recent studies on female sexuality have demonstrated that women are aroused a lot by many things, but they may not be consciously aware of it. They do not necessarily pick up on the arousal cues. I help women reconnect their hearts with their genitals, which is a very old but very simple practice. There are moments throughout the day when I will activate an aroused state, but I don't take it to an orgasm. I go back to work again, in that arousal. I do a few breathing exercises, and feel the connection with my vagina. When practiced correctly, arousal does not involve sexual tension, it is more of a grounding in your innermost self as a sexual being."

Practicing Together

If you are in a relationship, you can both bring the fruits of your practice and explore how making love together can be a way to cultivate brilliance. Once again, remember these same practices can be used for all sorts of outcomes. They can deepen intimacy and love, they can improve your health, they are even reputed to help you live longer. We are going to focus here only on how sexual cultivation affects brilliance.

I like very much the practice developed by my friend John Gray, which he calls "Polarity Sex." I would not suggest you do this every time you make love, because it might get a bit mechanical, but if you practice polarity sex once a week, then you could do whatever you want, whenever you want, wherever you want, the rest of the week.

Polarity Sex has three stages. In the first stage the woman gives pleasure to the man. He can lie down and relax, while she strokes and massages his body. She can include touching the penis with her hand or lips, but always moving his arousal to spread down into his thighs and abdomen, expanding the area of arousal beyond the genitals. You only need to do this stage for about five minutes. It is important that he gets aroused without ejaculation.

The second stage of polarity sex focuses on her pleasure, and lasts much longer. Now that he is feeling warmed-up and energized, he has the motivation and desire to serve his partner fully. It is best to start with gently stroking and touching her body: her thighs, the sides of her body, the arms: light featherlike movements are best. It is best to take 10 minutes or longer before you even move to any of the erogenous zones. Most women, when they experience touch in this way, will utter gentle murmurs of pleasure, or sighing. Then it is time to move to gentle breast massage. The breasts have more nerve endings than any other part of the body. Cup the breasts with your hands in a gentle rhythmical clockwise direction, including occasionally pinching or sucking the nipples. You can also include kissing and gently sucking her lips at this time. It is best not to move to the vagina until she is naturally well-lubricated. Then the man gives pleasure to the woman with his tongue or his finger. Ideally the best way is to move the tongue in always changing patterns around the clitoris at the same time as one finger is slipped into the vagina and pressing quite firmly against the G spot, which is the slightly spongy tissue behind and above the pelvic bone. The man continues to give pleasure to his partner in this way either until she orgasms or until she says she feels fully satisfied. It is important never to put a woman under pressure to have an orgasm. Only then it is time for penetration, which is the third stage.

Often waiting this long before entry means that there will be less of the quick friction we sometimes associate with sex. It will be easier for both partners to either be still and breathe, or to enjoy more gentle rhythmic movement together. At this stage you may both experience a kind of "plateau" orgasm, which often extends through the whole body. You may feel a tingling of arousal all the way into your fingertips and toes and throughout every part of the body.

For a man, if you want to use this practice to enhance brilliance, it is really worth experimenting with not ejaculating. For some men that may sound a bit like going to the prom and never dancing, or going to the amusement park and never getting on the roller coaster, but this is simply a matter of experimenting and trying new things. Sex without ejaculation is different and takes getting used to. By focusing on fully satisfying your partner, you wake up the lover within you who can also give love to the world in so many ways.

Making love in this way is rarely a quickie: you may need to set aside 45 minutes to an hour to come to this kind of plateau full-body orgasm that spreads through the whole body.

If you practice in this way together you will know that it is time to finish not because of his ejaculation or her climax, but because you both feel as fully alive in your whole body as you can imagine feeling. Then he withdraws his penis, still erect. Of course you will find your own intimate way to thank each other for this journey to the stars and back. Now you take a quick shower, get dressed, and move from mega-tickle to mega- capture.

This is where you discover that the aroused energy that began in the genitals is now no longer just sexual. It has become total aliveness. It has become not just sexual arousal but creative arousal. You become a man or a woman on fire. Now discover what happens when you bring your attention back to writing the next chapter of your book, or planning the launch of your new product, or turning your attention to any kind of problem-solving. As a man, instead of being a guy with an erection you have *become* an erection, thrusting the gift of your brilliance with passion into the womb of a humanity desperately in need of being made love to with care and devotion. As a woman, your heart is on fire; the love that you initially felt with your partner can overflow its banks and pours through your breasts as empowered compassion for all that lives and breathes.

IF YOU ARE SINGLE

I imagine that after that rather explicit description of an alternative way of making love some people who are single might be feeling a little left out. The good news is that you can practice on your own, and it can be just as effective. For a man, practice self-stimulation, the big draw, and the microcosmic orbit and then when you can feel the aroused energy spreading to all of your body, take that into giving the gift of your genius. For a woman, in the same way after giving yourself pleasure and allowing it to spread, transform that pleasure into potent love through your heart. Let it flow through the channels you have mastered for creative expression, as a gift to all of your children, in all of their colors and forms.

FOR GAY COUPLES

Just in the same way that I am not an authority on feminine sexual energy, so I also have no experience of gay sex. I am not a good person to offer advice. But still, arousal is arousal, whoever else you invite to share it with, and many of the same principles will apply. The key with any of these practices is the same and is very simple. Let yourself get turned on, alone or together, then find your own way to spread that hot energy through your whole body and let it express itself as your gift of brilliance.

CHAPTER THIRTEEN

DISCOVER YOUR BRILLIANT DIET

The foods you eat and the liquids you drink have an enormous impact on the quality of your life. Primarily they affect your physical health, and how long you can expect to live, but they also affect your emotional state, your relationships, and the clarity of your mind.

Because this is literally a life-and-death topic, there is a seemingly endless torrent of advice available, on the Internet and everywhere else, about how you should eat. To say the least, it can be confusing and frustrating. Click here and you'll be told to eat only raw fruits and vegetables ... click over here and you'll be told to cook everything ... click again and you will learn that you should only eat things grown within 100 miles of your home, and that are in season ... click again and you will find an endless host of companies offering prepackaged "superfoods" sourced from all over the world, delivered to you in shiny foil packages. Faced with so much conflicting advice, many people just throw their hands up in the air and eat ... whatever.

Diet becomes relevant to our conversation about brilliance because your brain needs nutrition in order to operate well. But digestion also consumes energy, so when your body is working hard to digest a big meal, it may contribute to fogginess. The simple key to having a body and brain that support the greatest flow of brilliance is to get the maximum nutrition with the minimum amount of digestive work.

THE HUMAN DIETA

I have talked to hundreds of brilliant people about what they consume, and what they do not, and what impact those choices have specifically on sustained mental clarity. I have not met anyone who has taken this question more seriously than Eric Edmeades, the creator of WildFit.

In 1991, in his early twenties, Eric was in very poor health. He had debilitating stomach cramps that made it impossible to function while they were happening, cystic acne that made it difficult for him to turn his head at times, throat infections so severe that his tonsils bled on a regular basis, and nasal infection so severe that he had not breathed through his sinuses in years. He was overweight. He had been to doctors and specialists, and taken all the pills and injections he had been told to. Medication at its best gave him a little respite from the pain and suffering, but then it would all come back again. His doctor had scheduled him for a tonsillectomy.

Then a friend casually suggested that Eric might consider changing his diet. "What the hell," thought Eric, "I'll try it for a month. I've got nothing to lose." Eric made some significant changes, including eliminating sugar, dairy, and red meat and increasing his intake of fruits and vegetables. Over the next 30 days he lost 35 pounds and all of his symptoms disappeared. He was a changed man. Eric went back to his doctor and announced that he wanted to cancel the throat surgery. To his surprise, his doctor was not remotely interested in what Eric had done to make the symptoms go away, he simply tried to persuade him to have the surgery anyway. "Oh come on, if you cancel it now you'll lose your appointment, you might have to wait four months for your next surgery booking ... and we can give you a discount, a payment plan ..." His doctor wasn't in the least curious about what Eric had done to so dramatically change his health. He was essentially a salesman for the knife.

Eric's uncle was an orthopedic surgeon. "How long did you go to medical school?" Eric asked him. "About ten years," his uncle replied. "How much of that time did you spend studying food and nutrition?" Eric remembers his uncle cocking his head to one side, in the way a dog does when it is confused. He looked at Eric and said, "I don't recall any." Over the next few years Eric asked that same question of every doctor he met, and got the same reply.

His health continued to improve. He experimented with vegetarianism, then veganism, then a raw food diet, pescatarianism, and many other approaches. None of them were perfect, but each and every one was a huge improvement from what he had been doing before. Eric became passionately curious about why none of the doctors understood these basics of nutrition. He also studied anthropology, archaeology, biochemistry: anything and everything he could find that would shed light on the connection between diet and health.

Several years later, in 1997, Eric was flying to Africa on a photo shoot for Virgin Airlines. Casually, he flipped through the in-flight magazine, and found an article about elephants in zoos. Back in the late 19th century, elephants used to live for only six or seven years in captivity. Zoo owners did not care much, because they recovered their investment in that time. But then, when people started to study elephants in the wild, they learned that they lived for seventy or eighty years. The article identified that there is a difference between an elephant's "captive diet" and an elephant's "wild diet." A light went on in Eric's head. "Immediately I saw that the term 'wild diet' was incorrect. What elephants eat in the wild is simply 'the elephant diet.' What they were eating in captivity was 'not the elephant diet.'"

Eric had a blinding epiphany. "I understood that every species on earth has a diet. The word comes from the Greek word *"dieta,"* which means "way of life." There is a natural way of life for every species, and if it veers from that, there are going to be consequences. We don't really know what ours is, because of the food manufacturing industry, and the pharmaceutical industry ... everybody has twisted the understanding of our natural way of living."

Shortly afterwards, Eric read an article by Stanley Boyd Eaton, M.D., in *The New England Journal of Medicine*, titled *"Paleolithic*

Nutrition," which had been the first attempt, in 1985, to trace back the natural way of life for Homo Sapiens. Eric lamented that there was really nowhere today to look. You can find out about the natural way of life of elephants by going into the savannah in Africa. But where can you go to find human beings still living in their original natural state? Where can you find human beings living "in the wild"? Eric continued to study and search.

He visited the Bloemfontein Museum in South Africa, and saw the original Middle Stone Age skull dating back 259,000 years, discovered by T.F. Dreyer in 1932. He visited the caves excavated by Dreyer, which human beings have continuously inhabited for more than 200,000 years. "Archeologists had dug down into the cave floor 10 or 12 feet, and they had put glass up so you could walk down wooden steps and see evidence of the cave litter for the last 200,000 years. When people live in caves, they don't take out the trash, they just toss it on the floor. So it was possible to see the culinary history of our ancestors." It was only later that his grandmother told him that T.F. Dreyer was her father: Eric's great grandfather.

But Eric was not satisfied with archaeology or anthropology; he was still hungry to find wild and natural human beings alive today. His opportunity came a few years later when he was running a leadership program, taking people up Mount Kilimanjaro, in Tanzania. His logistics partners there knew he was interested in anthropology, and offered to take him to Lake Eyasi, in the central Rift Valley, to meet with the Hadza tribe. "The science world overwhelmingly agrees that human life started in Africa, and that the Rift Valley is considered to be one of the most important paleoanthropological sites in the world. So this was the opportunity I had been waiting for. The Hadza have had relatively little contact with the outside world, they are the closest thing we can find today of human beings living in the same way that we did hundreds of thousands of years ago. It was not enough to just go for a visit, I got embedded with them, and lived with them for a while. I brought no provisions with me, I lived as they did. Our first day we went out hunting. We walked for 27 miles, it was 42 degrees Celsius outside. Our second day we did 17 miles: we had to cut it short because we killed a bush pig and we had to carry it back.

"It was perfect timing, I had been studying so much anthropology, archaeology and human migration around the planet, by the time I got there I knew what to ask, I knew what to watch for. I was able to pay attention to how they dug up food, how they knew where to dig, how they got honey, and how they hunted for food." Eric has been back to spend time with the Hadza on several occasions since, and as a result, he feels that he has answered some major questions about the natural human diet and way of life.

"Elephants eat 200 kg of grass and fruit every day, and drink 70 liters of water," says Eric. "If you change that, they will get sick. Cheetahs need about two and a half kilos of fresh meat, more or less every day. If they don't get that, they start to suffer consequences.

Leafcutter ants, remarkably, don't actually eat leaves at all. They cut leaves and bring them back to compost them, and they eat the fungus that they grow.

"Homo sapiens evolved out of Africa. They migrated, over hundreds of thousands of years, into Asia, Europe and the Americas. But they are not endemic to those regions. We have to go back and look at human beings who were living in the area we evolved from, living the way that we lived, to understand our natural *dieta*. It's important to get clear about time frames, and the evolutionary velocity for humans. How long does it take for us to change our processing capacity for food, and our nutritional requirements? Food has to be bio-available to us. There is riboflavin in your wooden desk, but it doesn't mean you can eat it, because you're not a beaver or termite. Today the food industry fortifies things with vitamins and minerals. But it doesn't mean that you can necessarily absorb them. There is calcium in cow's milk, but it is not bio-available to Homo sapiens. It is available to baby cows, we have not evolved the ability to digest it.

"If it turned out that human beings could change their DNA in a moment, the past would have no relevance. But it turns out that we can't. We are Homo sapiens. We require vitamin C, and iron, and certain fats and proteins and oxygen. Over the last two hundred thousand years, what have we predominantly been eating? Not McDonald's, not refined sugar, not cow's milk. Not wheat, or corn, or white potatoes. Not processed food, not GMO food."

So what is the authentic human diet?

The answer appears to include upward of 200 plant species a year, on a seasonal basis: leafy vegetables, root vegetables, nuts, seeds, as well as animal products like eggs, meat, fish, and honey. Any changes one makes to that mix, either by removal or addition, may well put stress on the entire digestive system, which may also negatively impact mental clarity.

In the wake of his discoveries, Eric has developed a global online learning community practicing the principles of living a more natural diet, called WildFit. Thousands of people now have taken his educational programs. People who were overweight report weight loss that stays off easily. People who were malnourished report weight gain. Others report alleviation of allergies, skin conditions, headache, and digestive trouble. But what is most important and relevant to us here is that his graduates report significant sustained mental clarity throughout the day. Eric is teaching people to use diet to become more radically brilliant.

"Think about your body as a number of independent systems that all operate together to create an optimal survival circumstance," says Eric. "You have the lymphatic system, the cardiovascular system, the liver, the heart, and the brain. Remember *Star Trek*? When the dilithium crystals are not working properly, Captain Kirk orders shutting off power to the nonessential controls first. 'Scotty, shut off power to the environmental controls, cut power to the gravitational systems ...' When we become de-energized, through a combination of bad nutrition and lifestyle, the body will cut nonessential stuff first. The immune system gets depressed, digestion becomes sluggish, the muscular repair system shuts down. If you were the engineer choosing which systems to put onto reduced power, where would the brain be on that list?

"I have asked thousands of people this simple question. Most answer, 'At the end.' When someone gets tired and foggy at 4 o'clock in the afternoon, it suggests that every other system in their body has already slowed down dramatically. When mental clarity is diminished, it is the end of the line. All the other vitality in the body has already been depleted."

If you are really serious about adopting the perfect diet to support brilliance, the best solution would be to study with Eric. He has been kind enough to make an introductory video for the readers of this book, with more details about the ideal way of life for humans. You can watch it here: radicalbrilliance.com/wildfit.

CHINESE AND AYURVEDIC DIETARY WISDOM

Master Chunyi Lin has come to very similar conclusions, via a very different route. To maintain optimum mental clarity and brilliance with diet, he emphasizes three points. First, eat food that is in season. Eating seasonal fruits and vegetables puts our bodies more in harmony with the environment, and therefore causes less digestive stress. Second, he suggests primarily eating "local" food, grown within 100 miles of where you live. Third, Master Lin emphasizes the importance of eating most of your food early in the day, with the most substantial meal, breakfast, occurring when the stomach meridian is active, between 7 and 9 am. He then recommends a substantial lunch close to noon, and a light meal in the evening, close to sunset, consisting of a soup or a salad only.

Master Lin has studied the habits of ancient Chinese Masters, some of whom have reportedly lived for as long as 800 years. He reports that these specific foods show up repeatedly in their diets:

- walnuts
- olive oil
- goji berries
- kiwi
- tomatoes
- black sesame seeds
- black beans

Mary Jo Cravatta reaffirms Master Lin's suggestions. Ayurveda, too, recommends eating more substantial meals earlier in the day, as well as generally looking for foods that give maximum nutrition but are easy to digest. She adds to this avoiding cold food, like ice cream, which dampens the digestive fire. She further suggests taking some grated ginger in hot water before each meal to stimulate digestion and stimulate greater mental clarity.

I have talked to hundreds of other brilliant people about what they eat and drink. There is no absolute conformity to their answers, but all agree we should listen to our body and eat consciously, rather than from a place of craving, or conforming to a one-size-fits-all theory. What follows are some general principles that have frequently emerged in interviews. I suggest that you experiment with adding or eliminating one suggestion at a time, and observing if that change makes you more or less brilliant. Like this, you can slowly eliminate everything that fogs your clarity, and keep everything that gives you the best brain performance. If you want a simple jumpstart, I have included a sample meal plan at the end of this chapter.

BASIC DIETARY PRINCIPLES

1. Eat smaller and more frequent meals. To avoid the fogginess and low energy that frequently follows eating a large meal all at once, experiment with eating smaller amounts, five times a day. This can include breakfast, midmorning boost, lunch, mid-afternoon boost, and a light supper.

2. Simplify your Food Combinations. Our genetic ancestors primarily ate one thing at a time. After a hunt, they would eat meat, probably not accompanied by a nice Merlot, French fries or Béarnaise sauce. When scavenging for berries or nuts, they would eat their fill of what they found, not combine it with many other ingredients into a superfood bar. To minimize brain fogginess, combine protein with vegetables, or carbohydrates with vegetables, but not protein with carbohydrate. Sorry, no burger with fries. Eat fruits at a separate time.

3. Eat a Diet of Predominantly Vegetables. Eat 2 to 3 servings of vegetables per meal. This includes leafy green vegetables, like spinach, kale, and chard, as well as root vegetables like carrots, beets, and yams. Avoid white potatoes, as they contain a toxin that is difficult to digest. They were not indigenous to the area of Africa we originate from. Our online practice community contains a close to complete list of vegetables that humans have been eating for the longest time, and another list of vegetables to avoid.

4. Eat Healthy Fats. Contrary to much of the information that had been disseminated in the last decades, most nutritional experts now agree that fat is good for your brain. In fact, your brain needs healthy fat to be able to operate well. You can get the good fats you need from coconut butter, avocado, fatty meats, and nut butter. If you tolerate dairy well, butter itself is also a good source of fat.

5. Hydrate. Drink 2 to 3 liters of water per day, between meals, not with food. Upon rising, drink 16 ounces of water with a lemon squeezed into it, a pinch of sea salt, and a pinch of xylitol, and 2 ounces of aloe vera juice. Because of the way that most water is processed today, it has been stripped of the minerals found in spring water at its source. Adding salt and a natural sweetener makes it easier for your cells to get hydration from water.

6. Eat Fermented Foods. Many of the important brain chemicals that allow us to feel inspired and to think clearly, like serotonin and GABA, are actually produced in the gut. If you have used antibiotics in your life, even as a child, your natural gut flora may be imbalanced. This can cause indigestion, bloating, and gas, but also fogginess and mood swings. Eating fermented foods like sauerkraut, miso, kefir, and kombucha can restore the balance of healthy bacteria, which you may quickly experience affects your capacity to be creative.

7. Eat Eggs for Breakfast. In his book *How to stay Focused in a Hyperactive World*, John Gray devotes an entire chapter to eggs. Egg yolks, he tells us there, are packed with every nutrient needed for optimal brain functioning. They are rich in the amino acid tryptophan that creates serotonin. They also full of tyrosine, which is the precursor for dopamine production. Egg yolks are one of the few foods that contain vitamin D, without which the brain cannot utilize brain hormones to increase healthy focus. Egg yolks also filled with all the B vitamins, also necessary for creating healthy brain chemistry.

Many people are still concerned that eggs contribute to high cholesterol levels. Several studies done at Harvard University have proven that the beneficial cholesterol in eggs will not raise your cholesterol levels. If you have high blood pressure, eggs have even been shown to lower it. Many brilliant people eat 2 to 3 eggs every morning, 5 to 7 days a week. The beneficial nutrients in eggs will be most easily absorbed when they are eaten with greens, rather than potatoes or other carbohydrates.

8. Eat your Largest Meal at Lunch. After having a cooked breakfast of three eggs and greens, to maintain peak brain performance the biggest meal should be in the middle of the day. That is when the sun is highest in the sky and, according to the ancient wisdom of both Ayurveda and traditional Chinese medicine, it is when we have most digestive power.

The ideal lunch would be 2 to 3 cups of vegetables or salad together with a protein, which could be chicken, turkey, fish, red meat or, if you are vegetarian, tempeh or beans. Eat fish for lunch twice a week, because of the omega-3 oil it contains, which is an essential nutrient for the brain. Add some healthy fat to this meal, which could be the fat already in the meat, or you could add avocado, olive oil, coconut oil, or grape seed oil.

Since this is the heaviest meal of the day, try to organize to take a 20-minute nap after lunch. This will likely allow you to feel refreshed and alert in the afternoon. Such a nap should be absolutely no longer than 30 minutes, or your body will go into a deeper sleep cycle that will cause you to be drowsy for the rest of the day.

9. Eat a Light Supper Before the Sun goes Down. Many people have trouble with this suggestion, and it is really up to you whether you can or want to make it work. We talked about this already in the chapter on sleep. If you have been in the habit of eating a large dinner after dark, as many people do in big cities, and if you sense that your brain is not operating at its peak potential, this may be the little change that makes the biggest difference. Experiment for a month with eating soup only in the evening, before the sun sets, and not eating anything afterwards. Then see what happens. If it makes no difference, you can always go back. But it might make all the difference, as it has for me and many of my friends, and it might be the most important thing you get from this book.

Here are four great ideas for a light evening supper.

- Chicken Soup. You can prepare it once a week, or even once every two weeks and keep it in sealed Mason jars in the fridge.
- Kidgeree. An old favorite from the Indian subcontinent, very easy to digest with a balance of essential nutrients. Quick to cook.
- Bone broth. Also something you can prepare once or twice a month, and then keep it in jars in the fridge. Chop in a few vegetables in the evening, and you are all set.
- Vegetable Soup with Miso and Coconut Butter. Prepare in the blender.

For those who want to go deeper and practice in a more committed way, I have included recipes and video demonstrations for these preparations in our Global Brilliance Practice Community.

10. Snacks Between Meals. To keep your blood sugar levels stable, which will also allow you to feel emotionally balanced and mentally clear, it is a good idea to eat a snack midmorning and midafternoon. Experiment for yourself and see how this works for your body type and weight. Here are some snacks that work well:

- **Almond milk/Coconut milk/Cacao/ Carob/Maca/Date drink.** Blend for 30 seconds.
- **Fruit:** apple or pear or banana or a handful of blueberries.
- **Nuts.** Best to soak them overnight, which makes them easier to digest.
- **Blue corn chips or flaxseed crackers.**

Again, I have included more detailed instructions and video recipes in our online practice community.

FOODS TO AVOID

We can also look at this topic from a different angle, and think about a list of what to avoid in order to experience brilliance. Here is the list of the most common foods brilliant people have mentioned to me that you are better off without, if you aspire to make the greatest contribution to your grandchildren's grandchildren.

White sugar. This includes anything in which white sugar is the main ingredient, like carbonated drinks, candy, and pastries. Kombucha, mentioned above, is an exception because the sugar is used up in the fermentation process. Not sure? Google "negative effects of white sugar," and read some of the 2.6 million articles the search produces.

Milk and other Dairy Products. Many nutritionists today estimate that more people are allergic to milk than realize it. Try eliminating milk from your diet for a month, and see if it makes a difference. Yogurt and Kefir may be exceptions, because they are fermented and the lactose has been broken down.

Wheat. Eric Edmeades recognizes gluten as a plant's natural defense mechanism, a poisonous substance to human beings. He tells us that wheat did not grow in the area of Africa from which we evolve. Take the same approach: try eliminating wheat for a month and see if your digestion improves, and if you also notice increased mental clarity.

Peanuts. Although other nuts like almonds, cashews, hazelnuts, and walnuts, have been part of the human diet since prehistoric times, peanuts originate from South America, and have only been introduced into our diet in the last few hundred years. Many people notice that by eliminating peanuts their health and mental clarity improves.

Processed food. Of course, the entire gamut of chemicals that get added to food sold in packages today have almost no history at all in human evolution. They have mostly been introduced to our diet just within the last few decades. Experiment with eating fresh fruits and vegetables and protein from naturally raised sources, and see if you notice the difference.

Regular Alcohol Use. While the occasional drink with other brilliant friends may be useful to getting the creative juices flowing (see chapter 19) daily or even regular use of alcohol will cause a buildup of toxicity in the liver, and contribute to moodiness and often aggression.

A Sample Meal Plan

I have noticed that whenever I have read a book or an article with suggestions about what to eat and what not to eat, I get impatient. "Okay, okay, enough of the theory, just tell me specifically what to eat for breakfast, lunch and dinner. I'll try it out and see how I feel." If you feel the same way as I do, here is the sample meal plan I stick to fairly closely when I'm writing a book, creating an online course, or otherwise involved in a creative process.

- **On rising:** 16 ounces of lukewarm water with a lemon, a pinch of salt, a pinch of xylitol, 2 oz of aloe vera juice, and probiotics.
- After morning practice, around 8 a.m.:
  Three eggs cooked with greens (5 days a week)
  Avocado or a generous helping of other healthy fat
  Oats or buckwheat (2 times a week)

- Midmorning snack, around 11 a.m.:
  Almond milk/coconut milk/cacao/carob/ maca/date / drink
  ... or
  Apple or banana or pear ... or
  A handful of goji berries, and a handful of cashew nuts ... or
  Any other snack which lifts you up and takes minimum digestive energy.
- Lunch, between 12:30 and 1:
  Two servings of vegetables, including roots, leafy vegetables, legumes,
  Chicken, fish, lamb, beef or beans
  A helping of healthy fat
- 20-minute nap after eating
- Afternoon snack:
  Tibetan Magic with shilajit (see next chapter)
  Sassafras / Roobos Tea / Xylitol / Super Yang Jing / Deer Antler Drops Drink
  Or any other healthy snack
- Supper, half an hour before the sun goes down:
  Steamed veggies in a blender, with coconut oil ... or
  Chicken soup or ...
  Bone broth soup or ...
  Kidgaree.
- No food after dark

Have fun experimenting, and remember to trust the wisdom of your own body more than any theory, including everything written here.

CHAPTER FOURTEEN
MOST BRILLIANT SUPPLEMENTS

The majority of brilliant people I have interviewed over the years use some form of nutritional supplement, in addition to the dietary recommendations outlined in the previous chapter. Sometimes people ask, "Why should I use nutritional supplements out of a bottle? Aren't they just chemicals, artificial and difficult for the body to digest? Isn't it enough to eat good food?" There is certainly validity to asking these questions. When we isolate nutrients from the foods in which they naturally occur, we do run the risk of reduced bio-availability. So once again, the important thing is to experiment slowly, one thing at a time, and see if it makes a difference. I have listed below, in descending order of importance and popularity, the nutritional supplements that most experts have agreed are most likely to make the most difference to your brain being in the optimal state for clarity and brilliance. Please be aware that I am not a medical practitioner, and I am not qualified to give medical advice. What is listed here is simply to report on what my interviewees found helpful. Please consult with your medical advisor before purchasing supplements.

John Gray is known the world over for his groundbreaking book on relationship, *Men Are from Mars Women Are from Venus*. That book has sold more than 60 million copies in 40 different languages, and has hovered near the top of the bestseller lists for two decades. Not as many people are aware that John is also one of the most well-researched and eloquent authorities alive today on the effect of nutritional supplements on the brain. He has developed his own formulas called MarsVenus Wellness, and his 2015 book *Staying Focused in a Hyper World* is packed with information about the causes of Attention Deficit Disorder and natural ways to heal it. Although the book was written primarily to address the epidemic of ADHD, it is also completely relevant to people like you and me who want to welcome more brilliance into our lives, and it contains much more information than we could fit into our chapter here.

I am indebted to John for most of the information that follows in this chapter, as well as to Daniel Schmachtenberger, the founder of Neurohacker Collective, and the creator of Qualia, which we will discuss later.

THE TOP 10 SUPPLEMENTS TO ENHANCE BRILLIANCE

Here they are, in descending order of importance. If you only have the budget and the bandwidth to take one thing, take #1. If you can expand to two, take #1 and #2, etc.

#1 Minerals

Both John and Daniel agree, as do most of the other people I have spoken to, that the most important supplementation for the brain is bio-available minerals. Due to the industrialization of farming in the last 70 years, as well as the introduction of chemical fertilizers and pesticides, the topsoil has been largely stripped of the essentials trace minerals to be found in fruits and vegetables. If you eat from your own vegetable garden, as we do, and you had the soil tested for mineral content, the need for mineral supplementation could be a little less. But why take the chance?

Minerals act as cofactors for other important metabolic processes in the body. This means that they often don't do anything on their own; they are "helper molecules" that help other nutrients become active and functional. Both Zinc and Magnesium are good examples. They are both cofactors in the efficient production and use of vitamin D. Our brains do not function well when deficient in this vitamin, but our bodies cannot utilize the vitamin properly when these cofactor minerals are deficient.

Generally, we cannot utilize minerals in their raw state. Galvanized Zinc, for example, may be applied as a coating on your car battery nodes, or on chain fencing, but you can't just scrape it off and eat it. Magnesium is the fourth most common element in the earth, and the 11th most abundant by mass in the human body. It is essential to all our cells, and to some 300 enzymes. But in order to assimilate this essential nutrient, it must be bound to another element, usually an organic compound, called a chelant. Hence you can purchase magnesium threonate, magnesium citrate, or magnesium hydroxide as a supplement, but not Magnesium alone.

When you were a small baby, you got these essential minerals in your mother's milk, which is rich in orotic acid. More and more researchers today are recognizing that this may be the most efficient and the most natural form of chelation: to bind minerals to the very same carrier which a mother produces to feed a baby. Dr. Hans Nieper, a German physician, was a pioneer in the discovery of mineral oretates and determined that magnesium oretate, lithium oretate, or potassium oretate is significantly more bio-available to us than in other forms. He was the victim of a campaign by drug companies to discredit him in his lifetime, but many of his theories, particularly about oretates, have been further developed since his death. When John Gray read this research, he had trouble finding a good mineral supplement bound to orotic acid, so he did what John Gray has always done in his life: he created his own. You can buy Mars Venus Super Minerals, one designed for men and one designed for women, from his website (marsvenus.com) or on Amazon.

#2 Probiotics

John Gray reminds us that all of the naturally occurring brain chemicals, like serotonin, are created in the gut. "People who can't focus," he says, "who suffer from ADHD, autism, dementia, or who are depressed or anxious, very frequently have both an imbalance in their brain function, and also imbalances in digestion. It may be irritable bowel, bloating, gas, stomach ache, or diarrhea. These are all symptoms of imbalanced gut flora."

Dr. Andrew Newberg even suggests that brain cells reside not only inside the skull, but also in the heart, and in the gut: we actually have three brains. The lining in the intestines is made of the same gray matter as the brain.

A well-balanced gut flora, known as the "microbiome," effects the production of nutrients, molecules, enzymes, and vitamins that will then lead to optimal brain function: they synergize together to digest our food and put it into a form we can utilize.

"Probiotics is the new medicine of the future," says Gray. "Antibiotics kill some of the original probiotics that are essential, and that were passed on from mother to child, from mother to child, from mother to child. "

The solution is quite simple and easily available: to take a daily probiotic supplement until the microbiome is restored to a healthy balance. There is a catch, however. Not all probiotic strains are the same. Many of the products you find in your local health food store do contain multiple strains of healthy bacteria, but they are no longer alive.

Three probiotic products stand out above the pack for having live active and viable strains of healthy bacteria:

HMF Forte, by Genestra Labs, contains 10 billion CFU per capsule. It must be shipped in a cooler bag, and then refrigerated. It has been tested by several independent labs to have one of the highest amounts of live bacteria among probiotic supplements.

Enterogenic Concentrate by Integrative Therapeutics is a blend of prebiotic and probiotic ingredients, highly concentrated human-strain microflora. It is well-tolerated by most people, and provides both beneficial intestinal bacteria and growth factors shown to promote healthy recolonization. It does not require refrigeration, and in fact they guaranteed the viability of the microflora at room temperature through the expiration date.

Bravo Yogurt. This comes in three sachets that you need to mix together into cooked milk at home, and then consume morning and evening, so it requires both cooking and refrigeration. The manufacturer claims that it contains 42 different strains of probiotic with colostrum, which within weeks will replace the original microbiome in your gut. John Gray claims "it has had miraculous results for people in terms of better brain function, better energy, better digestion. I lost a lot of weight in the belly." Bravo is available from marsvenus.com

#3 Potential Vitamins

This is not just an ordinary multivitamin. It was originally developed by Dr. Jerry Schlesser to support schoolchildren to improve academic performance and behavior. Anthony Elementary, a failing

K5 school in Leavenworth, Kansas was in deep trouble. The school never met any standardized testing benchmarks. Police were called in to manage out-of-control kids at least once a week. Violence statistics were nine times the state average, with high rates of absenteeism for both teachers and students. The school was about to be shut down.

For one year, the kids were given two tablets of Potential Vitamins every day. That was the only thing that changed. After one year, Anthony Elementary exceeded standardized testing benchmarks, and tested #1 in the district in math and #2 in English. There was a 97% reduction in office referrals for disciplinary problems and a reduction in absenteeism. The school was awarded recognition as a "Top School" by the Confidence and Education task force, and won an award for excellence from the state governor. It was the subject of a PBS special called "How to Turn Around A Failing School."

Potential is completely different from mass market vitamins, because it does not include the artificial colors and flavors that have been shown to adversely impact behavior and brain chemistry. It contains beneficial antioxidants from ORAC (Oxygen Radical Absorbance Capacity) super fruits and berries: bilberry, blueberry, cranberry, grape, elderberry, raspberry, rose hips, blackberry, pomegranate, and red Concord grapeskin. These fruits provide essential antioxidant supplementation from natural food sources, reported to be beneficial for healthy brain and nerve function, memory and neurocognitive performance. Although this product was originally developed for school kids, both John Gray and I, and many of our friends, take this every day, and you might be interested to try it as well. [mykidspotential.com]

#4 Vitamin D3

Vitamin D3 is an essential nutrient; every cell in your body has a D3 receptor site. It is critical to the health of your brain and nervous system, as well as the cardiovascular and immune systems. D3 is an important cofactor in the absorption of calcium. To have good memory and mental clarity you need a sufficient supply of calcium, but you also need to be able to absorb it. Vitamin D3 is essential for that.

We naturally get vitamin D3 from being in the sun, when most of the body is exposed for two hours every day. That is how most of our ancestors lived. Today, not all of us can manage that, especially during the long dark northern winters. Even for people who can get enough sun, today many people are afraid of getting skin cancer, so we use sunblock which prevents your body from making D3. The solution may be to use a supplement. John Gray prefers Source Naturals, and feels that 2000 to 10,000 IU a day is safe.

#5 Omega 3 Oil

In order to have good memory, the brain cells must be able to communicate with each other, quickly and easily. As we get older, our nerve cells become smaller, the vessels that carry nutrients to the cells and blood decline, and we often suffer from inflammation. As a result, the brain produces fewer neurotransmitters. Memory and cognitive function suffer. Omega-3 fatty acids, particularly Docosahexaenoic (DHA) have been determined to promote efficient electrical signaling between nerve cells, reduce inflammation, and improve concentration and fight memory loss. A study in *Neurology*, published in 2014, found that postmenopausal women who had higher levels of omega-3 fatty acids EPA and DHA also had larger brain volume, the equivalent of preserving the brain for an additional two years. Smaller brain volume has been linked to Alzheimer's disease and to the effects of aging. The body cannot manufacture omega-3 fatty acids, it needs to absorb them from food sources.

Fish is one of the best sources of omega-3, but they also carry risk of mercury and other heavy metals. Here are two great sources of omega-3 fatty acid as a supplement.

Vectomega is a relatively new form of omega-3, derived from wild salmon to support healthy heart and brain. It contains up to 50 times higher triglyceride fish oil than other omega oil supplements, because the fatty acids are bound to phospholipids instead of triglycerides, making them more stable. Vectomega is produced with enzymes and cold water, using no heat, pressure, or solvents. As a result, you don't get an upset stomach or "fish burp," which omega-3 supplements sometimes produce.

Liposomal DHA. Empirical Labs manufactures a fantastic source of omega-3, as liposomal DHA. It needs to be refrigerated. Liposomes are one of the most efficient ways of carrying nutrients all the way to the cells.

#6 Liposomal Vitamin C

Vitamin C is the most important vitamin you can take for your health. Without vitamin C we don't just suffer impaired health: we die. When animals get sick they naturally produce 200 times more vitamin C in the body than it needs. We are one of the few species that cannot make our own vitamin C; we have to get it from food. Glutathione (which we will discuss in a moment) is naturally produced by the liver, and causes us to reuse vitamin C, to recycle it. But the use of fever-reducing drugs, particularly in childhood, keeps our bodies from making enough glutathione.

The difficulty with maintaining sufficient vitamin C levels is that it gets flushed out of the body very quickly. You can make sure you have an abundant supply of vitamin C in your diet by eating foods like citrus fruit, red pepper, and kale, and that may be enough if you are in good health. But once you get sick, you may need as much as 200 times more vitamin C than when you are healthy. One way to get additional vitamin C into your body is with powdered supplements, like synthesized ascorbic acid, or more sophisticated products like EmergenC, which are fortified with other vitamins and minerals. But because most of its gets flushed out of your body, you may need to take many large doses a day when you are sick, in order for even a little of it to get absorbed, which can cause diarrhea. The alternative, which is much more effective, but for most people somewhat impractical, is to take vitamin C through an IV drip. Doctors who administer this say that you absorb much more vitamin C than with powdered supplements, but you have to go to a clinic to have it administered.

The recently innovated solution to this problem is "Liposomal" vitamin C. This means that the vitamin (and the same could apply to any other nutrient) has been enrobed in phosphatidylserine, under intense pressure, so as to make it enormously more available to the body. Empirical Labs [empirical-labs.com] produces a fantastic range of liposomal products. They cost a little more than off-the-shelf supplements, but you can tell the difference.

When John Gray and I were writing the book *Conscious Men* we got pretty enthusiastic, and put in long hours together. Sometimes we would work on the book till two o'clock in the morning, and then we were up again at seven a.m. to play some more. John has seemingly limitless supplies of energy, and although he's six years older than me, I have trouble keeping up. Sometimes I would wake up in the morning at his house, feeling very groggy. Then he would whip me up a magical concoction in the kitchen. Into his blender he would put some coconut water, some high-potency probiotics, and then less than a teaspoon from each of six bottles that he kept in his fridge. I had no idea what they were. But, after he blended the mixture for 30 seconds and handed me the glass, I could not believe the effect it had. It was like watering a dry plant, and watching it spring back to life in seconds. I could literally feel my brain getting clearer, my eyesight getting brighter, and my energy picking up ... in real time. The secret ingredients? Empirical Labs' liposomal vitamin C, glutathione, B12, DHA, CoQ10, and Reversatrol. If you really want to discover what liposomal supplementation can do for you, buy these six products for a month, and make a drink like this each morning. See if it does for you what it did for me.

#7 MCT Oil

Medium Chain Triglyceride (MCT) Oil is extracted from the caprylic acid found in coconut oil. It rapidly metabolizes into ketones, giving almost immediate energy to the brain, without requiring glucose from dietary sugars and carbohydrates. It is a low-density oil with excellent absorption properties. The bottom line is that you get the energy from the oil, without it converting to fat. MCT Oil has been demonstrated to improve athletic performance by increasing lean muscle mass and supporting athletic recovery time. For brilliance, it supports mitochondrial energy, because it supports cognitive performance with hardly any of the strain on your liver associated with other fats. It also has potent antimicrobial effects, helps support healthy digestion and immune function. The best brand you can get is called Brain Octane, and is produced by the same people who make Bulletproof coffee. [bulletproof.com/Brain-Octane]

#8 Glutathione

Glutathione is one of the most important molecules you need to stay healthy and prevent disease, but it is also essential to the production of brain chemicals. Glutathione is produced naturally all the time by your liver; the highest concentrations are found in the liver, pancreas, kidneys, and even in the lens of your eye. It is rich in sulfur, and so is a highly effective antioxidant, which reduces free radicals and heavy metals throughout the body. In a young and healthy body, there is no need for glutathione supplementation, because the liver produces it. It only becomes a question if the liver is sluggish or unhealthy. The primary reason our bodies stop producing sufficient glutathione is because of the use of fever suppressants like acetaminophen. Drugs which encourage the body to reduce fever simultaneously encourage the liver to stop producing glutathione. Regular alcohol use would have the same effect. If you suspect that your liver is under stress, and therefore not producing enough glutathione on its own, the best supplementation would be Empirical Labs' liposomal glutathione. You probably only need to take it for a short time, until your body can produce enough glutathione on its own again.

#9 CoQ10

CoQ10 is an extremely important coenzyme which allows your body to utilize oxygen in the process of making energy. If you don't have enough CoQ10, you feel tired and sluggish. It is the ultimate anti-aging supplement. "People often think that they are getting old, and so they have less energy," says John Gray, "but it's the other way round. In fact, if your body is producing less energy, it leads to the symptoms of aging." CoQ10 is absolutely essential for both brain health and muscular health. It is the essential nutrient your body requires for healthy mitochondrial functioning. The mitochondrial sheath protects almost all cells, particularly brain cells, and is responsible for the transmission of energy through the body. Once again, the combination of CoQ10 with liposomes is an excellent way to transport this delicate nutrient to all parts of the body. Liposomal CoQ10 bypasses the digestive track to go straight to the cells. You can take it with collagen peptide as a way to rebuild muscle mass.

#10 Grape Seed Extract

In France and Italy, people have always eaten the seeds in grapes, and they also go into the wine. Some people suggest that this might account for the extraordinary intellectual and philosophical contribution these countries have made. Grape seed has a concentration of proanthocyanidins, also found in pine bark extract. It is a kind of flavonoid, containing ketones, which makes it not only a highly potent antioxidant, protecting the body against free radical damage, but is also excellent for staying focused and having high comprehension, energy and calm. A dose of 300 mg a day, combined with 600 mg of vitamin C, will potentize the vitamin C as well as Vitamin D, and has been linked to improved transmission of energy in the brain. John Gray recommends Natural Factors brand as the most effective.

THE MAGIC MIX

Nootropics really require to be discussed in a class of their own. The word refers to any kind of smart drug or cognitive enhancer that directly and primarily improves cognitive function, memory, creativity, and motivation. It is a field that has become increasingly popular in just the last few years, but it is also an extremely controversial topic. Neuroscientists, psychiatrists, and doctors have all weighed in on the debate about whether such substances are ethical, as well as voicing concerns about adverse side effects. The main problem is that almost all substances that give immediate cognitive enhancement are also stimulants, like caffeine, Adderall and many energy drinks, which can also have long-term negative effects on health.

What appears so far to be a close to perfect solution to this conundrum is the advent of *Qualia*, developed by Daniel Schmachtenberger and his team at the Neurohacker Collective. Qualia comes in two very beautiful black bottles, with text printed in gold ink. Just the aesthetics will improve your day! Step One you take upon rising. It has an immediate effect (noticeable within 30 seconds) and contains a blend of ingredients which immediately stimulate clarity and productivity. But what is even more ingenious is that it also has a Step Two, which you take with food at breakfast or lunch. Step Two has no noticeable immediate effect. It contains nutrients to support the brain to rebuild neural pathways conducive to long-term cognitive enhancement. Almost everyone I know at this point is using Qualia, with unanimously beneficial effects. People swear by it. I'm not going to say more about it here, but please do stop by and listen to a personal message from Daniel about how he created Qualia and why it is so effective both in the short term and long term. They also offer a discount to readers of this book, like you. [radicalbrilliance/qualia]

SUPPLEMENTS TO TAKE ON AN AS-NEEDED BASIS

Everything we have mentioned so far has been suggested to have beneficial effect for more or less anyone who uses them. Now we will turn our attention to some supplements that are useful, but on an as-needed basis. Once again, please understand that I am simply reporting to you on what some brilliant people have told me helped them. Before you use any of these supplements, please make sure to consult your healthcare provider.

Lithium Oretate. Developed by Dr. Nieper, John Gray reports that the prudent use of this supplement helps to balance mood. It is present in Mars Venus mineral supplements, but if you notice yourself having significant mood swings, you might like to take extra. John tells us that one or two tablets a day will be enough for this purpose. He recommends the Advanced Research brand, available on Amazon.

Digestive enzymes. Once again, the neurotransmitters essential to our pursuit of brilliance are mostly created in the gut. If your digestion is not working well, if you feel gassy and bloated after meals, or even full after a few bites, your body may not be producing enough enzymes. There are three types of digestive enzymes. Amylases break down starches into sugar molecules; proteases break down proteins into amino acids; and lipases break down break down lipids into fatty acids and glycerol. We produce these enzymes in the mouth, in the stomach, and in the small intestines. Unlike other mammals, we are unable to break down the cellulose in plant cell walls, often referred to as "fiber." Since it does not get digested, fiber passes through into the large intestine and helps to feed healthy bacteria. John Gray recommends Nieperzyme, made by Advanced Research, which are food and digestive enzymes formulated by Hans A. Nieper, whom we mentioned earlier in connection with oretates.

If you have weak digestion, the bottle recommends taking 2 tablets just before a meal.

Maca Root (lepidium meyenii) is one of a class of substances known as "adaptogens," which help the body to assimilate and deal with stress. It is often referred to as one of the world's great "super foods." It grows high in the mountains of South America, mainly in the high-altitude regions of Peru. It is mostly recommended for its positive effect on hormone balance, energy levels, and general good health. It has a higher calcium level than milk, in a highly bio-available form. We have talked elsewhere about sexual energy: if you notice that your libido is low, and that this might be negatively affecting your creativity, maca might be your best friend.

Tibetan Magic. This is an excellent tonic produced by Dragon Herb, one of the most reputable companies for distributing traditional medicinal herbs. It is marketed as a unique, anti-aging, adaptogenic energy drink designed for creative individuals. They claim that it increases oxygen supplies in the blood, which directly affects both physical and mental energy, and that it lifts the spirit, calms the nerves, clears the senses, and generally lifts life-experience to another level. It is a blend of Tibetan and Chinese tonic herbs that have a reputation for both immediate and long-term health benefits. The main ingredient is the Tibetan tonic herb *Rhodiola Sacra*, revered as the most sacred herb of Tibet for its ability to increase concentration and memory, physical endurance, and sexual performance and enjoyment. Tibetan Magic is blended with other supertonic herbs and with wild cherry juice (a powerful antioxidant).

I use it regularly, and every word they say matches my experience. Colter Merrick, The founder of Elixart, and one of the teachers in our brilliance practice community blends the Tibetan Magic with Pur Black Shilajit, cinnamon and cardamom essential oils and sparkling water. You can't do much better than this for an afternoon pickup.

Ant Soda. If you can handle it, another product from Dragon Herb might be the ultimate energy boost, particularly for men. The small print is (and take a deep breath before you read this), it is made from Changbai Mountain Ants. You heard me right: the primary active ingredient is ants. Yes, the creepy crawly little black insects. Once you get over the feelings of shock and distaste, you may be ready to read that this is one of the most powerful tonic substances known. Polyrhachis Ants are widely consumed throughout Asia because of their many known health benefits. A dropperful gives a quick "Chi" boost to the brain and body, making it the almost perfect afternoon pickup remedy. Mix it with some berry concentrate and sparkling water. [dragonherbs.com]

Gabatrol. If you have trouble sleeping because of overwork or feelings of anxiety, many people have reported benefits from the use of gabatrol. It is claimed to be one of the few GABA products that successfully reaches the brain. If you plan to use this, drop by and watch a short video from Brian Cunningham, who created the product talking about how to get the best results. [radicalbrilliance. com/gabatrol].

Iodine. Iodine is a very important mineral that many of us don't get enough of today. It gets depleted in the body when we have absorbed too much chlorine, fluoride, and bromine. Your doctor can perform a blood test to measure iodine level, but there is also a test you can administer at home, by buying a solution of iodine and painting it on to a 3" x 3" area of your skin. Proponents of this test suggest that if the yellow color of the iodine solution disappears within a few hours, you are iodine-deficient. If it stays yellow for 24 hours, you have enough iodine. If you discover that you are iodine-deficient, John Gray recommends Iodoral by Optomox.

CHAPTER FIFTEEN

THE SUPPLEMENTS DADDY WILL NOT ALLOW

In 1943, a Swiss chemist in Basel working for the pharmaceutical company Sandoz took a jar down from a shelf in his laboratory. Let's call him Al. The jar had already been sitting there for several years, left over from research they had been doing on the fungus ergot for the treatment of contractions in pregnancy, but had found the results to be unsatisfactory.

It was extremely uncommon, almost unheard of, for a chemist to open up a substance for research that had already been abandoned, but this was 1943, the rest the world was busy killing each other in a world war, and Switzerland was neutral, so everyone had a lot of extra time on their hands. Al decided, as an experiment, to further synthesize the preparation. Later that day he felt "woozy" and had to sit down. His consciousness felt distinctly altered. He realized that he must have had got a tiny amount on his finger, and attributed this to the cause of his altered consciousness. So Al embarked upon an experiment. He decided to ingest a little bit more of the substance and see what happened. Bear in mind that pharmaceuticals are usually taken in milligrams: thousandths of a gram. For example, when you ingest vitamin C as ascorbic acid, you probably take a dose of 500 mg to 1000 mg, without any wooziness. Al wanted to be *extremely* cautious, so he took 250 micrograms [µg], a quarter of one milligram, or 1/4000 of a gram. With any other substance known to pharmacology, this would have had absolutely no effect whatsoever.

In fact, it had an extremely strong effect that lasted for three days. In the first phase (probably because even this small dosage was still too high), he experienced "everything in my field of vision was distorted as if seen in a curved mirror," but as it settled it down, "a sensation of well-being and renewed life flowed through me." The entire experience lasted for three days. Al was amazed, shocked, intrigued, and a little afraid. He lowered the dose even more, and then tested this on his secretary and other colleagues working at the pharmaceutical lab. Everyone experienced dramatic changes in consciousness, which often included feelings of deep insight and powerful self-reflection, as though "their eyes had been washed clean and they were seeing for the first time the beauty of the world."

This newly discovered substance was tested on animals, and then on humans in a clinical setting. It was determined to have useful psychiatric applications, so it was patented by Sandoz, and sold under the name Delysid. Over the next 20 years Delysid underwent huge amounts of research in more than 30 countries. It was widely used in a psychiatric setting, where in a controlled environment psychiatric patients would be temporarily alleviated of feelings of low self-worth, and could see their life in a fresh way and make new choices. It was used in prisons, where one dose reduced recidivism from an average of over 80% to an average of under 20%. It was tested by the Army. In addition to its application to treat mental illness, Delysid was also used by artists, musicians, and scientists, and was found to greatly enhance creativity. Among it's advocates were Cary Grant, Arthur Koestler, William Burroughs and countless others.

In the early 1960s, a group of Harvard professors became interested in *Delysid*. They had already been exploring similar substances from organic sources. An entire department was set up to investigate the impact of such substances, now known as entheogens, not just on treating mental illness, but as a gateway to accessing more integrated states of the human brain.

One such young researcher, then at Stanford, was a graduate student named James Fadiman, who later went on to found the Institute for Transpersonal Psychology. He is the author of *The Psychedelic Explorer's Guide* and is widely regarded today as one of the greatest living authorities on entheogens.

"Back in those days," he recalls," we conducted a study with senior scientists. The prerequisite for getting in was that you had to have been working on a specific problem for a couple of months and failed. These were people who made their living solving difficult problems and weren't familiar with failure, so they were very intellectually and emotionally invested. We told them that we were going to set up a situation where they would have a better chance at solving these challenging problems. We gave 100μg of this substance. Within a few hours, out of 48 unsolved problems, we had 44 solutions. We also gave them traditional creativity psychological tests and every participant improved. Not only did the subjects discover solutions in a few hours, but they reportedly remained more creative for a period of 4 to 8 weeks; there was an afterglow that slowly diminished."

There are volumes of studies like this, unparalleled in pharmaceutical research before or since.

In 1963 all this came to an abrupt halt. *Delysid* was made illegal, along with many other similar substances, both for psychiatric and experimental use in the United States, and the rest of the world soon followed suit.

The Swiss scientist in this story was, as you may have guessed, Albert Hoffman, and his "problem child drug" is Lysergic Acid Diethylamide, abbreviated as LSD-25.

THE WAR ON ~~DRUGS~~ BRILLIANCE

LSD is just one of a number of drugs which got swept up in the "war on drugs" that started in the '60s, and then got underway with full force in the 1980s. It has been frequently described as the most successful and coordinated global misinformation campaign in human history.

The "group think" we have all been indoctrinated into about "drugs" and people who are "on drugs" is so pervasive that it is actually quite challenging to find anyone willing to re-examine the facts. But nevertheless, that re-examination has been boldly and soberly taking place in the last years, and is now fully underway.

Imagine for a moment that you live in a community with other people: something like a small village, or a housing development. One day, one of your neighbors inadvertently and accidentally drinks a glass of toilet bowl cleaner, and becomes incredibly sick. She is rushed to the hospital, and has to have her stomach pumped. Of course, all her friends and family and everyone in the community are shocked, dismayed, and naturally want to take steps to make sure this *never* happens again, to anyone. Ever.

"Well, let's see now, Mary drank toilet bowl cleaner. Toilet bowl cleaner is a liquid. Whiskey, that's also a liquid. I also got very sick when I drank half a bottle of that stuff last year."

"Yes, and what about cod liver oil?" someone else chimes in. "I drank a bunch of that stuff once, and I was on the toilet all day. That's a liquid too."

"Yep," now weighs in the elected leader of the community, well into his eighties. "I think we can safely conclude that liquids are dangerous. We need to start a war on all liquids. Starting today."

Whoa! Wait a minute, slow down there! Water is also liquid, so is orange juice, they are not harmful. And that whiskey you talked about, half a bottle made you sick, but a splash in the bottom of a glass with some ice could have been quite pleasant. But it's too late. Everyone has their hands in their ears now, and they are all chanting together, "La la la la la la... We can't hear you," very, very loudly.

Dr. Fadiman comments, "There was no scientific basis to the decision to make LSD and other psychedelics illegal. The United States was in a cultural crisis. A lot of young people didn't approve of things the United States government was doing, such as Vietnam, especially drafting young people into the war. Psychedelics were part of that counterrevolution. So those in charge thought, 'These people are trouble. They are using this substance. We don't like their views, so if we make the substance illegal, they won't use it as much, and they may be less trouble.' Of course the logic was faulty, because the use did not decline, and the political pressure did not change."

"I am for science and medicine," Dr. Fadiman continues, "I'm not for dogmatic evidence-less legislation. I prefer science-based laws. The fact is, micro-dosing LSD has proven terrific for people with treatment-resistant depression. Why should people not be allowed to have medications that heal? Here in the United States we are having an opioid epidemic. In states where there is now medical marijuana there are not only fewer opioid deaths but there is also 15% less opioid prescription. Many people on opioids, when given the opportunity, use marijuana instead because it's safer."

"Since LSD was made illegal, 26 million Americans have taken it," Dr Fadiman goes on. "These are the US government's figures (the government annually asks all kinds of people to answer anonymously what kind of illegal things they have been doing), so the total is undoubtedly low. There have been about 400,000 to 600,000 new users each and every year; it is very hard to suppress something when there are that many new people taking it every year, and it is available. From my point of view, making LSD illegal is like trying to ban the color red."

Dr Rick Doblin is the founder and executive director of the Multidisciplinary Association for Psychedelic Studies (*maps.org*), which has been responsible for implementing dozens of psychedelic drug studies around the world. Says Doblin, "The key problem with the drug war and prohibition is that we are trying to ascribe properties to the substance, when what is really important is the relationship between the person and the substance. There is no such thing as a good drug or a bad drug. It's the relationship between how we approach a drug, and what it's used for that makes it good or bad. Not the drug itself."

There is a simple reason why I chose to include this topic in this book. Empiricism. I have come to conclusions about what precipitates brilliance by interviewing more than 420 extremely brilliant people over the last 20 years. By no means all, but a significant number of them, have used one or more of the substances referenced below, sometimes just once or twice in the past, and sometimes more recently and more regularly. What is most important: a significant number of these people described this experience as one of the most the most important of their life, and pivotal to the generation of brilliance.

Let's shift from listening to scientists for a moment to hearing from a highly creative contemporary musician. Alex Ebert is a Golden Globe winner, and the founder and lead singer of *Edward Sharpe and the Magnetic Zeros*. "Almost everyone I know has benefited from entheogenic substances, including myself," he says. Ebert believes that in the past, taking these substances was interpreted as a sign of irresponsibility and rebelliousness. "People like Timothy Leary threw the issue in the mainstream culture's face. These days the attitude towards all of these drugs is shifting. I know a lot of people in the business world who have done acid, and speak freely about it. It is not in anyone's face, there is nothing rebellious about it, it is about self-discovery. We have to tip our hats and be thankful that this is entering the mainstream culture.

"We have lost so much of our coming-of-age traditions. There are no walkabouts, no sun dance, none of these things. People are discovering their own ways to have self-realization moments that include the edge of fear. You are jumping into an unknown crucible, where you have a reckoning with yourself, your fears, and ideas of self-control. It makes available to us the classic arc of self-realization, coming to terms with things, having an amazing time, and then walking away with some takeaways that improve your scope and widen your sense of who you are in the context of the world."

SORTING POISONS FROM ELIXIRS

I have spent the last twenty-five years of my life training coaches and offering one-on-one coaching, and I have been extraordinarily lucky to have some amazing students and coaching clients over this time. Top-Notch. In the summer of 2016, I was leading a one-week Radical Brilliance Laboratory in Corfu in Greece. One of the participants was a professor of pharmacology at a university in the Netherlands. Her job was to coordinate between Big Pharma and the local health authorities, to determine which drugs were really helpful, and which were just profiteering. She knows a lot about how to evaluate substances objectively. Also in the room were two psychiatrists, a lawyer, and a doctor. The rest of the assembled dignitaries were also no dummies. Another of my coaching clients has a senior position in the World Health Organization.

This group wanted to talk about entheogens, so we did a little experiment together. We asked ourselves this question: *If the government had a justification to make a substance illegal, what would be the factors contributing to that decision?* My erudite group got busy discussing this among themselves in small groups, and after about an hour came up with these criteria:

- *Is the substance addictive?*
- *Is it harmful to your own health or potentially lethal?*
- *Could it cause aggressive or dangerous antisocial behavior?*
- *Could it be harmful to others' health?*

- *Is it a danger to children and teenagers?*
- *Does it precipitate crime or social problems?*
- *Is it polluting to the environment?*

Then we took a fresh look together at a range of substances that could somehow change your consciousness, irrespective of whether they are currently deemed legal or illegal. The results were very interesting.

Heroin always gets very low marks in such an evaluation: it is addictive, it can easily kill you, it does precipitate crime, especially once made illegal. An equally low score went to cocaine, and methamphetamines. But alcohol, tobacco, and many prescription opiates, although considered legal, also came off badly. There are other substances which, although considered illegal, are not addictive, have no negative health effects, do not cause aggressive or antisocial behavior, and when used at an appropriate dosage and under supervision posed little to no danger to the user or others, in fact seem to have great benefit. A similar fresh reevaluation of the drug laws has been discussed widely in the last years.

This is clearly a conversation that needs to be had. In the 1960s, homosexuality was still illegal. It sounds crazy today: you could actually go to prison just for being gay. Today we celebrate gay marriage. And 160 years ago white people were busy buying and selling black people as slaves in America. Today slavery has been all but eradicated from the face of the earth. Marijuana was first made illegal in 1913; now it has been legalized for both medical and recreational use in many parts of the world. Perhaps sooner or later other substances will also be reevaluated for their potential usefulness, particularly in the pursuit of brilliance. Time will tell.

Before we go on, here comes an important disclaimer. I am absolutely not suggesting here that you should do anything illegal. I am not advocating the use of any particular substance, and I certainly don't work with illegal substances myself in coaching or seminars. The information provided here is simply that: information for you to do with what you want.

MOTIVATION IS KEY

Let's remember that this is a book about brilliance, not about drug policy. We are only talking about entheogens to the degree that they have helped some people to access brilliance. There are plenty of other reasons why people use consciousness-altering substances. Here are just a few of them:

- **Medical.** Does the substance have any potential capacity to alleviate disease? Cannabis, for example, has recently been shown to have a wide range of medical benefits, including as an anti-carcinogen.
- **Psychiatric.** Has the substance been shown to alleviate the symptoms of mental illness?
- **Spiritual.** Some substances have been used ceremonially for thousands of years, to open people to a connection to a higher power, or a feeling of oneness with everything. For

example, peyote has been used by the Inca in this way, and Ayahuasca has been used by Amazonian shamans.

- **Recreational.** This covers a wide range of possibilities, and is mostly why governments feel justified to intervene. It means people getting high just for the fun of it, or sometimes to escape the tedium of a mechanical, loveless world.

- **Enhancement of Brilliance.** This is what we are exclusively interested in here. Has this substance been used effectively to change the way the brain operates, either for a short window or over a more sustained period, so as to help you to access and bring forth the greatest gifts which can further the evolution of humanity?

WHAT WORKS TO ENHANCE BRILLIANCE?

We are going to ignore the first four categories above: medical, psychiatric, spiritual, and recreational, not because they are not important, but because they are not within our mandate. Let's just focus on which substances enhance brilliance. When we reevaluate in this way, only a few stand out as potential candidates. Seen through the brilliance filter, and based on all the interviews I have conducted, we can organize consciousness-altering substances into three groups.

1) No obvious effect of brilliance, and often otherwise harmful. This would include addictive barbiturates, addictive opiates like heroin and opium, cocaine, and methamphetamine. No contest:

bad news. These substances are highly addictive, extremely harmful to health, and there is no credible evidence to suggest they have ever enhanced brilliance in any way.

2) Mind-changing but not necessarily in the direction of brilliance.

These are substances that change your state, but we have little or no reports of enhancement of creativity or cognitive capacity. Marijuana, for example, chills you out, relieves anxiety, can give you the giggles or the munchies, but it is rarely spoken of in the context of brilliance. Says Dr. Fadiman, "No one has ever said, 'I had this incredible breakthrough on marijuana.' Some people feel they like they are more creative: particularly musicians, graphic artists, and painters, but it is not the drug of choice for Silicon Valley entrepreneurs to have better ideas that can be implemented to make the world a better place."

Ayahuasca has become quite popular around the world in recent years, and certainly gives a deep dive into the subconscious mind, often its darker aspects. But again this experience does not bring back consistent reports of the kind of brilliance we are exploring here. Dr. Fadiman says: "Ayahuasca has a much greater body load than psychedelics, including vomiting and diarrhea. Many people also describe it as having an 'agenda.' This means that people talk about having dialogues with Ayahuasca, they say 'Grandmother Ayahuasca told me I should not do that anymore.' Nobody ever talks about Grandmother LSD. As far as I know, very few people have taken Ayahuasca for resolving intellectual problems, or break-throughs into brilliance."

Iboga and Ibogaine also give you a deep soul-searching look at your shadow, hence could be useful for a very thorough dive at 9 o'clock, but there are no reports back that they directly enhance innovation or brilliance.

3) Substances that have consistent and frequent reports of enhancing brilliance.

Dr. Doblin defines the word 'psychedelic' as 'mind manifesting': bringing things that are submerged to the surface so that you can then put them to a whole range of uses. There are four substances that reportedly make a significant contribution to creating original works of art, advancing science, or supporting individuals in en-hancing their gifts. Most of them work on the 5-HT 2A receptor site, a sub-type of seratonin.

LSD. Dr. Doblin explains, "We know enough about the LSD mol-ecule to know that if you take it at 9 in the morning, most of it is gone from the body by 12 noon, yet the peak of the experience may come at 1 o'clock. It starts a cascade of effects in the body or brain, for which the substance is only a catalyst or a co-factor. This effect continues over time, long after the drug has left the body." This explains why Fadiman's subjects in the 1960s reported on enhanced creativity for several weeks after a single dose.

Dr. Fadiman comments: "I like to tell writers that lower doses of tryptamines like LSD are fantastic for first drafts of a chapter: when you are faced with a blank screen or a blank page. A lot of people are able to sit and focus and write in a way that is very hard for them otherwise. People report that they can focus their attention voluntarily for a longer period of time, and stay in flow states more. The other side effect is relief from procrastination: if there is something that you know you need to do, but you have some emotional or practical obstacle to doing it, even with tiny micro-doses you find you can just do the task anyway."

Dr. Doblin agrees: "People's verbal associations are broader. A wider set of associations for ideas, beyond the logical, helps you to come up with new creative options. Dr. Robin Carhart-Harris, at Imperial College London, talks of the pacifying effect of LSD on the default mode network, sometimes associated with what we label as "ego." Bypassing this brings a greater sense of connection and broader perspectives.

Steve Jobs frequently stated that his many LSD trips were hugely significant to his work. The Beatles generated arguably their best music thanks to the use of LSD. Silicon Investor Tim Ferris recently told CNN, "The billionaires I know, almost without exception, use hallucinogens on a regular basis. They are trying to be very disruptive, to look at the problems in the world and ask completely new questions."

2CB. Synthesized by Berkeley chemist Alexander Shulgin and his wife Ann, the phenethylamine 2-CB has similar effects to LSD, but is reported to be softer, and more conducive to creative activity. Although less widely used, many brilliant people reported to me that 2-CB seems to be close to the perfect substance for our exploration of enhancing brilliance. People report that it gives them the clarity and problem-solving associated with micro-dosing LSD, but it also supports a warmth that allows them to feel a dedication to, and love for, humanity and to feel inspired to make the greatest difference to the world. Like LSD, 2-CB is not addictive, is non-toxic, causes no antisocial behavior, and no short or long-term physiological damage. Only bad news? Daddy has said "No."

Psilocybin Mushrooms. This is the only completely organic substance on the list. People using Psilocybin in conjunction with creativity report a significant feeling of connection with nature, and the capacity to feel informed by the intelligence of trees, plants, and the planet as a living being. Besides this, the subjective effects are extremely similar to the two substances mentioned above.

MDMA. This is not to be confused with the street drug Ecstasy which, although it contains MDMA, is usually laced with other substances like amphetamines. Pure MDMA has been used in clinical trials with Iraqi vets suffering from PTSD. Three therapeutic sessions using MDMA reduced stress to within normal levels. No other treatment for post-traumatic stress disorder has come anywhere close to this kind of effectiveness. Many people reported to me in interviews that MDMA has had a powerful effect on brilliance, because it gave them the experience of opening their hearts and feeling much greater levels of love and compassion which then inform their work. People also reported dramatically enhanced self-forgiveness, self-compassion, and psychological learning and maturing.

IMPORTANT CAVEATS

A hammer can be used to build a house; it can also be used to smash something beautiful. A knife, used by a surgeon, can save someone's life; it can also be an instrument of violence. None of the four substances listed above could be said to be universally helpful to anyone under any circumstance.

In his book *LSD My Problem Child,* Albert Hofmann, Ph.D., laments the misuse of the drug he once saw had great promise, prior to its recreational use in the early 1960s. There are several factors which people report on as significant for these substances to enhance brilliance, instead of a wild and sometimes bumpy ride.

Substance and Dosage. Wild trips on LSD, where people think they can fly, or hallucinate, are often induced by dosages from 250 µg to as high as 400 µg . "Micro-dosing," on the other hand, means using around 10 µg. That size of dose, Fadiman reports, leaves the user fully functional and not impaired in any way for normal kinds of activity: no effect on the perceptual field, no hallucinations. It simply allows someone to feel like the best version of themselves, to have good ideas, and to be able to execute them effortlessly.

Fadiman comments: "Psychedelics are like stations on the radio. A high dose of 400 μg will give you an intense spiritual experience: your sense of being a separate person melts. One man said: 'I could see I was in a cage, but then I realized that the key to the door was locked from the inside.' A medium dose of around 200μg can be used in psychotherapeutic contexts. A lower dose of around 100μg is useful for scientific and creative breakthrough. The micro-dose level is where you have a really great day, but you are fully functional. One young computer programmer told me, 'I only micro-dose when I have a coding problem.' Another said, 'I do machine design. When you are designing a machine, you have a lot of parts that are in motion. To have greater pattern recognition, micro-dosing is very helpful. I can follow more parts of my machine than without it.' We can fairly accurately know what is going to happen, if we know the dose."

"Micro-dosing has seen a huge surge in the last few years," Fadiman continues. "We previously had almost no research on it, because until a few years ago it didn't exist. It has surged because it is safe, it doesn't interrupt your day. If you look at the risk-to-benefit ratio, micro-dosing looks really good to most people."

Dr. Doblin reflects, "When we micro-dose, it is because we want to be more open in certain ways. LSD is like training wheels on a bicycle. Later you can operate at the same level without the training wheels. It's a process of integration: you learn how to be more creative, how to challenge your assumptions, how to be receptive to incoming thoughts that question the norm. In a sense, you have rewired your brain. New circuits get strengthened over time, as old pattern responses get weaker. Albert Hoffmann, before he died, told me that the most important area of research to explore with LSD is low-dosing. There is a fundamentally different effect than with higher doses."

"You cannot overdose on LSD. You can take thousands of micrograms; it will affect you for quite an extended period of time but it is not going to hurt you physically. Classic psychedelics are more powerful psychologically but much safer physiologically than many other substances."

Clearly many other psychologists, researchers, and consultants agree. One of my colleagues, a master coach who also works with executives and leadership teams and is in high demand in Silicon Valley, estimates that 30% of his clients in IT companies are microdosing regularly. They do it because it works.

Setting. People who report using these substances to enhance brilliance are not using them at a party or a rock concert, but in a controlled and often quiet environment where they can focus on giving their gift, as well as what gets in the way. Dr. Fadiman notes that since the early research conducted by Timothy Leary, Richard

Alpert, and others at Harvard, researchers have greatly expanded their understanding of what makes entheogens effective. "Now we use a standard room, with the right furniture, the right lighting, and a man and a woman guide, one on each side. If you are in a safe, trusted setting with one or more people who care for you, you already know things are going to be good, and the right setting will intensify it. 'Safe and comfortable' means either a room that feels comfortable, or a natural setting, but without additional people. Except for the guide, there should be no strangers."

Supervision. Some of these substances, particularly MDMA, yield much better results with proper supervision and interaction with a guide. When someone is there to ask the right questions, to keep your attention focused, they help unlock your gifts. Doblin comments, "I would advocate taking psychedelics with somebody facilitating: in the sense of protecting your space, in case there's a fire, a phone call, or someone comes to the door. By yourself, there's a certain part of your brain that is on reserve for survival questions or for interaction with others. If you've got a sitter to handle all of that, you can let go of those portions of your brain, leaving more brainpower to just think about whatever problem you are trying to solve."

Dr. Fadiman has been such a guide, and writes in some detail about the best way to do so in *The Psychedelic Explorer's Guide*. The guide only needs to interact with the explorer if they appear to be veering off track from their original intention. "A guide is agenda free, they know the territory, and they feel positively towards the person."

Mindset. Hofmann emphasized that psychedelics tend to enhance whatever is already inside you. If you experience underlying depression, fear, or self-loathing, those feelings may emerge under the influence of the drug. If you have a bunch of great ideas percolating and ready to be tickled and captured, it will emphasize those. He believed that many of the accidents and aberrations that happened with LSD in the '60s were because people used it without supervision, and with an unfavorable psychological history. Fadiman adds, "Psychedelics are definitely not for everyone, higher doses are even less so." But since the '60s a great deal of additional research sponsored by *maps.org* has also been done on how to use psychedelics effectively to enhance psychotherapy and heal trauma. Dr. Doblin says, "You can have a very difficult history, but if you're in a setting that is very supportive, with qualified people you trust, you can make tremendous progress."

Intention and Dedication. Finally, entheogens respond to the attitude brought to them. If the intention is to get high, they can take you there. If the intention is to have great sex, psychedelics have been touted as the ultimate aphrodisiac. If your intention is to bring forth great ideas to contribute to the evolution of humanity, then the judicious, responsible, and appropriate use of entheogens may occasionally be a useful key.

A SANER FUTURE

Who knows? Perhaps in some future and more evolved state of humanity, we might reconsider our prohibition of these substances and see if they have a place, when used responsibly, in the enhancement of brilliance. Dr. Doblin is a great believer in the total lifting of prohibition for all substances, as was done in Portugal in 2014. That resulted in reduced drug use, less hospitalization, and dramatically lessened incarceration per head of population. He comments, "I think the whole system of prohibition should be thrown out the window. We need to have honest drug education on the subject of harm reduction. The more dangerous the drug is, the more important it be legal. When dangerous drugs are illegal, and people have problems with them, they feel scared that they will be stigmatized if they come forward and seek help. In the US, we prioritize prison over drug treatment as a society."

CHAPTER SIXTEEN
BRILLIANCE BEYOND BELIEF

We discussed earlier how the 9 o'clock phase of the cycle is characterized by healthy self-doubt: by recognizing the limitations of our humanness relative to the huge mysterious force which gives us all life. In this sense, it is healthy to have a phase of your day or your week where you can accept your limitations, learn from your mistakes, and intend to do better next time.

But there is an enormously important caveat to this that we will explore now. Something else can be easily confused with the healthy self-doubt we all visit sometimes at 9 o'clock. We all also have conditioned limiting beliefs, almost like a kind of faulty programming in the software. You will notice these bugs showing up mostly between 12 and 3 o'clock. Almost everyone has original brilliant ideas from time to time, but when these ideas start to sprout and take form, they frequently bump up against habitual, unconscious, and deeply ingrained thought forms, and so die before ever seeing the light of day. These habitual thought forms are sometimes called "conditioning," or "programming," or "negative self-talk."

You are probably already very familiar with what we are talking about, but here are some common examples of pervasive and unconscious beliefs that interfere with the sprouting of original brilliance:

> *I'm not good enough*
> *I'm not ready yet*
> *No one will listen to me*
> *I will be punished*
> *I'm not okay as I am*
> *I'm not beautiful*
> *People don't like me*
> *There is something wrong with me*
> *There's not enough time*
> *It's too late*

We could go on and on listing such thoughts for the rest of the book. And that is all they are ... thoughts ... very small mice armed with megaphones.

How we address and overcome these bugs in the software makes all the difference to the real expression of freedom. Once we recognize that we are all subject to this kind of limited and constrained self-talk, and that it deeply inhibits the flow of brilliance, there are two very different ways of addressing the problem.

The first is to try to change "negative beliefs" into "positive beliefs." This is the huge industry of positive thinking, affirmations, creative visualization, manifesting, and the "law of attraction". If you adopt this approach, you might recognize a thought like *"I'm not good enough,"* and then find ways to constantly repeat and affirm the opposite: *"I am good enough;* in fact *I'm great, I'm terrific, I'm a winner, I'm a champion!"* You could journal these improved thoughts, write them on the bathroom mirror, sing them, say them to your friends, have them say them back to you, have them printed on your clothing or tattooed on your body. You could create an entire lifestyle out of affirming and proving *"Look at me, I am definitely, unambiguously, loudly and gloriously GOOD ENOUGH."*

The second approach is not to try to change one belief into another, but to see the fundamentally limiting nature of *all* beliefs: whether labeled as negative or positive. Then you can relax the need to clutch to either one, and relax into a natural state of presence, innocence, and wakefulness. This means learning how to dissolve beliefs, without replacing them with something else. Human beings live in a prison cell of their own creation. But most people are happy to rearrange the furniture in the prison cell, and then to call that freedom.

When we transform *"I'm not good enough"* into *"I am good enough,"* or when we try to camouflage *"nobody likes me"* with the assertion *"everybody likes me,"* we are still staying within the small confines of the mind, but now with these limiting beliefs spray-painted gold and shiny. This may lead to the appearance of high self-esteem, it may even yield material results in the world, but it is not the way to foster brilliance. Because we are replacing one thought with another, there is no space for original creative impulses to rise out of the mysterious silent source from which all new thoughts arise. We are clinging to repeating thoughts, and so staying on the surface of the mind.

The first step in finding freedom from limiting thought forms is to understand this fundamental distinction. Once it is clear, there are many simple tools available to free us from these constraining beliefs, and return us to a life of brilliance.

THE XPILL

Robert Richman is a "culture strategist." He cofounded Zappos Insights, dedicated to educating companies on the secrets behind Zappos' great success with customer relations. A few years ago, he was preparing to go to Burning Man, the massive annual festival in the Nevada desert where tens of thousands of people come together for a few days to celebrate art and higher consciousness, as well as contribute to each other in myriad other ways, all without the exchange of money. Inspired by the movie *The Matrix,* Richman asked himself, "What if the Red Pill could be real?" He decided to dedicate his Burning Man experience to this question.

He could not find a red pill, so he bought Cinnamon Spice Tic Tacs, put them into eighty yellow prescription pill bottles, and brought them to Burning Man. Once settled in, he approached random strangers and asked them, "Do you want to take the Red Pill?" He discovered that some people had instantaneous realizations simply by taking the "pill." They recognized unnecessary, limiting beliefs, let them go, and discovered a much deeper potential. But others experienced fear. "Get that thing away from me. I like my reality as it is." All this, from eating Tic Tacs. Participants started trailing after him in the desert, wanting to get their red pill.

After Burning Man, Richman did not think much more of it, until two weeks later when he got a call from a psychologist. She asked if he was the guy giving out the Red Pills at Burning Man, and he said he was. She told him she had kept one of the bottles, and had been giving them out to her patients. They were having big break-throughs. Could he send more?

Richman had to rethink things—a psychologist was getting trans-formational results from red Tic Tacs. "Okay," he said to himself, "let's see how far we can take this." Using red vitamins this time, he sent a message out on his Facebook page. "Hey, do you want to take the red pill?" But this time he asked people to commit to an intention. "Take the pill and swallow it, with an intention in mind, and let's see what happens for the next 30 days." One by one, people were able to achieve their goals and become free of limiting beliefs and thinking, all from the ritual of taking a red vitamin pill with a focus. As he scanned the comments that accumulated on his Facebook page, he noticed the one common denominator: distrac-tions seemed to fade away.

Richman went to a vitamin company and had his own supplement manufactured, which contains nothing but rice powder. He changed the color from red to purple. So was born the XPill, perhaps the most widespread and mind-boggling experiment ever on the power of the placebo effect. Richman discovered that it is possible to help people to break through seemingly impenetrable resistance, just through a decision, a commitment, and a purple pill containing rice powder.

Richman discovered a thing or two about how resistance works through this bizarre experiment. "The most important thing I have learned is that resistance exists on a feeling level. We can have all kinds of stories as to why we can't do the things we want to. These stories may or may not be true, but it is holding on to these stories that relates to the feeling. The XPill is simply a way to get straight to the truth, at a feeling level, and then we discover that the story is different.

"This is all happening on a very unconscious level. Let's say you have a desire to write a book. You sit down, and something gets uncomfortable for you. That's when we start procrastinating. We get busy with other things. We make up stories as excuses: I had to take care of my kids, I don't have enough time, I don't feel well." We find something else to do instead of staying with the bigger intention that we had to write. We make up a story. The XPill is simply a ritual, a way to allow the feelings to come up, to be with them, and then to reprogram the stories we hold on to."

According to Richman, three elements make this work: the pill, the process, and the people. "This comes out of both my own research with the XPill as well as research done at Harvard University at the Institute of Placebo Studies," he says. "First, it's a pill. You swallow this pill, which means you cannot take it back. You are on the ride. Your unconscious mind gets behind it. It's one thing for me to want to write a book, it's another thing for me to swallow a pill and feel all the emotions that suddenly surge. Second is the People behind the pill. With all placebo studies, it matters who the doctor is, and it matters who the people are surrounding you, and what they believe about you. The XPill works much better when other people are involved, reflecting back to you, asking questions, acting as a witness to your intention. Third is the Process. We have developed a process that focuses on the 'why.' 'Why do you want this outcome?' 'What will you get?' 'Are you doing this just to get something else, or is it intrinsically valuable in itself?'"

Richman has discovered that sometimes the way to overcome resistance and embedded beliefs is simply to unplug them. "What we really want is often quite simple. We just make up a whole bunch of obstacles, and once we have made them up, they become real in our imagination, and we go to war with them. I sometimes compare this to imagining that you are holding a weight. You've been holding that weight for a long time. What would happen if you dropped it? A lot of this comes down to willingness and curiosity. Taking a pill is a symbolic act of willingness and commitment, even if you don't know what is on the other side."

ASKING POWERFUL QUESTIONS

The first step, which is sometimes all that is needed, is to be able to clearly recognize that a limiting thought is just that: just a thought, without any power to do anything, and much more arbitrary and optional than we realize. Here is a series of questions I have been teaching to coaches for years to help their clients free themselves from the grip of limited thinking.

- **Identify the limiting thought or belief.** This is where it is very helpful to have a friend or a coach to help you. Phrases like "I'm not good enough" or "things are very hard" weave their way into how we speak and think, often without any recognition that they are thoughts and not reality. The first step is to ask the question "What was that?" and to be able to recognize that it was just a thought.
- **Would you wish it on a child?** If you have children of your own, or nephews and nieces, ask yourself, "Would I wish this belief on my child?"
- **Would you choose it from a menu?** If you went into a restaurant, where they had many different thought forms to choose from, would you choose this belief, consciously and deliberately, from the menu?
- **Have you signed any contracts to keep it?** Of course this is a rhetorical question, but nevertheless a powerful one. Is there any law in the city, or the state, or the country where you live that obliges you to stay in relationship with this be-

lief? Have you signed any contract that you must think this way? [Of course you haven't; no one ever does that. But it is powerful to remind ourselves of this fact.]

- **Could you let it go?** Who would you be, what would your life be like, if you simply made a fresh choice to release your allegiance to this way of thinking?

This line of questioning, just on its own, often creates enough of a distance from the faulty thinking in the mind to allow brilliance to flow again. Remember, we are using these questions to dissolve and abandon beliefs, not to replace them with shiny, glittery, positive new ones. Brilliance flows in the absence of allegiance to any kind of dogmatic thinking, positive or negative, not by improving it.

Is It True?

This is another fun game you can play alone, or with a friend. Often we get caught in these beliefs and don't even notice when they happen. You could set an alarm on your phone, to go off at irregular intervals (after 2 hours, then reset it for 3 hours 15 minutes, then reset it for one hour, etc.) to remind you to ask this question. Even better, ask your partner, your children, your friends, and your goldfish to regularly ask you this question. It is very simple. Whenever you find yourself thinking or saying, "*I'm not good enough … There's not enough time … I'm going to fail …*" ask yourself the question, or have someone else ask you the question, "Is it true?"

For this question to work powerfully we need to remind ourselves of the difference between fact and opinion. In order for something to be factual, every sane person on the planet would agree that it is true. Whenever sane, conscious people disagree about things, we are in the realm of opinion.

A great example would be "Paris is the capital of France." Anyone who understands what the words mean would have no argument that this is a factual statement. Other examples of facts would be "Tuesday is the day after Monday, the Pacific Ocean is to the west of America, or the Yen is the national currency of Japan."

On the other hand, "French people are arrogant" is not a fact, it is an opinion, for the simple reason that not everybody would agree. Particularly the French would have a problem with that statement.

Facts are simply true or untrue. Opinions (or beliefs) are neither true nor untrue; instead they are useful or not useful. Simply being able to recognize that a limiting thought is not a fact, not true, but an opinion allows you to then reevaluate whether it is useful and worth hanging onto.

If you would like to free up your mind to be more available for brilliance, get in the habit of frequently writing down the beliefs and random opinions that populate your day. Keep a list.

COULD YOU LET IT GO?

Limiting thought forms do not only exist in the mind, they are also feelings, which we experience in the body. For example, *"There's not enough time,"* a typical thought that can inhibit brilliance, is not only a logical thought that we think and believe, it is also something we feel and experience as a contraction, very often in the chest. As soon as your attention shifts from the thought to the feeling to the contraction in the body, you can ask yourself the simple question, "Could I let it go?" You could also rephrase this as, "Would I rather hold on to being right about this, or would I prefer to be free in this moment?"

RADICAL RELEASING

There are various tried and tested methods that go even deeper. Some of the thought forms which govern our lives are pernicious. Their roots are hidden and strong, in such a way that it is difficult to get free of them. Sometimes it is useful to use a more powerful method. There are many such technologies available. I have been training coaches for the last twenty-six years, and we have developed a method called "radical releasing." It is a very simple way of becoming aware of the "frequency" of a belief, consciously increasing that frequency, and then dropping back into limitless consciousness. Sometimes a picture, or a video, is worth a thousand words so, instead of describing this to you in more detail here, if this sounds intriguing, here is a page that shows you a demonstration of this method: [radicalbrilliance/rad-release]. On that same page you will find a link to a directory of some of the coaches I have trained, who would be happy to guide you through radical releasing for yourself.

This is an important component to living brilliance: to be able to get enough distance from your mind that it no longer enslaves you. Just "un-velcroing" the power of belief in this way allows you to explore what it's like to move from belief to a mind free of belief, in which brilliance can flourish.

RUSHING

Sometimes an effective way to move into brilliance without habitual thought forms tripping you up is to take action very quickly, so you literally do not have time to think. Here is Alex Ebert again. "People ask me how do you get your unique sound? I say 'rushing.' Sometimes I can hear the engineers that work for me chuckle, and, if enough months go by, they get flustered, because I have zero patience for protocol or process. *'Throw the mike up … give me the mike … I need it right now … because this moment is more important than making adjustments. I need to say what I have to say right now … I have to hit that snare right now.'* They hate it because their whole school of thought is to get something sounding right. But you know what happens when you do it the 'right' way? It sounds like everything else. It is through rushing that I end up having a sound that is unique.

"When I wake up and have inspiration, that is to be followed and to be completely honored. The ideas may stick around longer, but the inspiration to do them may start to evaporate, or start to mutate. I need to stay in this new world, and keep fostering it, and keep going with it, because otherwise I am going to lose the atmosphere that I am breathing: which is a new song, a new idea."

CHAPTER SEVENTEEN
HOW TO SIT

As you can probably tell by now, having a time of the day when you sit doing nothing is an integral part of becoming radically brilliant. I like to call this "sitting," because it is a word that does not immediately evoke scary feelings of inadequacy. Pretty much anyone who can stand up can also sit. Your dog can sit. But despite the fact that "sitting" is such an innocuous and unchallenging word, people often morph it into "meditation" or "spiritual practice," and that is where the trouble begins. Almost anytime I coach anybody and we discuss practices, I suggest they spend at least some small part of each day sitting doing nothing.

My instructions for sitting are extremely simple.

- Step One: Sit in a chair or cross-legged with your spine straight. Ish.
- Step Two: Set the timer on your phone for 20 minutes (or longer).
- Step Three: Put on a blindfold.
- Step Four:

There is no Step Four. There is also no Step Five. That's it. It is that simple: set your timer, put on a blindfold, and the rest is not up to you. Be curious, very curious, to see what happens next. It seems to me like no one could fail at something that simple. But a week after suggesting these simple instructions, when I ask my clients, "How did it go?" I often hear, "*Well, I'm not very good at it, it didn't go very well,*" or, "*I don't think I'm a very good meditator.*" These kinds of responses frequently baffle me, and leave me to the conclusion that it is worth spending some time clarifying what it means to just sit.

So imagine this. It is Sunday lunchtime. We made a nice meal, and Grandma is coming over. She has never been to this house before, not since we moved. Our driveway is a little hard to find. While preparing lunch, you ask me, "Is there anything I can do?" "Yes," I reply, "actually there is. Could you please take this folding chair, go to the end of the driveway, then sit in the chair, wait, and watch for Grandma to arrive." After about half an hour, she still has not yet shown up. It must be bad traffic, she slept in, or got lost. So I stride out to the end of the driveway, still wearing my very dapper-looking chef's apron, I saunter up to the chair you are sitting in, and I ask, "How you doing?"

"Not very well," you say.

"Why not?" I ask.

"I'm not very good at this thing," you say.

"What do you mean?" I ask, getting curious now.

"Well, I've been sitting here, watching, but there is a lot of traffic. I've not been successful in slowing the traffic down."

"*What?*" I ask you. "We didn't say anything about slowing the traffic down. I just asked you to sit and keep a lookout for Grandma."

"Well, yes, I can do that," you say, "but I don't think I'm really cut out for this sitting thing. I'm not really feeling blissful yet."

"*Blissful?*" I ask you. "Who said anything about feeling blissful? You just have to sit in the chair, and keep an eye out for Grandma. There is literally *nothing* to it."

As far as I am concerned, the instructions for sitting are just like that. Nothing more complicated is needed. Set the timer, put on the blindfold, and the rest is not up to you. Wait for Grandma.

The discerning reader amongst us might have noticed by now the subtle use of an analogy here. "So in the story about Grandma, what does Grandma represent?" asks the aspiring English-Lit major. And that is a good question. In fact, it is the very reason for using an analogy. There *is* an equivalent to Grandma arriving, when you sit, but, perhaps fortunately, it has no name and it has no form. It has no nationality. It has no voice. It cannot be described in words. But if you sit and wait, eventually Grandma comes.

TIME OUT

Dawa Tarchen Phillips was born in New York to a German mother and a father from Trinidad. When he was a young child, the family moved to Germany, where he was raised. "Even at five years old," he tells me, "I had a very curious mind and I loved to explore. Already then, I saw my life as a journey, or a path. Three questions preoccupied me as a child: 'Where do I come from?' 'Why am I here?' and 'Where am I going?' I didn't find answers in my conversations with adults, so little by little I lost interest in the questions. But then, in my early twenties I decided I was going to honor those questions. So I learned meditation, in the Vajrayana tradition of Tibetan Buddhism."

At age twenty-seven, Dawa made the unusual decision to enter into a meditation retreat for three years, three months, three weeks, and three days, a tradition in the Kagyu lineage. At the end of the retreat, Dawa made the even more unusual decision to do a *second* three-year retreat, bringing the total time he spent in undiluted meditative focus to six and a half years of his life. I have only met one other human being who has done the three-year retreat twice: a highly revered Rinpoche, the abbot of a monastery in Tibet. Today, Dawa is an ordained lama in the Kagyu tradition, as well as one of the foremost experts on mindfulness and leadership, which he teaches at U.C. Santa Barbara, and in several Fortune 500 companies.

In short, Dawa has earned the right to speak with some authority about sitting. I asked him the simple question, "Why do you sit?"

"The body is present, while the mind can be all over the place," he replied. "The body abides in the present, so it's a beautiful point of reference to bring our mind back into the present. If we allow the body to sit, it is easier for us to take it as a reference. When the body is resting it is easier for the mind to recognize it as a place it can come back to. This is what is meant by 'mindfulness.' That is why the body is such a useful tool for people who are beginning to cultivate awareness or some sense of presence. The body is already present, and it never goes with you when your mind gets distracted in worry about the future or gets trapped in some recurring memory. The body always stays here. It is a beautiful way to start practice, and to start to learn to return your attention to the present."

There are Not Two Minds

In order for sitting to be effective, it does not really matter if the mind is active or quiet. It is all the same as far as sitting goes. It does not really matter whether the body is restless, or itchy, or achy, or feeling great. It is all the same as far as sitting goes. The content does not really matter, it is all about the sitting and the observing. When you sit and observe (whether you are observing an agitated mind or a calmed-down mind), you are engaged in sitting.

"What are you doing?"

"I'm sitting. I'm not doing anything."

The more that you rest in just sitting, observing absolutely whatever happens without any precondition or expectation at all, you relax a little more into *being* that which is sitting and observing. You relax into being the observer of the thoughts, instead of the thoughts themselves.

And then, slowly, all by itself, without having to do anything at all, the flavor of that which is observing begins to release its perfume. Just by doing nothing, slowly you recognize the very nature of that which is observing, you realize your "true nature." Ironically, the more you have ideas of having to calm the mind, the more you postpone this true nature from revealing itself.

Sosan, the Third Zen Patriarch, spent quite a bit of time sitting and waiting for Grandma. He knew a thing or two about sitting. He said, "When you try to stop mental activity, your very effort fills you with activity." And Padmasambhava, another avid sitter, agrees: "Since merely allowing [thoughts] to settle into their own condition, without trying to modify them in any way, is sufficient, how can you say that you are not able to remain in true nature?" He went on to found Tibetan Buddhism, and did very well for himself, or so I am told.

Dawa explains, "The aim of any kind of practice is not to stop life or to stop motion, but to cultivate greater clarity around what is actually occurring every moment. In classical training, we use the word 'familiarization.' You practice to familiarize yourself with what's actually happening, with your own body and your own mind, so that you can become familiar with what it means to be alive, and what it means to be a human being. Where do the conditioned, unfree, and tethered parts of yourself lie, and where does liberation occur? Where are the free parts, where are the creative parts, where do the untethered parts of you lie? You develop greater choice and you can live a life that, over a period of time, often leads to greater fulfillment and also a greater sense of inner peace and inner freedom."

When you abandon any idea of having a calm mind, or feeling blissful, or even peaceful, or having some kind of peak state of enlightenment, something unwinds inside. The more you relax naturally, letting go of any goal, the more at home in yourself you become. This is why I suggest to everyone I work with, one-on-one or in groups, to start with just the sitting and the timer and the blindfold, and let the rest happen on its own. At the beginning, don't worry about how you breathe, or how straight your spine is, or feeling oneness with all things, or channeling Elvis Presley. Just set the timer, put on the blindfold, and wait for Grandma.

Once a week or two goes by and you find yourself naturally abandoning any ambition for some future state, there are indeed a few little playful modifications you can make, just for the fun of it. In our cycle, sitting belongs in the area between about 11 o'clock at 1 o'clock. These modifications each have their place somewhere in that area.

BODY-SCANNING

You can, in addition to just sitting and waiting, learn to very slowly scan your body. In our cycle, we would label this an 11 o'clock practice. In our Global Brilliance Practice Community, I provide a very detailed (and long!) guided audio to help you with this. Essentially you direct your breath first to the tips of your toes, and then breathe out with a gentle sigh. Then focus on the soles of your feet, and another sigh, then into your heels, and another sigh. You can do this very slowly over the course of anything from several minutes to an hour, working slowly through every part of the body, to the crown of your head. It supports you to let go of physical, emotional, and mental tension, and to relax more deeply.

INQUIRY

This is not really any different than the sitting and observing already described, it just brings a little more focused curiosity to it. After you have set the timer, and you are wearing a blindfold, you can simply ask yourself the question, very gently,

"Who is experiencing this moment?"

or you can phrase it as

"What is experiencing this moment?"

Bear in mind, this does not mean *"What am I hearing?"* It means, *"Who is hearing the sounds?"* *"What is the nature of that which hears?"*

It does not mean *"What am I seeing?"* (if your eyes are open) or *"What images are passing in my mind?,"* which is also a kind of seeing. It means, *"Who or what is aware of color and form and texture and shape? What is the nature of that which sees?"* It also does not mean *"What am I feeling in the body?"* including *"What emotions am I feeling?"* It means *"Who or what is aware of the constantly shifting and changing of body sensations and emotional energy? What is the nature of that which feels?"* This kind of inquiry, made popular in the modern world by the sage Ramana Maharshi, is still not doing anything, or trying to achieve anything, it is simply a way of directing the attention and becoming curious about that which is already here.

ENCOURAGE CREATIVE IMPULSES

The third modification when sitting is to develop an encouraging disposition toward creative impulses. If you are a parent, I am sure at one time or another you went through the experience of watching "the game." Personally, I have about the same interest in spectator sports as I have in recreational visits to the dentist. I'd rather do just about anything else in the whole world than sit and watch other people kick a ball. But, when it came to my boys, it was a dramatic exception. I went to every basketball game, every soccer match, every baseball game; in fact, every kind of game available, even though I almost always did not understand the rules. As soon as one of my little munchkins even came close to the ball I was on my feet screaming, "Yes, go, go, go! You got it, go for it!" I think a couple of other parents might have even tried to have me banned from the games, I was so loud, and so obviously completely ignorant about what I was watching.

You could take just the same disposition with the creative impulses that arise when you are sitting. They are the children of your true nature. You do not need to understand the rules, you do not need to have a highly developed connoisseur appreciation of art; simply, when you notice creative energy stirring, which will often feel like physical pleasure in the body, say a big, loud, embarrassing YES! to it. You might feel this as a light energized feeling of enthusiasm in your chest. You might feel it is a tickle in your throat, like you want to laugh, or scream, or sing opera. Whatever it is, say yes to it. Encourage it. Give it space. Let it move and breathe.

MASTURBATION MEDITATION

The fourth valuable enhancement to meditation, which I highly recommend, is masturbation. "You what now?" I hear a few people say. "I don't think you've got a very good proofreader there buddy; that was *definitely* a typo." Nope, you heard me right. I'm talking about playing with your naughty parts as a practice to enhance brilliance. If you are a man, I am suggesting that while sitting on your meditation cushion, spine straight, surrounded by serene statues and incense, you whip out Mr. Happy and fire him up. If you are a woman, I suggest that you dig down deep into the exotic garden of pleasure, or cup your breasts and massage them. We talked about this a bit already in the chapter on brilliant sex. But for most people, it is such an unfamiliar concept that it bears repeating.

I live in the little mountain town of Nevada City. Only 2500 people live within the city limits. It is more or less just one street, with little tributaries leading off it. The nearest town is a little bigger: Grass Valley has 9000 inhabitants. But, when you drive from Nevada City to Grass Valley, there is really no gap in between, there is no uninhabited area. If you walk from Nevada City to Grass Valley, you will not notice a moment when you pass from one to the other. You see houses, more houses, more houses, shops, shops, houses, gas station, houses. And somehow, quite invisibly, you are no longer in Nevada City, you are in Grass Valley. In just the same way, the distinction we draw between sexual energy and creative energy is really artificial. Sex arousal, excitement, happiness, creative flow, compassion, eloquence, these are all different flavors of states of arousal, and once we relax our thinking about it, one just bleeds very naturally into another.

Consequently, when you bring some erotic arousal into your sitting practice, it will quickly and naturally spread into other kinds of arousal throughout the body. You will feel more alive, optimistic, energized, and free.

There are a couple of small caveats. First, if you are a man, you definitely do not want to ejaculate. Stimulate your penis just enough to feel aroused energy, and then stop and relax and breathe and let the aroused energy that you have awoken spread to other yet-to-be-erogenous zones. Second, do not look at pornographic images, either on a screen on your mind. Learn to practice moving energy (literally "Chi Kung"), without being tied to desire for something outside yourself. Third, if you are a woman, find a way to connect your heart and your vagina into the same arousal. Some women say this can be best accomplished by massaging the breasts and touching the vagina simultaneously. Strengthening the heart/vagina connection is the best way to coax the aroused energy to flow into creativity.

THE PROOF OF THE PUDDING

Finally, how are we to know if a sitting practice is effective or not? How do we know if it is working? Let's return to the man who has done the research, Dawa Tarchin Phillips: "The sign of authentic practice is how much kindness, how much compassion, how much humanity, and how much wisdom there is in the way that a person goes about their life. In the way they relate to others: the way they work toward contributing to the betterment of life and the reduction of suffering in the world. Those are the real indicators of an authentic understanding of our true nature, when a person starts to express kindness and compassion toward others and toward oneself. Then actions begin to lead to better outcomes."

CHAPTER EIGHTEEN
PRAYER, DEVOTION, SURRENDER

The title of this chapter might take a few readers by surprise. Okay, now I get the picture. He lures us in with some enticing talk about brilliance ... productivity ... innovation ... but it's all just a front for some kind of conversion to a religious cult. The reason we need to talk about feelings and experiences which border on the religious is the same reason we needed to cover entheogenic substances and sexual practices: because if we want to objectively understand the factors that enhance brilliance, we can leave no stone unturned.

You may remember that when we first explored the Brilliance Cycle, we understood together that truly original thoughts are most often subjectively experienced as not coming from you, as a result of figuring things out in your mind with effort, but really coming *through* you from something deeper than your own cognitive process. We talked a lot already about sitting in silence, and stillness, and waiting for an impulse to arise on its own, and then gently fanning the flames with both attention and intention. Now we need to return for a deeper dive to inquire where these impulses are coming from. Remember, we already contemplated this question with the analogy of the bubbles arising in the Coca-Cola. When you have an idea that you did not hear from somebody else, when you have an idea that is original, fresh, and new, that has never been thought or expressed before, where does it come from? What is its origin? If we are honest with ourselves, we really do not know, do we?

The impulses of Radical Brilliance are not just randomly, chaotically, arising out of nothing, with no apparent connection to the circumstances of life. These impulses often provide practical solutions to real problems, and are often exactly the right brilliant impulse to move humanity forward to its next stage of evolution.

A phenomenon known as "multiple discovery" recognizes that many scientific discoveries and inventions have been made independently, and more or less simultaneously, by multiple scientists and inventors. For example, Isaac Newton and Gottfried Wilhelm Leibniz independently formulated calculus in the seventeenth century. Laser beams were developed independently by Gordon Gould at Columbia University, by researchers at Bell Labs, and by the Russian scientist Aleksandr Prokhorov. Endorphins were simultaneously but independently discovered in the US and in Scotland in 1973.

Many of the brilliant people I have interviewed speak of it like taking dictation, or "downloading" from some unknown source that appears to be intelligent, benevolent, creative, sees things in a bigger perspective than we can see them ourselves, and often has an outrageous sense of humor. This leads us to recognizing the footprints of a visitor we have never directly seen. It is as though you wake up every morning in your house, and there is a beautiful painting. You have never seen the painter, you only see the painting. But the hand of the painter is obvious.

CELESTIAL ARCHEOLOGY

Edward Sharpe and the Magnetic Zeros has been lauded for more than a decade as a truly original and fresh voice of contemporary music. Critics struggle to find an appropriate label or genre—the band cannot be pigeon-holed. As with Leonard Cohen, lead singer Alex Ebert described receiving lyrics and melodies that, soon after their arrival, no longer feel like "his," rather like a parent learning to accept the autonomy of each child. "I call it 'celestial archaeology,'" he told me. "You find the wing of an animal, then you go into space and you come up with the leg, with the spine. You keep dusting off the beast until you have put it together, and it can wing you anywhere in the universe. When you find those kinds of songs, they always work. They already existed out there in the ether. They have to be put back together by the band. Whenever you dust them off, there they are: animated, and they take you, as long as you give yourself over to the experience."

Ebert elaborates, "There are only two measurements of brilliance that I trust as pure. The first is the elation I experience upon witnessing my own works of art, which I generally experience while in the midst of making it. The second metric is that, after having made it, I don't recognize it as mine. When you experience brilliance, it feels sublime, and as if it came from somewhere else, not from you. This is the Celestial Archaeology."

JUST SAY YES

Where do these impulses come from, both the creative instinct within, and the geometrical complexity and intricacy often found without, in nature? The longing to answer this question initiates the dimension of human activity and feeling variously referred to as devotion, worship, or surrender. This is why we have temples and synagogues and churches and other sacred places. It is the origin of why human beings bow down in devotion and awe. We have a sense of something deeper than thought: something that is not just empty, but mysterious, intelligent, humorous, loving, benevolent, and creative. It is something far bigger than our minds, which yet is moving through us.

Michael Beckwith was a pre-med student at the University of Southern California when he first had a revelation of something luminous beyond his own mind. This insight deepened and returned many times. One day, sitting in his living room, he started to pray silently. "I want to know what my destiny is. What am I supposed to do in the world?"

At that exact moment the phone rang. A woman's voice on the other end said that they had been at high school together. She was going through a struggle. She prayed for help. Then she saw Michael's picture in the high school yearbook, as well as his number, and felt guided to call him. Michael counseled her that day, and continued for several more phone sessions. Soon she referred others in need. That was how his work supporting people who were struggling began. Years later, Beckwith would realize that he did not even have the same phone number as the high school number she called. Not only that, his new number was unlisted. This was the first time of many that he realized that something inexplicable was guiding his life.

For many years he worked with others one-on-one, but in 1986, he started to receive similar nudges "from the beyond," this time to start a community. "I resisted a lot," he told me, "but so many things happened in a short period of time, I realized that I was being squeezed into a new life. For example, at that time I had a crick in my neck, and couldn't totally turn my neck to the right. A chiropractor would adjust it, but a couple weeks later, my neck would be out again. When I finally said 'yes' to establishing a spiritual community as my next step of being of service, my neck popped into place on its own and never went out again. All my resistance to change had accumulated in my neck, but the moment I said 'yes,' it clicked in." That year, Michael and his wife Rickie founded the Agape International Spiritual Center in Culver City, California, which today has 9000 active members.

"There have been many iterations of hearing that voice, receiving that guidance, taking the next step in the evolution of my own soul," Beckwith continued. "It's always an evolution of how I give, how I serve in the world. I see myself as a servant. I give thanks every single day and before every presentation that I have the opportunity to be of service to the great God of the universe. I give thanks and I open myself up to be used by the spirit to be of service for anyone that I come in contact with. That is my mindset and my heart-set before I do anything. I am in great gratitude that I can be of service. Then I let that spirit show up however it is supposed to show up in that particular context."

WHO IS ON THE OTHER END OF THE LINE?

Although the subjective experience of "downloading" is very common, the way that we interpret or explain where we are downloading from is very different. The more we try to give it form, understand it, and explain it, the more it becomes articulated, organized religion. For some, the mystery can actually become quite dogmatic. But for others, the wisdom shines through, without needing to be understood or defined.

Some claim to be channeling messages from someone who was at one time a human being but is now dead, like Mother Mary or Jesus, Lady Diana or John Lennon. Others explain this experience of receiving messages in terms of a "higher self," a dimension of ourselves which is still you, but a much more intelli-

CHAPTER EIGHTEEN: PRAYER, DEVOTION, SURRENDER | 279

gent, free, and expansive version of you. And still others claim to be in touch with "entities" who either live on other planets like the Pleiades, or exist in another dimension altogether, like the Archangel Michael.

At the other end of the spectrum, there are plenty of people who subjectively experience this kind of downloading, while resting with both feet firmly planted in the recognition of "I don't know." This means, *"Yes when I get quiet and still, the sense of a separate me temporarily disappears, like a dew drop melting into the ocean, and it feels like something universal and beyond me has a chance to express itself, but I have not the first clue what that is. I can feel the effect of it, I know the beauty of it, the intelligence of it, I feel something like the love of it, but I don't know what it is. I don't know if it is a man or a woman, I don't know if it speaks English or Swahili or Russian, I don't know if it has any age. I don't know if it is just speaking to me, or in some mysterious miraculous way that I cannot understand, it is able to have conversations with everyone at the same time. I just feel the grace, and I step aside."*

Here is Michael Beckwith again. "It is a presence that is never an absence. Presence is formless, dimensionless, infinite, timeless, everywhere fully itself throughout all of creation. It is not merely in all creation. All creation is in it. It is everywhere. Humanity has the tendency to make images out of thought and imagination; people love to have some kind of visual representation of the formless. This creates an intermediary between themselves and the formless, which can be helpful, and can be hurtful. It can stagnate one's spirit to pay homage to a form."

"Oftentimes people give so much power to statues of the great deities that they forget that the presence that they are honoring is within them. So they give all this veneration to an external statue of an external deity, but forget to worship within their own hearts that light of beauty and intelligence and love. As magnificent as the universal presence is, it has to enter through our own consciousness. We have to accept it. When we have that 'aha' moment, that Satori moment of awakening, the moment of seeing not with the physical eyes or hearing with the physical ears, we catch something in consciousness that is formless. We are able to hear — beyond the ear — the inaudible, and see — beyond the eye — the invisible. Then the presence becomes more real to us than any form or any transitory temporality."

"The high side of religion is that it's leading people to that moment, to those moments of transcendence. The low side of religion is that it keeps people imprisoned in religiosity and forms and rituals that somehow keep them away from the presence. It's a balancing act we all have to do."

Once again, Leonard Cohen was for me the reigning champion of this kind of attitude. He told me on several occasions that he could feel his life is dedicated to being a faithful servant to that source beyond himself, but I never heard him once waver, either in conversations with me nor any interviews I have read, from his acknowledgment that he knows nothing about that to which he surrenders himself.

> *I make my plans*
> *Like I always do*
> *But when I look back*
> *I was there for you...*
> *I see my life*
> *In full review*
> *It was never me*
> *It was always you.*

These lyrics are from the song "There for you" on the album *Dear Heather*, which had just come out when I first met Leonard. I quoted those lyrics back to him, as well as the song "If It Be Your Will," and I asked him straight out, sitting there at his kitchen table, who, or what, the song is addressing. Who is the "you"? "Well, that's the thing," he answered me. "We don't know. We can't know. I don't like to talk about the things that I'm unqualified to talk about."

When we recognize the unavoidable truth that there is something coming through us, something that is intelligent, coherent, humorous, beautiful, and creative, we often feel inspired to voluntarily remove our hands from the steering wheel, and to call out, "You take the controls." That is the feeling of worship, the feeling of devotion, even when you don't know who or what you are devoted to.

WHO WROTE THIS?

I remember many years ago I was at the house of my teacher, H.W.L. Poonja, in India. People used to frequently write him poems. It was a cute and endearing thing. Someone would write a little poem, he would read it, his eyes would get teary, he would whisper, "Beautiful, beautiful." Then everyone would feel very emotional. The writer of the poem would then be revered as the reincarnation of Rumi. For a day. One day a few of us were sitting around in his living room. He was reading his mail. I casually wrote a little poem. It went something like this. *"Please take this body. It is not very useful, it is wiry and skinny and nervous, but please take it and use it. Please take this mind, it is chaotic, all over the place, but please take it, and use it."* When I was done, I folded up my poem, and slipped it among his pile of unread letters. After about half an hour, he got to my poem. He read it very slowly, looked around for an envelope to see where it had been mailed from, and, due to the lack of any stamp or address, realized that it had been hand-delivered, from someone in the room. He looked around and asked, somewhat sternly, "Who wrote this?" I felt like a kid who had strolled into the cockpit of the airplane, playfully pressed a few buttons, and suddenly found himself hurtling into the sky.

"I did," I whispered, like a church mouse. He looked at me for an agonizingly long fifteen seconds.

"Do you mean this?" he thundered at me, his tone making it clear that this was not fooling around.

"Yes," I squeaked nervously. Again, he gazed at me, more like *into* me, for the longest time. Then he slowly folded the letter back up, and placed it in his "read" pile. He looked back.

"Okay then," he said.

That poem was written almost by accident. I was just looking for some momentary pat of approval from a father figure. But since I wrote that letter, my life has never been the same. Looking back, I see now that I was not giving my life over to him. I was giving my life over to whatever he had given his life over to. Once it has been handed over, you cannot take it back, and even if you could, you would not want to.

Amy Fox, who already talked with us about the importance of vacations, was diagnosed with cancer at the age of twenty-two. She spent a year in chemotherapy and radiation treatment. Just before her very last CAT scan, she knew that this could well be the end for her. She might get the bad news, and then it would be time to go. Let's hear her tell the rest of her story.

"I felt tremendously held by God, by life. I remember making a small and quiet prayer. I said, 'If you want to take me, take me.' I felt really at peace with dying. Then I said, 'If you leave me here, the rest is yours.' It was a sincere vow. I have spent the last thirty years trying to figure out how to hear the whispers of what is wanted in the wake of that vow. It is not always easy to discern how life wants us to serve. That stance of believing that 'it is more than me," and that my life is designed and dedicated to being of service, is a very deep wellspring of fuel. People often will comment on my energy, or my vitality, or my work ethic, which is quite extreme. It is all the byproduct of that vow I made when I was ready to die."

I encourage you to find your own personal way of expressing surrender, within the context of your own life. Use whatever symbols and theology work for you, or use none at all. I hope deeply that you will find a way to surrender to something bigger than your own mind, desires, and reactive feelings, so that something unique and non-imitative can express itself through you.

Take a moment now to put this book down, and write your own expression of this, in your own words, to your own icon of the formless Beloved One. Just like I did all those years ago, write a poem or a letter or a song in which you can offer yourself up to something which you do not, and cannot, understand.

CHAPTER NINETEEN
BRILLIANT FRIENDSHIPS

A friendship can be many things. It can be just hanging out, doing fun stuff together, alleviating loneliness, playing sports, or sharing mutual interests. Not every friendship allows you to bring out the most brilliant dimension in each other: it requires a certain kind of dedication and agreement that that is the intention.

I am a very lucky fellow, because I have many brilliant friendships. The example that stands out most for me is with my friend John Gray. He has popped up a lot here, like in a Waldo comic book, because he is in so many ways a living example of what we are talking about. He and I are both part of the same men's group, in Marin County, California. We meet once a month. I live about two and a half hours away, in the Sierra Nevada mountains. One month, I had been feeling a little sick, and I did not really fancy driving down to the meeting, and then driving back the same night. So I sent an email out to the whole group asking, "Does anyone have a bed for me for the night?" John was the first to reply. After the meeting, I followed his car back to his house. When we arrived, his wife Bonnie was on her way to bed. John asked me if I'd like to have a cup of tea, so we sat down in the kitchen and started to talk. First we reflected together about what happened at our meeting that night. After an hour or so, our conversation shifted to men's groups in general, and how they can be useful. Around midnight, our conversation shifted to what it means to be a man in today's world. When we looked up, we had been talking for hours. It was two a.m.

The next month, I still didn't feel like the drive, but I did feel like another conversation with John. So I bypassed writing to the whole group, I just wrote to John directly and asked if I could stay. The same thing happened, we went to the men's group, went back to his house, started to talk, and suddenly it was the middle of the night. We discovered we were saying things in these conversations that we had never said before, we had never read anywhere before, we were having original ideas together about masculinity. In fact, we were evoking brilliance in each other.

The third month the same thing happened again. But this time, I said to John, "Listen, I feel like we are on to something. We are bringing out in each other ideas that have never been expressed before. Why don't we record our conversations for posterity?" Those conversations became a book, published in 2015, called *Conscious Men*. It has been published now in twelve languages. The entire book was created out of those conversations: sometimes agreeing, sometimes disagreeing, sometimes arguing quite fiercely, sometimes laughing out loud. Brilliance emerged out of friendship.

I have a lot of relationships like that. In fact, most of my books and blog posts are the results of passionate and sometimes fierce dialogues with my wife, my sons, and my friends. When you find yourself bubbling in the 12 o'clock to 3 p'clock phase, I encourage you to rub shoulders with other brilliant people. The story I just told you is about a collaboration: working together to co-author a book. We will talk about co-creation later. But even if you do not co-create a work with someone, you can still develop powerfully brilliant friendships that will bring forth your gifts much more than could happen on your own.

The basic principle of having brilliant friendships is very simple: it has to do with intention. Schedule some time with a friend or colleague who has expertise in the same field as you. If you write political blogs, get together with another political blog writer. If you play the guitar and sing, jam with other musicians. If you are a gardener, meet with other gardeners. You get the picture. This can work equally well in person, or by Skype or phone. You can plan a car trip or a long hike together. The important thing is that you are clear that you are getting together not just to hang out, but with the mutual intention of fostering brilliance in each other.

TAKE A HIKE

My favorite and most frequent brilliance partner is my close friend Jonathan Robinson. He wrote the books *Communication Miracles for Couples* and *The Little Book of Big Questions*. He was, at one time, the youngest person ever to be licensed as a psychotherapist in California. He is interested in enhancing consciousness in the same way that I am. We meet at least once a week, either in one of our houses, or we go out to eat. But our favorite thing is to take walks together, with his two miniature golden retrievers. There is something about the movement of the body when you're hiking, the left, right, left, right, integrating the two halves of the body, which causes a balancing of the brain.

We usually adopt a fixed format. One of us will present an idea, or a "meme" for 5 or 10 minutes. The other one simply listens. The one speaking might outline the idea for a blog post, the overall structure of a book, or just a random idea. Then, after 5 or 10 minutes we enter into a dialogue together. When we are done with the dialogue, we switch over: the other one speaks for 5 to 10 minutes and then we dialog again.

There are three kinds of response you can give when listening to someone else expressing a new and brilliant idea.

Encouragement. "Yes, I love it. That's brilliant! OMG! You're amazing. Wow. Wow. Wow."

Skepticism. "Are you serious? I can't believe you are wasting my time with this. You don't seem to have thought this through at all. It is all very simplistic. You are still thinking thoughts I gave up twenty years ago. Everyone's heard this a thousand times before. Who is going to listen?"

Curiosity. "I hadn't thought of it that way before. Tell me more. Does this apply to everybody? What about the political implications? Is this likely to happen in our lifetime? I didn't understand that bit about... Tell me more about that ... What does that word mean?"

If you want to bring out the best in each other in a brilliant friendship, it is a great idea to become conscious of the ratio of these three kinds of responses, and to also notice your default setting. When coaching teams to interact with each other in this way, I have noticed that most people have an unconscious leaning toward one of these dispositions. Some people, for example, are unconditionally encouraging. That can be very helpful for a speaker who is feeling insecure or testing new ground, but it does not support the other person to be deeply challenged beyond what they already know. Some people are automatically critical as their first response. That is certainly a great preparation for what you will inevitably get from trolls when you publish blogs or post videos on YouTube: it can help the speaker to find their fire. But too much of it will dampen the fire and extinguish it. Some people are naturally curious and ask a lot of questions. This prompts the speaker to elaborate upon their ideas. But only asking questions can be a safe position, and avoids the possibility of useful feedback.

When you start practicing in this way, I suggest you make a mental note of your default ratio of encouragement, criticism, and curiosity. If necessary, you can jot it down on a piece of paper, and keep score.

290 | RADICAL BRILLIANCE

The best thing when listening to someone's new ideas is to avoid getting stuck in any one of these responses. The ratio I encourage people to experiment with in seminars and training is:

- 50% curiosity...
- 40% encouragement ... and
- 10% criticism.

Developing brilliant friendships in this way can enormously enhance your creativity. Once you have built this crucible of brilliance, you find yourself saying things and having ideas you would never normally express.

It is super important when you go for a brilliant walk with your brilliant friend to take along your voice recorder. Make sure everything gets recorded. There are things you will say, and an eloquence with which you will say them when talking to a friend, that you might never be able to capture again on your own.

BRILLIANT DINNER PARTIES

As well as fostering brilliant friendships one-on-one, you can also have a brilliant dinner party. As with any friendship, a dinner party can be many things. In order to have a brilliant dinner party, it needs the proper intention. Invite other people who are also dedicated to their grandchildren's grandchildren: people who are committed to our collective evolution. Seek out artist friends, writers, inventors, innovators, social architects. It is usually more interesting to have a balance of people with different talents and gifts. Make sure it is really clear that this is not just going to be a dinner, it is going to be a crucible of brilliance. The ideal number is six people, with eight the maximum.

I know that elsewhere in this book we have focused on the dulling effect of alcohol, particularly if it is used on a regular basis. But on this occasion, alcohol can be your friend. Have a little aperitif together before the food, and a couple of glasses of wine over dinner. It lubricates the practice that follows. Over dinner, you can simply completely enjoy being together, and allow the conversation to flow in a natural way.

When you are done eating, you can move into the more structured part of the evening: the radical brilliance party game. It takes about 10 minutes total per guest, so an hour for a party of six people. Each guest takes five minutes to express one strong bold original idea, just as we described in the one-on-one practice earlier. It should not be quoting somebody else, or something that you have read, it should be an original thought that has bubbled up out of nowhere. Then the rest of the guests get another five minutes for response. Remember the ratio of encouraging, critical, and curious. Now you will aim to create the ratio of 40%/10%/50%, but as a whole group. This is a little bit like jamming together with musical instruments. When you realize that as a group there is not enough encouragement, you add some. When you realize that could be more curiosity, you add that. Everyone together aims to maintain the balance of the 40/10/50.

It is a great idea to record both the presentation and the response, either on audio or ideally on video. In just the same way as we described above, you will find yourself expressing new ideas with an eloquence that might elude you at other times.

This is a brilliant dinner party: you will create some brilliant videos out of it, you will get some brilliant ideas with your brilliant friends, and you will find yourself saying things, and thinking things, and sharing things, using language where you will amaze yourself.

Of course, musicians who play together in a band know this all too well. Here is Alex Ebert again: "The feeling is like hopping a train. Once you're in the groove, it's quite easy to stay in it. You just have to stay present. You just keep staying present, keep being present, keep being real, keep following your instincts, and then it is suddenly happening. It is like catching a fish or hopping a train."

CHAPTER TWENTY
FEED YOUR BRILLIANT ROLE MODELS

One of the most powerful ways of enlivening brilliance is to have people in your world to whom you look up, and who inspire you. For our purposes here, a "role model" is someone who is alive today, acting as a beacon of inspiration to the world, in a way that you would like also to be doing in one or two or five years into the future.

In the early 1990s, I loved to tell people I was retired. I was in my early thirties, and through a combination of luck and hard work I had made enough money that I could live modestly without having to work again. When my wife (at the time) got pregnant with our first child, I realized that my savings would not be enough. Several seemingly qualified "financial advisors" appeared from out of the woodwork from every direction, offering me fantastic once-in-a-lifetime highly exclusive investment opportunities. I bit the bait. I invested my money in five different enterprises, and after a year they had all gone down the toilet. I had a family to raise, less than $20,000 to my name, and no gainful employment. I'm sure that many people at this point would have the wisdom to get a regular secure job, but I took a different route. I wrote a book. You might think that writing a book about the impact of non-dual awareness on psychotherapy might not seem like the most sensible plan of action when you are in financial dire straits. But sensible has never been my middle name. It took a couple of years to complete that book. I poured my heart and soul into it. The book came out in 1997 with the title *Relaxing into Clear Seeing*. But there was a small snag. No one had heard of me.

When the book came out, we were living in Marin County, California. Lots of people I admired were living in the area, tucked away in the hills. One of them was Barbara Marx Hubbard, who had written a book called *Conscious Evolution*. I had heard her speak at conferences many times over the years. I did not know her personally, but I had great admiration for her. Her message resonated more precisely with my book than anyone else I could think of, and her opinion of it would be more meaningful to me than anyone else I could think of. So I developed a dream, a wild fantasy, to get my book to this woman I admired.

Any time you reach out to someone you do not know, someone who has built a reputation and an organization, your first encounter will be with their gatekeeper gremlins. These are the people whose job it is to keep intruders at bay. The default setting for any gatekeeper in response to the question "I was wondering if it might be possible to…" is "NO." It does not matter what you were wondering about doing. It's still "NO." And sure enough, that was the message I got from Barbara's assistant.

But I persisted. And that is what this chapter is all about: persistence.

I wracked my brains for anyone who might know her. Remember, I had never written a book, and I was completely, 100%, unheard-of. My old friend Pete Russell, whom I had known from England back in the 1970s, was living on a houseboat in Sausalito. I went to visit him one day. It turned out he knew her, and he promised to make an introduction. I still remember the day when I got my phone call returned from Barbara (no email back then) saying she would be willing to look at my manuscript. I personally drove it over to her house in Greenbrae, and dropped it off in the mailbox.

The next morning, less than twelve hours later, I got another phone call. "I've read most of your book during the night," she said. "We have to meet." We did meet, that very morning. We took a long walk, and she told me how deeply she resonated with everything I had written. She gave me a glowing endorsement for the back of the book. She had many very useful suggestions for how to make the book better. That one instance of persistence, of not taking a "NO" from the gatekeeper gremlin, introduced me to many other people, and finally the book was published a few months later with endorsements from not only Barbara Marx Hubbard, but also Byron Katie, Coleman Barks, Lama Surya Das, Jack Kornfield, ... and dozens of other people. It all started with an unwavering determination to connect with one woman whom I admired.

I've known Barbara quite well now for twenty years. One of the things she told me early in our friendship was how she had got started with giving her gift.

"I was a mother of five, married to an artist, living in Lakeville, Connecticut, yet I felt like something was wrong with me. I had everything, what more could I possibly be wanting?

"Things changed the day that I invited Jonas Salk out to lunch. I told him everything that I thought was wrong with me. That I was feeling a sense of discomfort, depression, incompletion with my life. That there was something more I had to give, but I didn't know what it was. I remember saying to Jonas, 'I'm attracted to the future. I know I have a great thing to do but I don't know what it is. And this is really a crisis. There are so many things wrong with me, Jonas.' And he answered, 'Barbara, that's not what's wrong with you, that's what's right with you. You are an evolutionary woman. You are what's needed in the world, because you combine characteristics that the world needs.' So every single characteristic that seemed to be a problem suddenly lined up to be a virtue.

"Everything in my life changed after that lunch. It was a shift to a feeling of joy. I felt a sense of vocational purpose, which I had not had before. I became a futurist, although the word did not even exist back then. I joined the World Future Society. I had to find other teachers, other books, other things to study. I was very inspired by reading Abraham Maslow's book *Toward a Psychology of Being*, and I decided to find him. I was bold. You have to be bold. Don't just sit and wait for it to come to you."

I reached out to Barbara, my role model, and it changed my life. Barbara had reached out to Jonas Salk and Abraham Maslow. I often wonder whom Jonas Salk might have taken out for lunch, thirty years before. Who might have seen his potential? I was part of a long lineage of persistence and inspiration. And of nervous lunch invitations.

NOT TOO HARD, NOT TOO EASY

In order for any role model relationship to be an effective catalyst of brilliance, you need to choose carefully. If you choose a role model who is very accessible to you, or too close to your current level of giving your gift, it will not have the necessary stimulating effect. For example, your next-door neighbor, or a college friend would better qualify for a brilliant friendship than a brilliant role model. On the other hand, if you choose someone who is really inspiring but completely inaccessible, like the Pope, Bill Clinton, or Adele, the whole exercise will just become frustrating and disappointing. You need to find a middle ground: someone whom you could theoretically meet with enough persistence, and who would be genuinely inspiring to you.

NOW IT'S YOUR TURN

It is not so important how rich someone is, or even how famous; the important thing is to find someone who really inspires you: as close as possible, an embodiment of what you aspire to give yourself. When you find someone like that, be bold in reaching out and requesting (sometimes even demanding!) a meeting. Be persistent. This might be one of the best things you can do to amplify your brilliant impact on the world.

So why not do this today? Write down the names of a few people who are really inspiring to you. Remember: don't make them too easy, not a personal friend or a family member, but don't make them impossibly difficult either. Then get busy. Start with the contact form on their website, try to find an email, a phone number, an agent. If your role model is giving any kind of public event anywhere, whether seminar or a talk, travel to attend it.

Now, with trembling knees, it is time to request connection. You could ask to do an interview for a book or a podcast. If you do, remember to record it with good quality equipment. But there is something even better.

Remember that old saying which was drummed into your head growing up, "There's no such thing as a free lunch"? Everybody heard that, it somehow got ingrained into us all around the world. But it is not even true! In fact, the world is overflowing with free lunch. I think I might have even had more free lunches than lunch-es I had paid for. Nevertheless we have all been hypnotized into be-lieving that free lunch is as elusive as the gold at the end of the rain-bow. Consequently, it does not matter how busy or famous anyone is, no one can resist the offer of free lunch.

So when you do make contact with your inspiring role model, I sug-gest that you simply ask, "You have been an incredible inspiration to me. I have a few questions I'd love to ask you. May I invite you out to lunch?" I cannot remember ever being turned down when offering a free lunch. Make sure, of course that it's the fanciest place in town. Don't take your role model to Denny's; splash out a little.

WHAT TO ASK

Once you do sit down together, and you have ordered your food, you might be feeling a little flustered and stagestruck. So here are a few important questions to slip into the conversation:

- How did you get to do what you do? How did you get started?
- What is the most important advice you would give to some-one like me, wanting to make a bigger impact?
- What are you working on now? What is your passion today?
- What are the biggest mistakes you made? What would you not do again?
- I have this idea I've been working on … I'd really like to get your feedback and your opinion.

- Is there anyone you think I should talk to about what I'm working on?
- Remember to take a selfie with your role model, partly to remind yourself later of this life-changing event, but also put it on Facebook and Instagram because this is part of your shifting identity. *Hey, Facebook friends! No big deal, just another day in my life, having lunch with my bud Richard Branson. What's up on your end?*

Developing relationships like this with brilliant people who have already got their message out into the world will be an enormous boost for you to do the same.

CHAPTER TWENTY ONE
DON'T PLAN ON A BESTSELLER

Every potentially brilliant voice, like yours, sooner or later has to consider the relationship between brilliance and the natural and inevitable need to earn a living.

Until the advent of desktop publishing and the Internet, publishing was known as "the gentleman's profession." When I grew up in England, both of my parents were intellectual and creative people. My father was a journalist for the London Times, and later went on to write seventeen books. My mother was an editor at the publisher Faber and Faber; her desk in their Russell Square office was on the other side of the door from T.S. Eliot. I grew up in an environment where creativity—whether making films or writing novels, or poetry, or art—was not thought of primarily in the context of commercial success. Deals were made with handshakes, and the decision to publish was made entirely on the merit of the work — the quality of the word. What else could there possibly be?

I'll tell you what.

Today publishing, and writing, as well as music, art, and techno-
logical innovation, is a very different game to play. If you have a
book germinating in you, a publisher today will ask you about
your "platform," your marketing plan. How many Facebook fol-
lowers do you have? How big is your mailing list? How many hits
will a Google search produce on your name? Oh yes, and by the
way, the folks over there in editing will take a peek at your manuscript too.

NOT FOR THE MONEY

Bill Gladstone is a literary agent and the founder of Waterside
Productions in Cardiff-by-the-Sea in California. Among the best-
selling authors he has represented are Marie Kondo (*The Life-
Changing Magic of Tidying Up*), Eckhart Tolle (*A New Earth*), Jack
Canfield, Pamela Anderson, Jean Houston, Neale Donald Walsch,
and hundreds more. Over the last thirty years, his agency has sold
titles that have created more than $5 billion in sales, and gener-
ated more than $300 million for their authors. Clearly Bill is not
averse to a book doing well financially. However, he was quick to
emphasize in our conversation that dollars and fame must be the
by-product of a truly brilliant work, not the goal. He offered two
examples of this.

"Marie Kondo was obsessed since the age of six with order, neat-
ness, fashion, and design. These principles led her to take a very
spiritual approach to decluttering her house, in which you bless the

articles that you discard. This is certainly not something that was invented to make money, but fortunately for her, it did catch on in an amazing way and her book, *The Life-Changing Magic of Tidying Up*, has sold over ten million copies worldwide. Similarly, Eckhart Tolle did not ever anticipate a level of commercial success, nor was it particularly important to him. He was living in a $50-a-week flat in Vancouver, Canada, at the time he wrote his first book, *The Power of Now*, earning a whopping $15-$20 an hour as a meditation teacher. That book resulted from his desire to share a greater awareness that actually saved his life. He had been feeling suicidal, when he had a form of awakening and realized his true nature as distinct from what he recognized as his pain body. That insight is what drove him, not any idea that he was going to found *Eckhart TV* and that all these people were going to find ways of marketing him. In fact, he shunned all commercial opportunities until Oprah selected him.

"I always advise people to only go into publishing if God — or your equivalent of God — commands you to," Bill continued. "It is not something to do lightly. If you are a very energetic, intelligent human being, it is not likely that going into publishing will be the way that you can generate the most material benefit for yourself." The same would apply to being a musician, artist, or even an entrepreneur. "There are so many other professions that pay ten to 100 times more: you can be an investment banker, an advertising executive, you can run a big corporation. There are many other things you can do that will compensate you more materially. You should only write a book or go into publishing if you know this is your calling. You will be satisfied because you are expressing your truth, and that is your primary reward. The funny thing is, I am always telling people, 'Don't do it for the money,' and with that guiding principle, we have generated hundreds of millions of income for our authors.

"The reward for all the people we represent is not the money, it is the impact they have had. It is not just the lives of the people who read those books; it is the lives of the people who interact with the people who read those books. That is the way the world changes. If you raise the awareness of one reader, that person may change their behavior, in ways that raise the awareness of everyone in their network."

HOW TO RIG THE SYSTEM

Before social media and the Internet became so prominent in our lives, the primary means for a book to gain popularity was through reviews in newspapers and magazines, and word-of-mouth referrals. It was virtually impossible to rig either one of these avenues. A book reviewer writing for a reputable literary publication probably had a university degree in literature. It would be considered corrupt for any reviewer to recommend the work of a personal friend or business associate, let alone to be paid off to make the book more popular. In this way new books were measured against the highest standards, and only works with real merit could survive the test.

Today, you don't even need the approval of the editors at a publishing house to write a book. If you own a computer and some inexpensive software, one click will make you a published author. Anyone can write a book or make a movie, and in fact more people than ever are doing just that every year.

It is not only easy, but also quite commonplace, to rig the system. Anyone with a fairly mediocre book but savvy in the skills of Internet marketing can organize for "joint venture partners" to send promotional "e mail blasts" out to their lists, all within the same week, offering "bonus gifts" to buy on a certain day. Presto! Even a book with relatively little merit can now be called a "bestseller."

The last remnants of credibility left standing, until recently, were the New York Times and Wall Street Journal bestseller lists. Until a few years ago, they both seemed to be immune to these kinds of schemes. But no more. Jeff Bercovici reported in Forbes magazine in 2014 that there are several companies that will help you simulate the appearance of a book's popularity. They do this by "taking bulk sales and breaking them up into more organic-looking individual purchases, defeating safeguards that are supposed to make it impossible to 'buy' bestseller status." Such a scheme costs about $230,000. If you have that kind of money, it does not matter what kind of book you write, you can have a bestseller, or the appearance of one, anyway.

Wait, what is that rumbling sound? Ah, that was Ernest Hemingway turning in his grave.

MAINSTREAMING

If you write books, sooner or later you are probably going to talk to a literary agent or a publisher, either before or after your book is written. If you are a filmmaker, you are going to need to talk to a studio. If you want to launch a new product or start a company, you need to talk to investors. Everyone has to have a conversation with somebody someday about how this is going to sell. The conversation can be tricky. Some choose to ignore this topic completely. "No," they say," I just want to follow the creative impulse." They refuse to do any marketing or connecting with their potential audience, and remain unnecessarily unknown. Van Gogh, William Blake, Emily Dickinson, Thoreau, and many other brilliant minds died in obscurity. None of them paid even momentary heed to catering to the "mainstream"; in fact, one might say that the majority of radically brilliant people go out of their way to question and challenge mainstream values.

If you talk to a publisher or a literary agent today, you will be advised on how to make your work more "mainstream." "Remember, you are not your target audience," I have been reminded so many times by well-wishing mentors. Frequently, I have turned in a manuscript I thought was brimming with brilliant insights (just as our cat proudly delivers a dead squirrel to our kitchen as her contribution to the family shopping), only to be told that my book was "preaching to the choir." This kind of reminder can prove very useful. It trains us to develop discipline and rigor, to weed out prejudice, not make assumptions that are unproven, to seek out values that are universal, and to employ a language that is fresh and accessible.

To be more "mainstream" means to use language and appeal to values that not only apply to you and your close friends but that might also apply to a milk farmer in Wisconsin, or a construction worker in Texas. This language and value set has already been heavily influenced by corporate interests wanting to increase sales, and politicians wanting to consolidate power. This is done by steering the conversation toward fear of calamity and the desire for more "stuff."

"Mainstreaming" your work will often require you to massage your message into agreement with the shared assumptions that we are weak, undefended, the prey of imminent and merciless attack, and that our lives would be oh-so-much-better if only we had an upgrade to the iPhone, the computer, the car, the house ... your spouse, your body, your face, your personality: all of which can somehow be paid for. When you mainstream, you often write, make a film, or produce something, to appeal to that desire or alleviate that fear. It means thinking in advance about what will sell the most copies and bring the most money, and then creating something to achieve that goal. People can't be controlled, or sold endless new stuff, when they are feeling powerful, empowered, awake, or happy-for-no-reason.

There is a significant risk to this modern-day extreme sport of "mainstreaming." You put your creative life at the risk of a fatal accident each and every time you measure the worth of your work by dollars made, number of copies sold, Amazon rank, or New York Times position.

Edward Sharpe and the Magnetic Zeros is best known for their song "Home," which has been played on YouTube more than 80 million times. Founder Alex Ebert talked about how the song came to life. "When we wrote '*Home*,' I knew that this was something that had been missing from the cultural fabric of society for at least thirty years. That 'something' was 'earnestness.' We wrote '*Home*' with all of our hearts. It was a pure song. When Jade, who was lying on the bed, hopped up and sang "Alabama Arkansas ..." it was a pure moment, a pure expression. Later, listening to the song we had just created, I immediately recognized that it was going to serve a purpose: to fill an empty box that society had either abandoned or forgotten about. It was a love song that wasn't riddled with sexuality, a love song that was entirely earnest, not about a breakup, really just the earnest tones of true friendship."

I provoked Alex to think of other times when he has witnessed that quality in another artist. The first thing that came to his mind was Joaquin Phoenix's performance in *The Master*. "I had not seen something like that since Brando in *Last Tango in Paris*. I was completely electrified by his presence. This was a man on fire. I did not know if he was going to grab the camera, I did not know what was going to happen on screen at any moment. That is really what I look for in any artist. Are they eschewing everything that shackles them from their truest, most potent self? When you eschew those things, you are eschewing safety nets: posturing, posing, speaking a certain way. When you see someone dangling up there on the tightrope without a safety net, like Joaquin Phoenix, you can immediately tell there is no safety. That is always the most electrifying place to be."

AIM TO PLEASE YOUR MENTORS

To be radically brilliant and to also reach the people you can serve requires you to be able to understand and make conscious choices about the balance between deeply honoring and obeying the impulse of brilliant authentic creativity that flows through you, and how to play the games of marketing and media.

My one-on-one coaching with clients, and teaching with groups, focuses mostly on supporting people to discover and express their unique message, insights, and gifts that could only flow through them and no one else. If your unique gift is not given through you in this lifetime, it means that it will never be given. Quite often, people hire me as a coach to support them to birth, foster, and complete a book. From the very beginning, I always encourage people to NOT try to write a New York Times bestseller.

Instead I encourage my clients to think of ten to twelve people they admire completely, and whose respect means everything, and then to create their book with an aim to pleasing those specific people.

For example, I am writing this book for you now. I have no idea if it will sell dozens, hundreds, or thousands of copies. I have no way to know if it will remain obscure or find a wider audience. I would like to be happy either way. Here are twelve people whose opinion I do care about. If any of these people read the book and like it, I will feel more satisfied than reaching a #1 position on a bestseller list.

1. Michael Pollan
2. Tim Ferris
3. Lynne Twist
4. Chameli Ardagh
5. David Suzuki
6. Steve Kotler
7. John Gray
8. Jean Houston
9. Alex Ebert
10. Barbara Marx Hubbard
11. Charles Eisenstein
12. Malcolm Gladwell

I would like to ask you to do the same thing now. You are probably reading this book because you have a project going, or you would like to have a project going, to advance the evolution of humanity. Whose opinion would mean a lot to you? Think of ten to twelve people. Think of people who are already established, and whose work you admire the most. As you are crafting your work, keep the potential reaction of those people in your mind as the yardstick for truly giving the gift that you were born to give.

What would it be like for one or all of those people to say, "Yes! That is brilliant!" This will allow you to not just live in a vacuum of creative impulse, disconnected from any readership, but at the same time it will avoid you getting lost in only thinking about how you can make the most money.

If you stay true to the tender impulses of original creative impulse pushing their way to the surface through you, the satisfaction derived from that integrity makes financial reward and fame a secondary benefit. You might sell millions of copies, as Eckhart Tolle did by following this principle. You might remain obscure like Henry David Thoreau. Either way you will remain happily married to your Heart's True Song, rather than working the streets as a prostitute of the word.

CHAPTER TWENTY TWO
BRILLIANT MENTORING AND COACHING

If there is one common thread that binds together all of the brilliant people I have ever met, worked with, or interviewed, it is that they recognize that we are always more brilliant, more creative, and we shine more brightly when we support each other and work in collaboration. Brilliant people are not experts, they are lifelong learners. "In times of drastic change, it is the learners who inherit the future," said Eric Hoffer, in his book *Reflections on the Human Condition*. "The learned usually find themselves equipped to live in a world that no longer exists."

Until the early 1990s, the word "coaching" referred only to sports. Thomas J. Leonard is frequently recognized as the one who, with a group of friends, saw that athletics is one of the few areas of human activity that keeps getting better all the time. This is not true of music: you cannot say that music today is infinitely much better than in Mozart's time. It is also not true of painting; we cannot say that Leonardo da Vinci looks like an amateur relative to art today. It is certainly not true of religion. But every four years new records are broken at the Olympic Games. Human beings run faster, jump higher, and excel more in physical prowess every year. Thomas Leonard realized that this is true to a large degree because of the nature of the relationship between an athlete, or team, and the coach.

Coaching is very different from teaching. The teacher will demonstrate how to do something that can then be duplicated. A coach is someone who sees the potential in you, the possibilities of what you can achieve, and then is willing to be by your side, in a disposition of continuous encouragement, to bring that potential forth. A coach will say, "Tell me more about that ... that idea you just expressed."

Rudolf Steiner was the original founder of Waldorf education. The first school was created at the Waldorf-Astoria cigarette factory in Stuttgart, Germany, during the Second World War, where Steiner had been asked to start a school for the employees. Steiner instructed the teachers to perform a type of visualization each night before going to sleep. He told them to bring each of the children in their class into awareness, and then to think of that child not just as they are now, but in their fullest possible potential. My children were lucky enough to go to a school founded on these principles. My older son's teacher, Carol Nimick, followed this request of Steiner to his teachers each and every night. For the eight years my son was in her class, she evoked an image of each child in her class every night, and then contemplated the fullest blossoming of that child's potential. Today, all those kids are grown up. Some became artists, some writers, one has founded his own company. They are all doing "their thing." This is the power of coaching and mentoring: someone can see through your limited sense of yourself into your true potential and coax that, encourage that, celebrate that to blossom fully.

HOW TO CHOOSE A COACH

It is estimated that there are approximately 50,000 professional coaches in the world today. Of course, one coach will be better qualified than another. Someone just starting out will have less experience, less confidence, and less training than someone who has been coaching for decades. There are so many people offering coaching today and so many types of coaching that many people feel at a loss to know whom to choose. Here is a fairly simple and very reliable formula. The key is to find someone who has mastered want you want to get good at, and who is still passionate about that pursuit in their life today; it still gets them excited. So if you want to write a book, get coached by someone who has successfully written books, and who is still writing today, still challenged, motivated and excited.

Let's also understand who does not make a good coach. If you want to write a book, don't get coached by someone who has never written one, but strives to do so, just like you. That person cannot help you because they have not yet mastered what you hope to learn. They have not crossed the terrain between aspiration and accomplishment, and so are not familiar with the potholes and the open stretches. In the same way, don't seek out a relationship coach who is single or recently divorced. Get coached by someone who is currently living a passionate, alive, and engaging relationship.

On the other hand, don't get coached by someone who mastered what you aspire to some years ago, and is now bored with it. A good coach needs to share your passion. For example, someone who made a lot of money decades ago, and now is mainly interested in fly-fishing will not be a good financial coach for you. Once the passion has gone, and is just a memory, you can get remembered information and skills, but not the infectious excitement you need.

Gay and Kathleen Hendricks are among the world's best relationship coaches. If you are in a marriage and you want to make it even better, they are the perfect candidates because their own marriage is not only loving and happy, but they are both still very excited about it to this day, sometimes challenged, and always working to make it better.

Jack Canfield is one of the world's greatest success coaches. He has made hundreds of millions of dollars, so he knows how to cross the terrain. But at seventy-three years old, he is still passionate, excited, and constantly learning how to be an even better, and more multi-dimensionally successful, version of himself.

Dave Ellis wrote the book *Life Coaching* in 1998. He is also the author of *Becoming a Master Student,* which was the best-selling college textbook in all disciplines for over twenty years, having sold over six million copies. Ellis coached an economist from Bangladesh named Muhammad Yunus, who then went on to win a Nobel Prize. Ellis coached Lynne Twist, who then went on to found the Pachamama Alliance, and to participate in rewriting Ecuador's Constitution to protect the Amazon rainforest. Ellis has coached the CEOs and presidents of the world's largest nonprofit organizations, like Save the Children and CARE. Many people whom Dave Ellis works with go on to make huge contributions to making the world a better place. Let's hear what he has to say about coaching.

"I assist people to think what they have never thought, to open up their creativity and their imagination to see things in ways that they have never seen them, to say what they have never said, and then to write what they have never written. The result is to take actions you have never taken. What makes the biggest difference is an invitation, a challenge to open up and to begin to consider that which you have never considered."

Ellis elaborates, "The style of coaching I have developed started when I was working with college students in computer programming. Students would come to me with their program, lay it on my desk, and say, 'I want some help.' I would answer, 'I would be happy to help. Tell me what is going on.' The student would look through it. 'Here it is ... then I do this ... then it branches over here ... then it just seems to ... Oh, I see, I get what I did wrong now.' They would light up, thank me profusely, and leave. What did I do to earn that thanks? I did nothing but listen, and challenge the student to talk it through. I learned this from my father. When I was young I would come to him with a problem. 'Dad, I am stuck and confused, what do I do?' He would say, 'Let's research it.' What he meant was, 'You research it and I will listen and help and guide a bit.' He did not give me advice, he did not give me direction, he did not tell me how to do it; he just sat there and challenged me to think."

"A lot of times people say, 'Well I procrastinate, I know I want to do it, but I don't.' More often than not it is because the motive is missing, not the motivation. The root of motivation, energy, enthusiasm, excitement, involvement, and action is having a clear motive. Most people who say they are procrastinating are actually not in touch with their true heart's desire. What is it you actually want? When you wake up in the morning, clear about what you want, it is like a magnet. Motive is a magnet.

"My favorite expression is, 'Do not go there alone.' Even the Lone Ranger was not alone, he had Tonto. Partnership with somebody who is really there for you, really rooting for you, with your agenda as their agenda, is not always easy to find. But you can find it, we can all find it. Sometimes it is a dangerous place in here. We have wild and woolly thoughts. If you are going to go out into the wild and woolly woods, do not go there alone.

"A coach will assist you to self-reflect and self-direct. A great coach will not be brilliant for you but will leave you with the understanding that you are brilliant."

BEING COACHABLE

Getting maximum value out of a coaching relationship is not only about finding the best coach. It is also about finding the right disposition within yourself. Even the best coach in the whole world cannot help you unless you are also fully on board, and even a mediocre coach could be of great help when you are on fire. Remember the analogy to sports? It is just the same. A terrific sports coach cannot help you win the Olympics unless you are willing to train hard, show up for practice every day, and develop the right mindset.

A good first step in becoming coachable is to notice the "default disposition" that you might bring to coaching, which is very often the same disposition that you bring to life, out of habit. If you find it difficult to recognize this on your own, ask your close friends and coworkers for feedback, and request that they be really honest with you. Here are some of the "default dispositions" that many people fall into out of habit.

> **Skepticism**. *I'm not going to believe any of this until you prove it to me. You show me it's true, and then I will cooperate.*
>
> **Resistance**. *You can't get to me, nothing works for me. In fact, this is probably not going to work.*
>
> **Superiority**. *I know much more about this than you do. I'm incredibly highly trained and credentialed. You don't really know what you're talking about, you are incompetent.*
>
> **Knowledgeability**. *I've been studying this for years, I'm familiar with all the statistics.*

Passivity. *I really hope this is going to work. I need to make more money. How long will it take until your coaching is effective?*

Victimization. *I'd love for this to work, but my father was very cruel and authoritarian me when I was a child, and so I think it's left me with a strong tendency to sabotage everything. I'm scarred and damaged.*

Go with the flow. *I'm really open to wherever this takes us. I have no particular agenda or outcomes in mind. I'm really open to anything.*

Approval-seeking. *I did all the practices you suggested, and even more. I read all the materials you suggested, three times. This is amazing. You are amazing. I think you're the best coach anyone could imagine. I'm getting so much benefit from you. (Am I your best client ever? Please tell me I am...)*

Lighthearted and humorous. *Never been much of a productivity fiend myself, more of a beer and Doritos guy. But hey, what the f**k, try anything once. This whole coaching thing could be a bit of a lark.*

Comparison. *I was interested with what you said about talking to disowned parts to overcome resistance. I studied Gestalt with Fritz Perls back in the day, and I've read Hal and Sidra Stone's work. I'm quite familiar with sub-personality theory.*

Jump the Gun. *I'm feeling really great about this coaching, I'm totally fired up. Everything is great, I'm totally inspired and going for it. I really can't find any resistance, we've achieved everything I wanted in just two weeks.*

THE DISPOSITION THAT WORKS

Once you become aware of the default habits that you might bring to coaching, and that you also bring to life in general, the awareness itself causes them to dissipate. Then you can begin to consciously cultivate a disposition that works, one that makes you extremely coachable. Mostly, this requires the skillful balancing of seeming opposites:

Intention/Vulnerability. This means being at the same time very focused and determined about reaching the outcome, but simultaneously open to exploring what gets in the way.

Responsible/Receptive. This means being willing to take full responsibility for the process and the outcome, and at the same time being willing to listen to your coach and to consider aspects you might have overlooked.

Authoritative/Curious. This means fully owning what you know to be true and the fruits of your previous experience through experimentation, and at the same time wanting to hear feedback from your coach.

GET COACHED FROM START TO FINISH

Brilliant people who make extraordinary contributions frequently set up channels of support even before the inception of the project. First hire a coach, then decide together what the project will look like. Make getting coached the first line item on your budget, and the first thing you pay for once you have funding. People who get very high value from coaching commit to the same coach from before the project starts all the way through until it is completed. When you start to wonder if perhaps you don't have the best coach, treat this thought like you might deal with commitment phobia before the wedding, or even once recently married. It is natural for your commitment to wobble, but you do not have to turn that into actions and decisions. If you can find the right coach, and commit to staying with that person all the way through the project, it will almost certainly bring out the most luminous brilliance waiting within you.

CHAPTER TWENTY THREE
THIS ISN'T ABOUT YOU

Up to now, most of what we have explored about becoming more radically brilliant has, in one way or another, referenced the benefits to you. But there is another dimension to all this, which goes beyond you and your life and even your life purpose and your gifts, where the importance of you, and me, and him, and her, diminishes almost to the point of obscurity.

Most people today recognize that we face various crises of unprecedented proportions: global warming, terrorism, financial inequality, depletion and pollution of natural resources. The only thing they all have in common is that we do not have ready solutions to any of them. The future looks a little wobbly. Albert Einstein is often quoted to have said, "You cannot solve any problem in the same state of consciousness in which it was created." All of the problems we face today were created by one kind of thinking, and they will finally be solved by the intervention of a more evolved kind of thinking: by more people having brilliant ideas.

We have no indication that there has ever been a time like this before, where the activity of one species threatens to destroy not only our own habitat, but the balance of many other lifeforms as well. It is a big deal. If it was just the basement of your house that had dry rot, you could always try to get it repaired. If it was beyond repair, you could move, and the insurance might even kick in. If it was the neighborhood in which you live, you could move to another part of the city. You could always move to another city altogether, another state, even another country. But when it is the planet on which we live, the issue becomes more serious. Most of us have no reliable awareness of anything other than Planet Earth. This is it. This is home. This is all that we have stored in our memory banks.

In the late 1800s, as more and more people moved to big cities (because of the Industrial Revolution), there was a problem with too many horses on the streets. London had about 11,000 horse-drawn hansom cabs, as well as several thousand horse-drawn buses. Altogether, there were more than 50,000 horses in London transporting people around the city each day. This created major problems. The average horse produces up to thirty-five pounds of manure per day, which attracts flies and spreads typhoid and other diseases. A horse produces about two pints of urine per day. That's 100,000 pints of urine per day for the city. The problem came to a head when, in 1894, the Times of London (no less) predicted, "In 50 years, every street in London will be buried under nine feet of manure." There was absolutely no solution in sight. We were all doomed to be buried in sh*t. Much like some people feel about politics in America. Of course, no one anticipated Henry Ford and the manufacture of motorized cars at affordable prices. By 1912, that particular problem had been resolved. All that fret and worry was in vain. Of course, the internal combustion engine created an upgraded kind of problem, which perhaps Elon Musk and his friends at Tesla will now take care of. It has always been like this: we resolve and overcome our challenges and evolve to a more complex and integrated state by people having brilliant ideas.

YOU ARE IRRELEVANT. YOU ARE CENTRAL

While written records only go back about 5000 years, Homo Sapiens have been on this planet in their present form for about 260,000 years. Living organisms, in one form or another, have been here for 4 billion years. Our lifespan of 80 years is not even a blink of the eye relative to the entire story of the miracle of life on this earth: just one 50 millionth part of the whole story. If the whole history of life were the distance from San Francisco to Los Angeles, your or my entire lifetime would be less than a sixteenth of an inch of that journey.

This little rock is going around the sun, which is just one of 200 billion other suns, and that is just in the Milky Way galaxy. Astronomers estimate that there are more than 100 billion galaxies in the universe. When we contemplate these numbers, we may start to feel our smallness, the irrelevance of one individual life trajectory.

When you think of a huge river, like the Mississippi, or the Ganges in India, and think of one water molecule moving in the river, relative to the whole body and journey of the river, that one water molecule is irrelevant. If you scooped it out, the river would continue and be absolutely unaffected. And yet, with no water molecules, there is no river. Each individual molecule is a part of the movement of the river, but take that one molecule out of the river and it is still the river. It is just like that for you and me: your brilliance, your showing up, your living a life that allows brilliance to flow through you is a tiny, tiny part of the story of the evolution of humanity. In a way it is irrelevant relative to the whole story, but it is also essential. It is your brilliance, and his brilliance, and her brilliance, and their brilliance: all of it together is essential for humanity to evolve.

You are showing up not just for you to fulfill your life's journey, your life's longing, but you are also showing up for the sake of your children, your grandchildren, and countless generations. How do you think global warming will be solved? Probably not through an act of divine intervention, probably not through time just playing itself out. Most probably global warming will be solved through somebody, or some people, having brilliant ideas about the way we use energy. How do you think that economic imbalance in the world will finally be solved? Probably not through just waiting it out. Almost certainly somebody like Muhammad Yunus, who won the Nobel Prize for his work with microcredit loans, will have an idea so brilliant that it will solve financial inequality once and for all. How was smallpox eradicated? This all happens with individuals having brilliant ideas.

PRESERVING THE RAINFOREST

Lynne Twist has always been the kind of person who looks for meaning in her life beyond her own personal needs. Her father was her big love. He was the leader of a big band orchestra. He died when she was twelve, and then the music stopped in their lives. She became very religious. As a young teenager she silently and secretly went to mass every morning at 5:30 a.m. before school. Mother Teresa was her idol. Later, at Stanford, she protested the Vietnam War, and she was active in the civil rights movement. When she and her husband moved to San Francisco, they founded the Pacific Primary School because it was the only way they could ensure that their kids would grow up with African-American kids, immigrants, and people of different economic classes. In 1974 Twist took the EST training with Werner Erhard, and was profoundly changed.

"Transformation became the water I wanted to swim in for the rest of my life," she remembers. Soon after, she introduced Werner Erhard to Buckminster Fuller, whom she had already known for some years. Out of that first meeting was born the Hunger Project: a commitment to ending world hunger. "They knew that it was not a food issue, it was an integrity issue," Twist recalls. "I heard Bucky speak about living a life that makes a difference, for the betterment of all humanity; creating a world that works for everyone, where no one is left out. I became completely committed to that. I turned my life over to ending world hunger." Even with three young children, Lynne became responsible for 200,000 volunteers in the United

States, 40,000 full-time volunteers in Bangladesh alone, and offices in dozens of countries around the world. She raised more than 2 billion dollars to end world hunger, and became an expert fundraiser for other organizations as well.

In 1994, Twist was asked to do some fundraising for a project in Guatemala. Her job was to lead a group of donors to meet the native people. She led the trip with John Perkins, who had a considerable background with indigenous people. John told her he had just come from the Amazon, where he had been working with the Schuar people. They had told him about the Achuar, a neighboring tribe, who had previously had almost no contact with the outside world. Their land was being threatened, and they needed help. John asked, would Lynne be a part of that? "Thank you very much," Lynne replied. "But I'm too busy ending world hunger, and I do not work in South America. So thank you for your invitation, but you do that one on your own."

Later during that same trip, they attended an all-night fire ceremony with a shaman. He told the dozen donors to lie down in a circle, with their feet toward the fire, like a big wagon wheel. No medicine; he just started to drum, in a very rhythmic and beautiful way. He began chanting. Lynne remembers what happened next. "The chanting was so beautiful, so hypnotic. The sound of the drum, the crackling fire in the cold night air, the shaman's voice, was absolutely mesmerizing. At a certain point I felt my right arm turn into a giant wing. I absolutely had to extend it, then my left arm started to also turn into a giant wing, and I had to extend that also. Then a beak started to grow on my face. I had to fly; I could not lie there for one more second. I began to fly up into the air above the campfire; I looked down and saw the twelve people and the shaman. His drumming and chanting still in my ear, I flew into the night sky, all in slow motion, toward the stars, in a moonless night. It was so exhilarating. Then the sky grew lighter. I looked down. I was flying over this vast, completely unending sea of green, a magnificent, incredible forest. My gaze became so acute I could see all the way to the forest floor. I could see what was crawling around – little animals, little critters. Lifting my gaze, I could see very far off into the distance, over this endless forest with winding rivers. Then the disembodied faces of men, with orange geometric face paint on their faces and yellow, red and black feathered crowns on their heads, started floating up from the forest floor through the trees toward this bird: me. The faces were vivid and beautiful, and they called to the bird in a strange tongue. They would disappear back into the forest and then would float up again, call to the bird, drift back into the forest and disappear. These faces kept reappearing and disappearing, reappearing and disappearing into the forest.

"There was a very loud drumbeat. I opened my eyes. I sat up. I felt my arms, they were intact, there were no wings, I was a human being. I did not have a beak, I was myself. I looked around the circle and all the other people looked as discombobulated and confused as I was. Once we were all calmed down and centered, the shaman asked, through John Perkins, what happened for each of us, did we have visions? One by one people shared their visions. One had become a wolf, another became a snake. Every single person became an animal. When it came to my turn I shared my experience of becoming a bird. The shaman gave me an intense look. When John Perkins shared a vision very much like mine, the shaman gave him the same look. He asked everyone to go except for me and John.

"When we were alone, the shaman told us this was not a normal vision. We were being contacted by a culture, by people who were calling to us and we needed to go to them. John knew exactly who they were. 'Lynne,' he said, 'This is the Achuar I was telling you about. They are ready for contact. This is the contact. They are asking for us to come to them. We must go.' I said, 'John, I can't. I am ending world hunger. I need to be in Africa. I am going from here to Ghana!' I had no psychic space to take on another thing. I was maxed out. It was just too much for me.

"So I went on to Ghana where I had a Hunger Project board meeting. Eight Ghanaians, five men and three women, were our Hunger Project leaders. During the conversation, first one, then two, and then all five of the men started having orange geometric face paint appear on their black faces. Everyone kept talking, as if it was not happening. 'I am hallucinating,' I thought, 'that weird thing in Guatemala got me.' I excused myself and went to the ladies room so that I could pull it together. But as soon as I went back into the meeting, it happened again. Eventually I burst into tears right at the table. 'I've lost my center,' I said. 'I have been in too many countries, too many time zones, too much travel. I need to go to my room. I need to go back to the United States.'

"I packed my bag, went straight to the Accra Airport, and got on the first plane, which was to Frankfurt. All the way from Accra to Frankfurt I saw the painted faces; whether my eyes were open, or they were shut, waking or sleeping. Then I flew from Frankfurt to New York, I saw the faces all the way, and then from New York to San Francisco. By the time I got home I was a wreck. I thought I was losing my mind. It took a few days to reach John Perkins by phone. When I did, he was very clear. 'We need to put together a group of twelve people with a global voice that can be heard around the world. People who have open hearts, people who know that the rainforest is critical to future of life, people who know indigenous people carry critical wisdom for the long-term future of life, and people who will respect the ways of the shaman.'"

In 1995, Lynne travelled to meet the Achuar people for the first time, with her husband Bill, John Perkins, and nine others. They travelled down the valley of the volcanoes, over the eastern side of the Andes range to the edge of the Amazon rainforest, which is the same size as the entire United States, the same size as the face of the full moon. They flew into Shuar territory, and then made their way to meet the Achuar. The tribal leaders met them there, with their face paint, yellow and red feather crowns, and spears, and took them by canoe upriver and showed them where to build a campsite.

"The Achuar had seen in their dreams and visions that contact was inevitable," says Lynne, "so their very wise and unique decision was that they would initiate what they most feared— contact with the outside world—but in their territory, on their terms, in ways that they can control. They had a vision for their territory, to be never touched, to never have roads, to be governed by indigenous people. To stay pristine, not only for them and their future, but for the future of life. In order to do that, they needed modern world partners who would help them navigate a relationship with the modern world, and give them exactly what they need to preserve the territory, but no more than what they need.

"They had five years for us to prepare them, which is what they wanted, for this dangerous contact that they knew would come. They would have modern world friends, they would be ready for it; they would understand oil companies, the government, extractive industries; all that ultimately they saw would come. They did come, and the indigenous people have prevailed and kept them out. Bill and I realized it was clearly our destiny to connect with these people. That was the beginning of the relationship which became the Pachamama Alliance."

Initially Lynne and her husband raised $125,000 from that original group of twelve, enough to pay for a meager little office with an old typewriter and a rotary phone, and to start the work of protecting the rainforest. Today, the Achuar have legal title to every inch of 50 million acres, comprising 59 different communities, sometimes many weeks walk apart from each other. The Pachamama Alliance now works with indigenous people throughout the entire Amazon area, the largest freshwater source in the world, the lungs of the planet, and the source of the global climate system.

"We have been successful in preserving the entire region from oil company after oil company, mining company after mining company, ethnobotanists, lumber, all of the extractive industries that have been pushing enormous pressure on this area forever. The government itself has caved in over and over, and tried to get indigenous people to submit, but they have not. Nothing has happened to encroach on these lands. Nothing. That is a huge accomplishment."

"But the indigenous people have always known that the pressure on those forests is not really coming from oil companies, or rubber tappers, or their government, it is coming from the modern world's blind and unending trance for more of anything and everything. They asked us to not only work with them, but to go home and change the dream of the modern world: a dream of consumptive acquisition and more of everything, to a new dream. A dream of what we call environmentally sustainable, spiritually fulfilling, and socially just human presence on this planet. Maybe the biggest work of the Pachamama Alliance is our transformation processes and educational programs that awaken people from the trance and put them on a path for a new dream for humanity. We do that in 82 countries. That is a huge accomplishment as well. Hundreds of thousands, probably millions of people have participated in those programs."

Phew.

Lynne Twist is a bold and inspiring example of a life lived beyond "me" and "my needs." I asked her to reflect on what it means to lead such a life. "People want to make a difference with their life. That is the most profound way to live. That is what everybody longs for more than anything. Food, shelter, and all that, you do not have to have them first. It seems logical, but I do not agree with it. I have been with people in Bangladesh who had no shelter, who have not eaten for three days, whose primary commitment was to make a difference with their lives. That is really what people want. That is what gives life meaning."

"Taking care of oneself in order to be of service makes sense. Taking care of one-self just to take care of one-self does not give you satisfaction. People will give up anything to make a difference with their life, if they get a whiff of what it means to live a life that matters. Contribution does not have to be self-sacrificing. We sacrifice nothing, and we gain everything when we participate. For me, the greatest privilege is to participate in the transformation of life itself and the lives of other people. There is nothing I can imagine that would be more powerful and more fulfilling.

"I have lived what I call a committed life; a life that is governed by my highest commitments, not by my desires. If you live a life of commitment, where you give your word for something larger than yourself, you are constantly in a state of fulfillment. I am not saying that there are no struggles, no problems. It leads you to a life you could never have planned. It does not have anything to do with ambition. It has to do with surrender. You cannot surrender to get that kind of a life because that is cheating. You have to really surrender and somehow it is given to you."

YOUR VISION OF THE FUTURE

One of my coaches loves to help people plan for the future. He has you start off by planning your own future. What would you like to be doing, how much money would you like to be making, where would you like to be living, in two years? Then he advises you to make a five-year plan, and to align your actions today with what you want to create. But after that, it gets more challenging. He asks you to develop a 50-year plan: how would you like the world to be, how would you like us be living, 50 years from now? If you do that exercise when you are 20, you may get to enjoy the fruits of your vision. But if you create this at 60, as I am now, you may not live to be 110. You are envisioning a future you may not live to witness. What about 120 years from now? We can safely say you will be gone. But you can still visualize and intend how you would like the world to be in 120 years, and then align your actions today with that outcome. Now you are dedicating the way you live not for your own well-being, but for the grandchildren of your grandchildren. What would you like for them?

The construction on York Minster Cathedral began in 1220 and it was completed in 1472. It took 252 years to complete: eight generations. It has some of the finest stone carving in the world from medieval times. A stonemason might have spent decades carving an ornate depiction of a lion's head, or an angel, never to see the stone put in place in his lifetime. Hundreds and hundreds of craftsmen worked on the Cathedral but only their distant ancestors in future generations would see it completed.

This puts the dedication of brilliance into a different context. You can unplug from an exclusive interest in your own pleasure and financial reward, or the desire for fame and notoriety. Now you are dedicating the fruits of your actions to people who are not yet born.

I suggest you take some time to do this right now, for real, before you put this book aside. Do you have children? Do you love them? Do you want your children to thrive, to breathe clean air, to have the maximum opportunity to express their creativity and their love? Think of the world you want for them, and what small actions you can take today to contribute to the world you want for them. I would like to suggest you to write a short letter to your children, one they could read thirty years from now, summarizing what you wanted to create for them to inherit, and the steps you took.

Would you like your children to have happy families as well? Think of your grandchildren, whether they are born yet or not. What kind of life would you like for them? Do you wish them to breathe clean air or polluted? Would you like them to be able to drink from pure mountain streams, or to need multiple layers of complex filtration to be able to drink water? Would you like them to be able to travel the world and meet interesting people without fearing for their lives? Would you like them to be able to look people from other countries in the eye, and feel a shared respect, or would you prefer that they feel shame about the imbalance between the haves and have-nots? Now write a letter to your grandchildren as well, one that they can read many decades from now.

If you wish your grandchildren well, whether born or unborn, would you like them to also raise families? What kind of future do you wish your great-grandchildren? Write another short letter for them to read. And what about the grandchildren of your grandchildren? What future do you want for them? You are the grandparents of their grandparent. They are your great-great-grandchildren. What you create today, for better or worse, they will inherit.

Here is my letter to one of the grandchildren of my grandchildren. He or she will turn twenty-five somewhere between 75 and 90 years from today.

My Dear One,

I am the grandfather of your grandfather. My name is Arjuna, I was born in 1957 in England, and I write this to you now from California in 2017 at the age of 60. Of course I will have died before you were born.

First thing I want you to know is how much I love you and care about you. I have deeply loved my two sons, who I call by their nicknames, Abhi and Shuba. They have not yet had children, but I eagerly wait for the day they will arrive, and I know I will love my grandchildren too. One day they will have children, and one day one of those children will be your mother or your father.

I care deeply about the world you live in, and the quality of your life. In my lifetime we all lived quite foolishly: furiously burning oil without heeding the consequences, and often thinking of our own immediate and disposable needs instead of yours. I am sorry on behalf of my generation for not thinking of you more. We talked a lot about the damage we were doing to the earth, but we did not take a lot of action to change things. I have tried in my own way to pass on a better earth to you. We drive a hybrid car that uses little gas, and we have ordered an electric car. I never take a plastic bag in a store, because I know it is one more plastic bag whose consequences you will have to deal with later.

But most of all, my dear one, I have done all I can to help people to have brilliant ideas: those that can solve problems instead of creating more: the kinds of ideas that can make life better for you. I have done this for you. I have dedicated this book specifically to you, grandchild of my grandchild, in the hope that this will be the very best contribution I can make to a life that can be great for you.

I can look back four generations into my past, and recognize how much more we understand today than they did back then. And so you can look back as you read this and realize how much more you know than I do. You are a more evolved and mature human being than I have ever been, and I cherish you with all my love and blessings

With all my love to you,

You great-great-grandfather,

Arjuna

We are the ones, you and I and the people we know, who can make pivotal decisions. We can take actions that determine the quality of life for people not yet born. You are reading a book about radical brilliance. You must be someone who cares, someone who wants to make a difference. The way you dedicate your life and your time, from the moment you wake up in the morning to the moment you close your eyes at night, determines the clarity of your own consciousness, and is the very ground in which your contribution can take form. That, in turn, will affect the lives of more people than you and I can possibly imagine.

This is why we rearrange our lives to increase the possibility of being used by an intelligence beyond our own understanding. It is another layer of motivation to live brilliantly: so that you can also, in your own way and on your own scale, be a Louis Pasteur, a Copernicus, a Muhammad Yunus, or a Lynne Twist.

CHAPTER TWENTY FOUR
WANNA GET OUT OF HERE?

Congratulations.

We have come to the end of our journey together, and now it is time to complete our shared experience, and also to make some plans for what comes next.

Among the many qualities that brilliant people share is that they know how to celebrate victories and milestones, and also how to integrate learning so they can use it later. I am going to invite you now to join me in these kinds of practices here.

Let's start with integration. Brilliant people know how to sift through and integrate what has gone before in a way to build upon what is useful, and then to gratefully reject what is not. You can do that right now with everything you have read in this book.

Step One. Take a sheet of paper and write down anything and everything you remember from this book. Do a brain dump. This could include particular practices you remember, quotes from other people, as well as the basic map of radical brilliance. In this first step, just write down everything you can remember: the good, the bad, the ugly, and the irrelevant. Include what you liked, what you found irritating, what was new, and what seemed repetitive. If you need to, you can cheat a little bit and flip back through the book to remind yourself of some of the themes that were explored.

Step Two. Now evaluate everything that you have put on your list with a number, from 1 to 5, according to how relevant and useful it could be to you in your life.

1   would mean extremely useful, and helpful: something I definitely want to integrate and use right away.

2   would mean very useful, something I want to explore more, contemplate further and perhaps integrate at a later time.

3   would mean I could take it or leave it. This might include ideas that you were already familiar with before reading the book or ideas that have little relevance to your particular field of brilliance.

4   would mean mildly disagree. This would include practices, ideas, and voices you could just as soon have done without. This is in the category of, "The book was okay, but I could have really lived without that bit."

5   would be strongly disagree: I felt irritated, outraged, like my time was wasted by the inclusion of that element. I found it offensive and completely against my values.

You can do this exercise all in one sitting, or over a period of a few sittings.

Now go back to your list, and write only the 1s and 2s on a new paper. Throw away the paper with the 3s, 4s, and 5s on it. If you want to make this list in a spreadsheet, you could just sort them in descending order, and then delete any row that has a 3 or more. As you delete, or throw away, or even burn, you could say something along the lines of, "Thank you for offering, but not for me."

Step Three. The next step is integration. For each of the ideas, practices, or quotes from people to which you gave a 5 or a 4, contemplate, "How am I going to use this?" What action steps or commitments can I make to integrate this into my life while it is still fresh in my mind? Here is where you might like to involve an accountability partner or a coach to make sure you are in integrity and follow-through on your intentions.

This is an incredibly useful practice with any seminar, book, or service that aims to support you. If you swallow the whole thing indiscriminately, you are going to get indigestion. You might at first be a diehard follower, but sooner or later you are going to react the other way, and become critical and rejecting. The other extreme is to reject everything indiscriminately, but that way you never learn anything new or expand your repertoire.

The above practice will help you to sift through and integrate what is helpful and what is not.

GRATITUDE

We often think of gratitude as an emotion we feel in response to especially nice things that happened to us, but that is a passive relationship to gratitude. The event happened outside your control, and so did the emotional response. You can also, if you choose, integrate gratitude as a conscious and deliberate response to life.

Perhaps it is easier to understand this if we think of a different example than this book. If you attend a weekend seminar or training, there will certainly be some things you like and some things you don't like. Our habit of critical thinking, which is very pervasive in our culture, often leads us to focus on the things we didn't like, and to give "feedback" of how things could be better. But of course that means you are focusing your attention on all the things that you do not want to integrate, instead of the things you do. Gratitude does the opposite. Bringing your attention in a seminar or a training onto what was useful to you, and consciously giving thanks for it, integrates the material much more thoroughly. Gratitude is something like taking digestive enzymes when you eat a heavy meal. The food becomes more bio-available. Whatever you expressly give great gratitude for will become more brilliance-available and useful to you.

In the case of a seminar or training, obviously a more personal and physical experience than reading this book, you might want to give the seminar leader a card or flowers, or a gift. Of course you already paid your money for the seminar, so you might argue with yourself,

"Well, I have already given back."It is true that the payment takes care of the exchange of services. But if you noticed a little extra brilliance or generosity, beyond the call of duty, acknowledge that with a gesture of gratitude. It will benefit both of you.

If there are things that are useful in this book, you might like to just offer up a prayer of thanks to the mysterious force that gives us all life, for sending those things your way. If there was a quote or practice from somewhere else, you might seek that source out, you might go find their website, send a message, or even plan to study with that person more deeply. And if you appreciate something I have said, I would love to hear what worked for you on Facebook or on the Radical Brilliance website.

NEXT STEPS

Here are some ways that you could go deeper with me in the exploration of Radical Brilliance, if you feel attracted to do that. In this book we have described the principles that govern practice at each phase of the cycle. But we were limited in how much we could teach the practices themselves. This is partly because practices often require audio or video to be taught effectively, and also because of lack of space. You might like to join our Global Brilliance Practice Community, where you will get detailed instructions on audio, video, and in writing, on all 108 practices mentioned in this book, dozen of videos from brilliance experts, as well as access to trained coaches who can guide you in your practice.

If you'd like to get together and practice together in person, I hold Radical Brilliance Intensives and longer Brilliance Laboratories regularly in many parts of the world. Some are weekends and some are a week or longer. During a practice retreat, we utilize the tools of radical brilliance to activate and energize the different parts of the cycle. You can find a calendar of upcoming events at radicalbrilliance.com.

I have made frequent reference in this book to the benefits of being coached, and that is certainly one of the most powerful ways to squeeze all of the juice available from this approach. You could get coached by me one-on-one, or I could refer you one of the people I have trained. You can also get more information about one-on-one coaching at radicalbrilliance.com

Finally, we have a training program to prepare people to become Radical Brilliance coaches. This is not an entry-level coaching training; it requires some previous experience in working with people. If you are already a coach, or a consultant, or psychologist or a trainer, or if you work with people in any other way, this might be an option for you. The information is also available on the same website.

And now it is my turn to give gratitude to you.

Imagine if you threw a big party, with balloons and streamers, and delicious food and perhaps even a band ... and then nobody showed up. Wouldn't that be sad? After all the energy that went into preparing for people to have a good time, all of your effort was wasted. It would be seeing your friends having the very best time of their lives that would bring fulfillment and purpose to all your efforts of preparation. That is the real reward.

Because you read all the way to the end of this book, you have contributed greater depth, meaning, and purpose to my life. Thank you so much for that. Almost all the joy to be derived from writing a book like this is to be found in the real benefit that it has for other people. So thank you for reading. I would sincerely love to hear your comments on my Facebook page: facebook.com/arjunardagh. I do my best to read everything that is posted there, and to respond.

May the brilliant gift that was implanted in you, as you, in the moment of conception, fully bear fruit in the journey of your life. May you have the courage, the energy, and the humor to fully deliver that gift, leaving nothing held back in this short human life.

Barnet Bain

Made in the USA
San Bernardino, CA
09 December 2017